Towards Strategic
Staff Development in
Higher Education

SRHE and Open University Press Imprint
General Editor: Heather Eggins

Current titles include:

Catherine Bargh *et al.*: *University Leadership*
Ronald Barnett: *Beyond All Reason*
Ronald Barnett: *The Idea of Higher Education*
Ronald Barnett: *The Limits of Competence*
Ronald Barnett: *Higher Education: A Critical Business*
Ronald Barnett: *Realizing the University in an age of supercomplexity*
Tony Becher and Paul R Trowler: *Academic Tribes and Territories (second edition)*
John Biggs: *Teaching for Quality Learning at University (second edition)*
David Boud *et al.* (eds): *Using Experience for Learning*
David Boud and Nicky Solomon (eds): *Work-based Learning*
Tom Bourner *et al.* (eds): *New Directions in Professional Higher Education*
Anne Brockbank and Ian McGill: *Facilitating Reflective Learning in Higher Education*
Ann Brooks and Alison Mackinnon (eds): *Gender and the Restructured University*
Sally Brown and Angela Glasner (eds): *Assessment Matters in Higher Education*
James Cornford and Neil Pollock: *Putting the University Online*
John Cowan: *On Becoming an Innovative University Teacher*
Gerard Delanty: *Challenging Knowledge*
Chris Duke: *Managing the Learning University*
Heather Eggins and Ranald Macdonald (eds): *The Scholarship of Academic Development*
Gillian Evans: *Academics and the Real World*
Andrew Hannan and Harold Silver: *Innovating in Higher Education*
David Istance et al (eds): *International Perspectives on Lifelong Learning*
Norman Jackson and Helen Lund (eds): *Benchmarking for Higher Education*
Merle Jacob and Tomas Hellström (eds): *The Future of Knowledge Production in the Academy*
Peter Knight: *Being a Teacher in Higher Education*
Peter Knight and Paul Trowler: *Departmental Leadership in Higher Education*
Ian McNay (ed.): *Higher Education and its Communities*
Louise Morley: *Quality and Power in Higher Education*
Moira Peelo and Terry Wareham (eds): *Failing Students in Higher Education*
Craig Prichard: *Making Managers in Universities and Colleges*
Michael Prosser and Keith Trigwell: *Understanding Learning and Teaching*
John Richardson: *Researching Student Learning*
Stephen Rowland: *The Enquiring University Teacher*
Maggi Savin-Baden: *Problem-based Learning in Higher Education*
Peter Scott: *The Globalization of Higher Education*
Peter Scott: *The Meanings of Mass Higher Education*
Colin Symes and John McIntyre (eds): *Working Knowledge*
Richard Taylor et al: *For a Radical Higher Education*
Susan Toohey: *Designing Courses for Higher Education*
Paul R. Trowler (ed.): *Higher Education Policy and Institutional Change*
Melanie Walker (ed.): *Reconstructing Professionalism in University Teaching*
David Warner and David Palfreyman (eds): *The State of UK Higher Education*
Gareth Williams (ed.): *The Enterprising University*

Towards Strategic Staff Development in Higher Education

Edited by
Richard Blackwell and
Paul Blackmore

The Society for Research into Higher Education
& Open University Press

Published by SRHE and
Open University Press
McGraw-Hill Education
McGraw-Hill House
Shoppenhangers Road
Maidenhead
Berkshire
England
SL6 2QL

email: enquiries@openup.co.uk
world wide web: www.openup.co.uk

and
325 Chestnut Street
Philadelphia, PA 19106, USA

First Published 2003

A catalogue record of this book is available from the British Library

ISBN 0 335 21209 3 (pb)   0 335 21210 7 (hb)

Library of Congress Cataloging-in-Publication Data
CIP data has been applied for

Typeset by RefineCatch Limited, Bungay, Suffolk
Printed in Great Britain by Biddles Limited, *www.biddles.co.uk*

Contents

List of contributors

Cliff Allan is programme director for the Learning and Teaching Support Network, a post he has held since 2000. Previously he was head of teaching and learning at the Higher Education Funding Council for England. An Africanist by background, he has worked as a lecturer, management consultant and charity official.

Simon Barrie is a lecturer in the Institute for Teaching and Learning at the University of Sydney. He is responsible for the Institute's work in the evaluation and quality assurance of teaching in the University. His primary research interests are in graduate attributes in higher education.

Ian Beardwell was professor of industrial relations and head of the Department of Human Resource Management at De Montford University, UK when he wrote his chapter. Subsequently he was director of human resources and co-ordinator of institutional human resource strategy at the North East Wales Institute for a short time before, sadly, he passed away.

Martin Binks, PhD, FRSA is the director of the Institute for Enterprise and Innovation and professor of entrepreneurial development at the University of Nottingham, specializing in entrepreneurship and the financing of small and medium-sized enterprises. He is associate editor of the *Journal of Entrepreneurial and Small Business Finance*.

Paul Blackmore is director of the Centre for Academic Practice at the University of Warwick and was formerly at De Montfort University. He developed teaching accreditation programmes at both institutions. At Warwick he is responsible for the University's strategy and policy in academic staff development. His research interests are in conceptualizations of professional expertise and in the development of higher-level capabilities. He is a convenor of the Standing Conference on Academic Practice, a grouping of heads of academic development in research-intensive institutions.

Richard Blackwell is Senior Adviser in the LTSN Generic Centre, UK. Previously he was Director of Training and Staff Development at University of Nottingham. An industrial relations specialist by background, for 10 years he researched and taught human resource management, including at Coventry and Oxford Universities. He is a member of the research committee of the Staff and Educational Development Association and the governing council of the Society for Research into Higher Education. Recent publications focus on staff development and quality enhancement.

Caroline Bucklow is acting chief executive of the Institute for Learning and Teaching in Higher Education, having been its director of accreditation since March 1999. She was previously head of education at the British Computer Society, spent six years teaching at Coventry University and is an associate lecturer with the Open University Business School. She holds a Certificate in Teaching in Higher Education from Oxford Brookes University.

Paul Clark was director of quality assessment for the Higher Education Funding Council for England from 1993 to 1996, then moved to the Scottish Higher Education Funding Council as director of teaching and learning. Paul was chief executive of the Institute for Learning and Teaching in Higher Education from 1999 to 2002 and is now pro-vice-chancellor at the Open University.

Sir Graeme Davies is principal and vice-chancellor of the University of Glasgow. He is chairman of the Universities Superannuation Scheme Ltd. He sits on the Scottish Science Trust and the board of Universities UK. Previously he was chief executive of the Higher Education Funding Council for England and chaired the board of the Higher Education Staff Development Agency.

Jacqueline Dempster is head of educational technology in the Centre for Academic Practice at the University of Warwick. She has extensive experience in developing the use of information and communications technology in higher education both nationally and at Warwick. She manages a range of e-learning projects and is involved in establishing national development opportunities for learning technologists. Her research interests are in developing innovative e-learning practices at both curriculum and institutional levels.

Moira Fraser works for a charitable foundation. She was academic development adviser in the Centre for Academic Practice at the University of Warwick, with particular responsibility for developing approaches to research-based learning.

Marie Garnett is based in the Centre for Academic Practice at the University of Warwick. She has been working in educational development since 1991 and has a particular interest and expertise in issues facing fixed-term researchers.

Graham Gibbs is professor and director of the Centre for Higher Education Practice at the Open University. He has worked as a national co-ordinator for subject-based projects supported by the Fund for the Development of Learning and Teaching since 1997. Previously he was head of the Oxford Centre for Staff Development at Oxford Brookes University.

Ruth Goodall is currently director of the Higher Education Funding Council for England's Good Management Project, 'Learning the Habit of Innovation: Harnessing Technology for Strategic Planning'. She was formerly head of the Centre for Staff and Educational Development at the University of East Anglia with a particular responsibility for working with academic staff.

George Gordon is a professor and director of the Centre for Academic Practice, University of Strathclyde. A geographer by background, he has written widely on quality assurance, the scholarship of teaching, staff and management development in higher education. He has undertaken numerous research, evaluation and development projects, in the UK and overseas.

Mary Taylor Huber is a senior scholar at the Carnegie Foundation for the Advancement of Teaching, USA, where she helps guide the Carnegie Academy for the Scholarship of Teaching and Learning. A cultural anthropologist by background, she is also directing a research programme on the cultures of teaching in higher education.

Edward Lumsdaine, DSc, FASME, FRSA is currently professor of mechanical engineering at Michigan Technological University, USA and consultant to Ford Motor Company. He has many years of experience in industry and as a professor at ten universities. In 1994 he received the Chester F. Carlson award for innovation in engineering education from the American Society for Engineering Education/ Xerox.

Kathy Maclachlan is a lecturer in adult education at the University of Glasgow. She had responsibility for setting up Learning Works in the University and has conducted research into various aspects of the scheme. Her other research interests lie in adult literacies and workplace learning.

Martin Oliver is a lecturer in the Department of Education and Professional Development at University College London, a role that includes leading an MA in learning technology research and undertaking staff secondment projects. His research interests include curriculum design, evaluation and educational theory, usually in relation to learning technology.

Stella Parker is dean of the Faculty of Education at the University of Nottingham. She has worked for almost 30 years in both further and higher education in adult and continuing education. Her publications include papers on science education and lifelong learning, and she is co-editor of the *International Journal of Lifelong Education*.

Michael Prosser is Associate Professor and director of the Institute for Teaching and Learning at the University of Sydney. Prior to that he was the foundation professor and director of the Academic Development Unit at La Trobe University. His primary research interests are in student learning in higher education.

Bob Thackwray has worked with the Higher Education Staff Development Agency since October 1994. Prior to that he was head of educational development at the University of Luton. Bob has published widely on staff development, in particular on Investors in People. He is a nationally registered Investors in People assessor and adviser. He holds a visiting professorship with the University of Hertfordshire.

List of abbreviations

CASTL	Carnegie Academy for the Scholarship of Teaching and Learning
CEC	Commission of the European Communities
CPD	continuing professional development
CUTSD	Committee for University Teaching and Staff Development
EDS	employee development scheme
FDTL	Fund for the Development of Teaching and Learning
HEI	higher education institution
HE	higher education
HEFCE	Higher Education Funding Council for England
HESDA	Higher Education Staff Development Agency
HRM	human resource management
ICED	International Consortium for Educational Development
ILTHE	Institute for Learning and Teaching in Higher Education
ITL	Institute for Teaching and Learning (University of Sydney)
JNCHES	Joint Negotiating Committee for Higher Education Staff
LTSN	Learning and Teaching Support Network
NCIHE	National Committee of Inquiry into Higher Education
NIACE	National Institute of Adult and Continuing Education
OECD	Organization for Economic Co-operation and Development
QAA	Quality Assurance Agency for Higher Education
RAE	research assessment exercise
RCI	Research Careers Initiative
SD	staff development
SEDA	Staff and Educational Development Association
SHRD	Strategic Human Resource Development
SHRM	strategic human resource management
SRHE	Society for Research into Higher Education
TQM	total quality management
UCoSDA	Universities' and Colleges' Staff Development Agency
UEA	University of East Anglia
UNESCO	United Nations Educational, Scientific, and Cultural Organization

Preface

This book has been written for senior staff in higher education institutions, heads of department and school, and professional staff developers. It explores ways in which staff development can become more strategic. In our view institutions still do not take the development of staff expertise seriously enough, and often do not go about it in an effective way. It is not seen as a major university function, but is often merely support for teaching. That which is labelled 'staff development' will often deal with some categories of staff but exclude others, and will usually not be central to the organization. Warner and Palfreyman's (1996) brief treatment of staff development, in their otherwise authoritative account of higher education management, is typical of its peripheral position in the eyes of institutional managers.

There is clear evidence that some aspects of staff development are being accorded greater importance. Ingrid Moses' study of educational development units in Britain, America, Australia, West Germany and Sweden showed a shared feeling of being marginal (Moses 1987) which Phil Candy, writing almost a decade later, declared was no longer the case (Candy 1996). Certainly a detailed and useful study of educational development units in the UK, carried out in 1995 and again in 2000, showed a significant increase in staffing levels and influence (Gosling 2001). However, overall, staff development has yet to become strategic in its conception or its effects.

This is not a lament for the overlooked staff developer or an appeal for funding or respect for that body of people. Rather, we believe that staff development as a function is a pale shadow of what it might be. It needs redefining, and it needs to attract a larger number of able people to it if it is to help institutions meet the challenges they face.

On the face of it there is a convergence of interests: senior staff want to improve organizational effectiveness, while staff developers want to influence organizational policy. However, for many managers, staff development as currently conceived is not a major contributor to organizational effectiveness while, for some staff developers, such a close engagement with policy delivery may be uncomfortable and involve 'a loss of innocence' (Buchanan and Badham 1999: 230–1). Moving towards strategic staff development will of course involve a number of challenges and will in many ways be problematic.

Terminology

The concept of staff development in higher education is itself difficult to frame. There are surface problems of terminology, since a range of terms is in use, none of which has an entirely settled meaning. Terminology varies from one community to another, and will continue to do so.

We have chosen the term 'staff development' as the broadest possible term available, referring to development for all categories of staff in all their work roles and throughout their working lives. Webb (1996: 1) defines staff development as 'the institutional policies, programmes and procedures which facilitate and support staff so that they may fully serve their own and their institution's needs'. The definition is useful, both in its inclusiveness and in its reference to the tensions between individual and institutional needs, although it does overlook the increasingly important dimensions of discipline and department.

Thus staff development is not only about academic staff, and certainly not only about teaching and student learning. Obvious though this sounds, it is worth saying. The majority of those who have been given a formal development remit in universities appear to have teaching as their main or more often sole focus of attention. The history of US faculty development is focused on teaching (Lewis 1996: 26–7). In the UK, the growth of the educational development community has been impressive, so that some claim that it is now 'a recognised field of study and a recognised professional role in most institutions of higher education in the UK' (Gosling, 2001: 75). Australian staff development too is characterized by recent fast growth, variety in levels and patterns of provision, and a teaching orientation (Hicks 1997: 56). However, development for research, management and a range of other activities is increasing, and there is a growing interest in how these interrelate, so we would prefer to retain a broader meaning for the term. In this we are in accord with a mapping of Australian and New Zealand usages (Fraser 2001: 62). We also note that academic staff are less than half of the workforce, and that professional administrators, secretarial, technical and other staff have needs to do with the changing demands of their roles, some of which are only indirectly, if at all, related to teaching and research.

While the authors have tried to use the term 'staff development' consistently, we do acknowledge that there are particular issues that relate to the development of the academy only. Authors occasionally use the term 'academic practice' or 'educational development' when appropriate (see Andresen 1996: 40). 'Faculty development', is used in a related way in USA, but is not sparingly employed here.

The term 'non-academic' is avoided since it seeks to describe a large group of people as what they are not, and so 'support staff' is preferred. By senior staff (or managers) and institutional leaders authors mean vice-chancellors, presidents, rectors, their immediate deputies and assistants and registrars, sometimes referred to generically as 'senior administrators' (for example, in the USA). Department and heads of department refers to the basic academic unit, whatever its name, and its head.

Finally, the term 'development' is not without problems. It may be rooted in positivist notions of advancement, through the application of scientific rationality, to some improved state. Thus a rational organization works in an organized way to better its practice. It also has patronizing overtones. In its customary interpretation, it is the staff who are developed through the institution's provision. Many developers are themselves uncomfortable with the term, as Fraser's (2001: 56) survey shows. There is an ethical dimension in professional development: 'Who develops whom, in what ways and on what authority?' (Harvey and Knight 1996: 157).

Plan of the book

In putting together an edited book such as this, editors inevitably find they have to be selective. It is not an easy choice, because there is such a wide range of possibilities, all of which seem worthy of inclusion. We have had to make our own judgements about what are and will be central and continuing issues, and have elected to look beyond the current policy agenda. The chapters we have chosen focus not on immediate policy issues but on what we believe are likely to be enduring themes: accreditation and standards; the subject or discipline dimension; and investing in all staff.

We are conscious of some apparent omissions: globalization and the growing international competition between developed Western institutions for new markets, such as Asia, are clearly important and may have major implications for staff development in some institutions. Beyond e-learning (represented here by Chapter 12) it is unclear how far the various potential effects of globalization will in fact occur and whether more than a minority of already internationally renowned institutions will be seriously affected. Another unknown is the so-called 'demographic timebomb' (Kogan *et al.* 1994) of an ageing academic population which apparently presents a substantial human resource challenge to higher education in the developed world, particularly when, as in the UK, a simultaneous expansion of the system is planned. Its resolution may be mainly through pay and rewards and other human resource activities, involving staff development only indirectly, for example in the growth of part-time staff and in the changing roles of academic and support staff that may be implied (see Chapters 2 and 13). However, the need to attract scarce high-calibre staff to higher education employment may prompt institutions to pay greater attention to staff development provision as a means of making themselves more attractive to potential employees.

Since we intend that this book will be of interest to senior staff as well as staff developers, contributions come from within and beyond the staff development community. The result is a broader range of voices than would usually be found in a book on staff development, and this is deliberate, reflecting the focus on strategy. Also, we did not want simply to update the previous book in the series, much of which remains highly relevant today (Brew 1995). As we wished to ensure that each chapter kept staff development fully in view and had something practical to offer, we asked each author to list key learning points for consideration by institutions, by departments and by staff developers at the end of each chapter.

The book is divided into four parts with short introductions by the editors. *Part I* is designed to set the scene for the rest of the book. It begins by discussing the meaning of strategic staff development and its implications for universities and colleges. A second chapter looks at the changing roles of higher education staff, especially academic staff, and argues the need for a new articulation of academic professionalism. Two chapters cover key themes of lifelong learning and entrepreneurship, both of which are likely to be of increasing institutional significance, although one of them perhaps sits more easily with the traditional outlook of staff development professionals than the other.

Part II focuses on extra-institutional themes, initiatives and provision. The subject and discipline dimension of staff development provides a theme of growing significance. Two chapters consider the very different approaches embodied in the creation of a publicly funded 'network' in the UK and the development of 'disciplinary styles' in the scholarship of teaching and learning through voluntary effort in the USA. The professionalizing and accreditation activities of the Institute for Learning and Teaching in Higher Education identify themes that are likely to endure, and increasingly find expression in a number of education systems. Staff development initiatives that involve all staff are represented by a chapter on Investors in People, a UK government-sponsored initiative, which has generated some international interest. A chapter on management and leadership offers an overview of this area, focusing in particular on extra-institutional interest and provision rather than on detailed case studies of universities' and colleges' own efforts.

Part III deals with intra-institutional issues, treating them in a thematic way. The chapters focus on: developing communities of practice at departmental level; promoting research-based teaching; and embedding new technology on learning and teaching into practice. A further chapter deals with support for often overlooked but critically important research staff.

Part IV provides case studies which take up aspects of key themes identified earlier. The late Ian Beardwell provides a case study from De Montfort University, that exemplifies the social practice approach to learning, creating a research culture where none existed previously. Graeme Davies and Kathy Maclachlan's chapter is concerned with studying the application of inclusive lifelong learning principles to draw in staff normally reluctant to engage in staff development, demonstrating a range of mainly intangible benefits to the organization (in this case the University of Glasgow). Mike Prosser and Simon Barrie focus on quality assurance at the University of Sydney, and illustrate how a student learning approach may underpin quality assurance arrangements.

Part I

Setting the scene

In this opening part of the book we have resisted the temptation to repeat familiar material about globalization, massification, resource constraint, managerialism and other related aspects of the context for higher education. Many other writers have dealt with these issues very ably elsewhere. We take it that all our readers will be aware of these general trends, many of which are clearly world-wide, although they may impact rather differently from one system to another. Instead contributors to this book offer responses to that context, exploring its significance for staff development.

We discuss, in the opening chapter, what might be meant by strategic staff development as an institutional function, suggesting that prevailing conceptions of the purpose, scope and methods of staff development are narrow and inadequate. The second chapter is a counterpart to the first: attention shifts from the development function to the staff themselves. Specifically it is argued that higher education institutions need to review the roles that their staff play. In particular, the traditional role of the academic is now under considerable pressure and in need of redefinition.

We have chosen two other themes that we believe will be of enduring importance. One of them is lifelong learning, which is included here for two reasons. First, the traditional concept of the young undergraduate undertaking three or more years' study immediately on leaving school is seriously outdated. In many education systems, including the UK's, mature students are now in the majority and provision extends well beyond the undergraduate degree for young adults. The widening participation and access agenda suggests that these trends can only deepen. The implications for what is taught and learnt, as well as how and when, are immense, and are only just coming to be appreciated. Second, higher education staff are lifelong learners too, and some of the same reconsideration that is now being given to curricula can also be applied to the design and delivery of staff development.

The second theme is that of enterprise. Increasingly seen by some as the third activity being undertaken in universities, alongside teaching and research, this is a field to which staff developers have traditionally paid little attention, and some may indeed find that it does not sit comfortably with their own values. It is an excellent example of an area that senior staff in higher education see as important, but which is not yet supported by most staff development functions. Whether helping learners to become enterprising or developing academic entrepreneurship, staff developers need to engage with this agenda.

1

Rethinking strategic staff development

Richard Blackwell and Paul Blackmore

Introduction

Strategic staff development (SD) has no settled meaning and is unlikely to acquire one. 'Development' suggests change, and a recent survey of staff developers' approaches to change identified 12 separate orientations (Land 2001). Individuals operating from some of these orientations, for example the interpretative-hermeneutic orientation, might even question the desirability and legitimacy of 'strategy' in SD. However, most would agree that if SD is to be effective it must engage with its sponsoring institution's key concerns. Some staff developers have long bemoaned their lack of influence over policy and the extent to which they are not trusted with new initiatives (Weimer 1998). On the other hand institutional leaderships, increasingly under pressure to move towards more 'tightly coupled' – even corporate – organizations (Weick 1976; McNay 1995) can be forgiven for wondering about the contribution that their SD functions make to achieving institutional goals and priorities. There is a perception of a tendency

> to repeat exactly the same mistakes that have made SD marginal to the management of universities. Imbued with an evangelical desire to convert others, they seem to have no concept of acting strategically (i.e. to maximize their own university's effectiveness) at all.
> (Ramsden, personal communication 2002; see also Ramsden 2003, chs. 10 and 11)

This book explores the possibilities of achieving strategic SD. The contribution of this chapter is to take a pragmatic approach, focusing on major trends in discussion of organizational learning and taking into account the interests of the primary readership of the book (senior staff, heads of department and SD professionals). The chapter seeks to review four major approaches to strategy in organizational learning, indicating their assumptions, strengths and weaknesses in a higher education (HE) setting. This review begins with more organizationally focused and managerial approaches, before turning to social learning theories and the debate about professionalism in SD. It identifies the need for greater organizational focus than has hitherto been the case in many SD functions, a message reinforced by a number of the chapters in the book. Towards the end, it addresses itself to those SD practitioners and others who may feel uncomfortable with this argument, considering possible positive roles and ethical stances.

Diverse contexts and histories

The argument that follows is in broad-brush terms. There are a number of caveats and qualifications that need to be made at the outset. First of all, national HE systems vary considerably and, although globalization is thought to be encouraging convergence, for example between the UK and USA, important differences remain. In particular, the state continues to have a much more direct role in the UK, Australia and elsewhere than in the USA, creating mandated change some of which is arguably to the advantage of SD – an example of this is the quality agenda in the UK (see Gosling 2001). Within national systems there remains a great range of institutions, with the USA demonstrating the greatest diversity and overlapping of institutional types. Although most systems have their elites – the Russell group in the UK, the Ivy League in the USA and the Group of 8 or Sandstones in Australia – much variety exists within and between these elites and their national settings. In the UK, 'post 1992' universities, previously polytechnics under the control of local government (normally an elected 'council'), developed separate 'educational development' units during the 1970s to cater for the specific educational needs of academic staff, students and the new technology of the time. At that time, in theory, other categories of staff were integrated into the internal labour market of their local council and catered for by its training function. A similar separation appears to be the norm in the USA (faculty development and professional development) and Australia (where unit names vary considerably). In the UK, the split between provision for academic staff and provision for other staff tends to have continued in the post-1992 sector, whereas it is much less common amongst 'pre-1992' universities. Recent growth in SD in the UK, related to official 'quality' agendas, seems, however, to have been associated with a dispersion of SD and somewhat disturbed this pattern (Gosling 2001). More generally, the common distinction between pre- and post-1992 institutions in the UK masks considerable differences, Scott (1995: 44–7), for example, identifies 12 sub-sectors. In short, many institutions have highly specific local traditions, as do their departments, and SD arrangements that work in one context do not necessarily transfer well into others.

Strategic engagement is at least to some extent a matter of the 'inner' institutional context and choice. In some contexts strategic engagements with important initiatives may not be offered. Weimer (1998: 109), for example, lists a string of educational reforms in North America over a decade which did not come the way of SD units. In the Australian context, by contrast, Hicks (1998) maintains it is possible to earn a place at the table by establishing one's credibility. Within these constraints, choices may be possible. One can choose not to engage in strategic SD at all, in the sense of activities closely aligned with institutional policy development and implementation. Later in the chapter, we shall offer some thoughts about how a contribution to organizational learning can be made.

Strategic human resource development

A useful starting point is the literature on strategic human resource development (SHRD) – see Garavan (1991), Garavan *et al.* (1998) and McCracken and Wallace (2000). This approach focuses on creating a learning culture through mutual and reciprocal relationships between SD and corporate strategy. It sees SD as both responding to and shaping corporate strategy as it develops. In this model there is a continuum from the organization with no learning culture, characterized by an administrative and delivery approach to 'training', through to an organization with a strong learning culture, strategic approach to SD and a function focused on strategic change. Nine characteristics distinguish SHRD (McCracken and Wallace 2000):

1. Relationship to organization goals (poor integration through to a shaping role).
2. Top management support (little support through to leadership by top management).
3. Environmental scanning (little environmental scanning through to senior management scanning in SD terms).
4. SD plans and policies (few plans and policies through to developed strategies and plans).
5. Relationship to line management (little commitment through to strategic partnership).
6. Relationship to human resource management (HRM) or personnel (lack of complementarity through to strategic partnership with HRM).
7. Role of staff developer (training role in contrast to organizational change consultant).
8. Cultural engagement (a training role not embedded in the organizational culture at one end of the spectrum and at the other SD both embedded in and able to influence the development of organizational culture).
9. Evaluation (little emphasis on evaluation through to a focus on cost-effective evaluation).

It is easy to criticize models such as the SHRD model, not least for its assumption of an end-point rather than seeing development as emergent (Lee 2001; McGoldrick *et al.* 2001). Certainly the list of characteristics needs to be interpreted; the notion of line managers is problematic in academic areas despite 'new managerialism' (Deem and Johnson 2000), although perhaps the notion of strategic partnerships with heads of department less so. Many in HE would want to add an additional point: staff, including the extent to which staff are involved in strategic partnerships with the SD function (for example, through their organizations or in the planning, execution and evaluation of activities intended for peers). Indeed, there is a vein of literature in the UK which sees the essential role of SD as being to balance 'top-down' and 'bottom-up' impulses. This involves taking initiatives to satisfy both levels and handling sometimes conflicting demands, signalled through perceived roles such as that of 'diplomat' (Smith 1992; Elton 1995). SHRD is, however, a useful heuristic device and highlights the role of top management and integration with organizational goals in conventional thinking. It is worth noting that a recent international study of HE chief executives found that they were much more concerned with broad values and goals, with establishing agreed vision, than with classical corporate control and planning (Bargh *et al.* 2000). Indeed, it has been argued that achieving such shared values and common understandings underpins successful change management in HE (House and Watson 1995), which gives a special meaning and importance to point 1 (above) in SHRD. Staff developers would seem to have little trouble endorsing broad values and goals, especially if they are framed in terms of creating facilitative, continuous learning organizations. More problematic may be roles in implementing specific policy prescriptions developed by senior managers, and the ability to influence the formation of such policies. It is likely that staff developers would need to 'deliver' on their general mandate and key central policies before a role in policy formation would be enabled. As Hicks (1998: 112) says: 'I would contend that if you, the developer, do it well, more power is granted to you to influence the broader institutional agenda setting process'. In other words, to move along the continuum of influence, staff developers first need to demonstrate their value to the organization at a lower strategic level.

The relationship with HRM (or personnel) is a matter of some debate. Some SD activists are hostile to HRM, on the grounds, *inter alia*, that it involves association with a low-status activity (Elton 1995) and/or too close association with 'management' (D'Andrea and Gosling 2001: 68–9). Below we deal with the issue of structural location; here it is enough to note that there are encouraging signs that the status problem is being addressed (Blackwell and McLean 1996a) and a range of practical reasons for working together. At one time it may have been possible for academic staff developers, catering only for tenured academic staff, to dismiss employment relationships as of little concern, but not today. There are a growing number of ways in which progress in SD requires parallel and simultaneous facilitative action in employment relations. The growth of contract staff and of a large peripheral 'casualized' teaching work force employed on a hire-and-fire basis makes it difficult to undertake development activities without bumping into contractual matters (career prospects in HE or payment for attending events, for example). Pressing the case for rewarding excellent teachers (Elton and Partington 1993; Gibbs and Habeshaw 2002) in the UK or for equal recognition for the scholarship of teaching and learning with research in USA must entail review of reward structures (D'Andea and Gosling 2001: 74) and forming implicit or explicit alliances, including with HRM. A greater desire for teamworking across staff groups, and the enhanced emphasis on the role of heads of department, inevitably raise employment and reward issues as well as SD needs. This is not to say that SD function should be subsumed by HRM, but rather that the function is an increasingly important 'loosely coupled' internal partner.

A final point to note about SHRD approaches is the explicit recognition of environmental scanning as a key function – the notion that developments in the external environment may have a big impact on the organization and its SD function. This factor, together with the need for the organization to have proactive scanning such that it is positioned to address issues independently in advance rather than reactively respond, is not always recognized in more introspective discussions within HE. The growing pace of and staff sensitivity to external change (Blackwell and Preece 2001) suggest this is an important function, which SD may undertake with senior staff.

The learning organization

The SHRD model is concerned with the creation of a strong learning culture, albeit within a rationalist and planning framework. The learning organization literature in particular stresses the need for reflexive, flexible individuals who are constantly learning and developing (and therefore flexible, creative employees). Writers who see higher education institutions (HEIs) as or becoming learning organizations relax the planning assumptions and see learning as much more complex and unpredictable. The notion appears particularly appropriate for relatively non-hierarchical, diverse knowledge-intensive organizations needing to adapt to a constantly changing world. 'An essential characteristic of a learning organization is that it facilitates the learning of its individual members and continually transforms itself' (Tann 1995: 46). It is flexible, facilitative, takes a long-term approach, welcomes variety, diversity and consequently contradiction and paradox. At the organizational level it seeks to go beyond 'single loop learning', focused on improvements that are found within existing paradigms, to 'double loop learning', concerned with challenging the assumptions of existing paradigms, the theories in use embodied in practice (James 1997) and looking at new possibilities. 'Triple loop learning' is the even more radical questioning of the principles on which the organization is founded, sometimes required at times of dramatic change, it is argued (Tann 1995: 48–51). The role of SD is summed up in Tann's (1995: 55) view that the typical staff appraisal interview might shift from asking 'what courses did you attend last year; to what did you learn last year and what is your learning plan for the present and future?'

Duke has applied these ideas to the 'ideal seeking' university and its management in which 'delegation, trust, valuing of local expertise down the line, nurturing teams and giving credit' characterize management (Duke 2002: 66). Staff development 'will support learning on the job and in teams through work. It will provide mentoring, formal training, and reflective evaluative review and planning (away-day-type activities) which allow learning and tacit knowledge to be identified, shared and extended in pursuit of the university's objectives' (Duke 2002: 118). James (1997) has presented a less ambitious, decentralized variant of the model which is not linked to 'ideal seeking management'. It sees organizational knowledge as embedded in existing practice, in theories in use locally, which are the focus of inquiry-based collaborative examination by staff. An organizational issue is identified after wide consultation, and the issue or problem is tackled through experimentation in context-specific ways within departments and the maximum cross-institutional collaboration is built into both the work and disseminating outcomes. The learning strategy is explicitly based on organized serendipity and feedback. The approach is exemplified by an apparently successful attempt to enhance the students' experience of the first year at University of Melbourne, Australia. Following survey and focus-group investigation of student views, nine departments were involved in seminars and workshops. A report was produced and widely circulated throughout the institution, and the approach was praised in a national report on quality assurance (James 1997: 37–9).

There are some well-known objections to the learning organization concept, including its relative lack of clarity about how continuous learning by individuals is translated into organizational learning and the practical limits to flows of information, for example around defensive individual behaviours and sensitive policies (see James 1997). Taken together, these approaches seem to go some way to addressing these criticisms, although micro-politics is always likely to limit information flows. Projects such as that at Melbourne require senior staff tolerance of risk-taking and occasional failure, including by SD practitioners (some would say celebration of failure as a learning opportunity). The counter danger of external pressure for accountability turning HEIs into more defensively structured and bureaucratic organizations inimical to organizational learning (Tann 1995: 55) also needs to be recognized, especially by government and external funding agencies.

Communities of practice

Some scholars have taken the notion of learning from practice even further, and argued that the most effective form of learning is that which arises from 'legitimate peripheral participation' in daily practice (Lave and Wenger 1991). Here the emphasis is upon groups with common values, engaged in common working practices: teams or work groups, normally departments in HEIs. In this conception, learning is conceived largely as 'what we do around here'; is tacit in nature; and is distributed across the community (for further discussion, see Chapters 10, 12 and 14). This approach, emphasizing situated learning and sensitivity to contingencies and context, sits well with the primary source of academic identity, the discipline (Henkel 2000), the diversity of discipline cultures (Becher 1989), and the preference which professionals themselves have expressed for informal learning (Becher 1999). Opportunities for learning in everyday practice can arise from seeing; reading; doing; and disturbing assumptions (Knight 2002b). Appropriate SD includes subject and professional body participation, team awaydays and meetings (Knight and Trowler 2001). Malcolm and Zukas (2000) have launched a spirited critique of conventional SD for teaching from this perspective too, criticizing what they perceive as the dominant uncritical and decontextualized approach to student learning.

One problem with this social learning approach is the rather rosy, uncritical view of 'communities of practice' that it sometimes implies. To an outsider, it may not always be obvious that a healthy community of practice exists and that informal learning is doing more than reinforcing taken-for-granted assumptions (single loop). Such learning may reinforce 'dysfunctional' local traditions (Boud 1999) and perpetuate historical inequalities and prejudices (Billett 1999). For individuals in workgroups the 'lived experience' of group membership may be very different from the way it is portrayed to the outside world (in formal documents, plans, etc.). There is sufficient international concern about workloads and stress (Kinman 1998; Rhoades 1997; Maslen 2002; McInnis 2000b) not to be too sanguine about this.

A second concern is the implied exclusivity of the 'community'. Much of the literature focuses explicitly or implicitly on the interests of full-time tenured academic staff only. Yet around these core staff are large numbers of fixed-term contract staff (see Chapter 13) and part-time teachers engaged in activities critical to core functions. Their membership of 'communities of practice' is in reality highly problematic and may require more formal SD (see Knight 2002b: 95). Furthermore, there are large numbers of staff, in most large institutions a majority, who are not academic members of staff but fulfil functions which support primary academic purposes – cleaners, gardeners, porters and security staff, and, nearer the core, secretaries, technicians and professional administrators. Some of these are in separate organizational structures (if not contracted out) but many are not and they tend to enjoy much more traditional hierarchical line-management relationships. Many do not have sufficient autonomy in their jobs to engage in development without the explicit agreement of their managers. Second, in times of rising demand and financial constraint, teamworking across staff boundaries has some potential for increasing productivity and creating more interesting, enhanced jobs for support staff. The changing nature of the academic role, discussed in the next two chapters, implies an erosion of the traditional boundaries between some jobs and academic work and more collaborative working. Developing communities of practice around such collaborative teamworking may provide important gains to the individuals concerned and their organizations.

The community-of-practice literature implies a decentralized focus on academic units, their needs and development. In healthy communities of practice, the role for the SD function would appear to be largely in terms of providing, directly and indirectly, consultancy and support for internal learning activities. Possibilities include reciprocal peer working such as the teaching development projects and the writing for publication group established at the University of Technology, Sydney (Boud 1999), although the extent to which academic staff are prepared to view developers as peers may be problematic (Gosling 2002). Other roles may include providing the necessary challenge and intervention to enable 'double-loop learning' and to avoid continuation of any historical prejudices. When new teams or departments are being formed SD personnel may help prepare the ground and context for the emergence of (newly defined) communities of practice and an inclusive learning culture. A focus on supporting those with a key role in developing and sustaining learning in teams and local communities of practice, notably heads of department, seems particularly important (see Chapters 9 and 10).

At the HEI level the emerging orthodoxy around communities of practice as the site of situated learning disturbs traditional reliance on initial training programmes for new faculty (important as that is) and formal short courses for volunteers. It suggests that supporting informal learning processes, the bringing together of socially distributed learning into explicit discussion at departmental level and below (with research teams, for example) assumes much greater importance. There is, however, a potentially wider role. Knight and Trowler (2001) note that only liberal arts colleges in the USA approximate to a community of practice at the organizational level (others might add small specialist art and design colleges in the UK), and other HEIs are more like constellations of communities. This suggests a role in working horizontally across these communities to make connections and spread ideas and practices (see Chapters 5 and 6), and to broker inputs and exchanges designed to ensure 'double-loop' learning. There may also be a role in developing tools and guidance to avoid constant local 'reinventing of the wheel' and ease the path of innovation. In short, a strategic co-ordination and resource provision role is implied.

Structures for staff development

In conventional thinking, structural arrangements should be derived from strategy. In practice, however, organizations rarely have a blank sheet of paper to write on and changes in organizational strategy may be imperfectly reflected in structural arrangements. Separate functions focused on learning and teaching and on academic staff interests appear common in the USA, Australia and some UK institutions. A recent survey of 'educational development' units in the UK (Gosling 2001) indicates a growth in their number in the late 1990s; increased staffing partly as a result of the Teaching Quality Enhancement Fund of the Higher Education Funding Council for England; and a growing remit. Although the definition of educational development used was somewhat restrictive (interestingly, use of the term 'educational development' in the name had fallen from 57% in 1995 to 23% in 2000), the data on institutional location and reporting lines is instructive: 38 per cent were stand-alone central units, while the remainder fell into eight categories, the largest of which were HRM (17 per cent) and education departments (13 per cent). However, reporting lines show much more consistency: 51% report to a pro-vice-chancellor (mainly) or the vice-chancellor/principal (and a further 8 per cent to registrars, powerful heads of administration in pre-1992 universities) (Gosling 2001: 78–83).

The variety of institutional structures reported by Gosling seems to reflect a complex of factors, including variation in institutional types and histories; shifting policy priorities; political power plays within institutions, for example by new pro-vice-chancellors; and growing policy emphasis on enhancing learning and teaching. Although evidence on relative effectiveness is thin, it may be that in relatively flat, loosely coupled systems this diversity makes good sense and allows for a 'good fit' with local particularities. Functions in apparently less favoured positions for connecting with academic cultures, such as HRM, as noted earlier, and education departments (low academic status), may be able to function perfectly successfully in propitious conditions. These conditions appear to include that they are allowed sufficient autonomy to be able to act and to be perceived to act independently; that they adopt appropriate partnership approaches designed to serve 'top', 'middle' and 'bottom' interests; and that they are sensitive to the cultures of disciplines. Other conditions are that they receive visible and sustained support from institutional leaders (in this respect the data on reporting lines are significant) and that they are led by individuals able to gain the trust and respect of senior staff, unit heads and individual members of staff (Blackwell and McLean 1996a: 167–9). The least promising arrangement, from a strategic point of view, would appear to be the lone staff developer, often seconded part-time from amongst the staff and operating in isolation – that is the 'shop floor' model that predominated in the pre-1992 universities in the UK until the 1980s (Matheson 1981; Smith 1992).

Turning to reporting lines, the worries about being too closely associated with 'management' through association with HRM within the SD community, noted earlier, are out of proportion to the data and suggest a selective myopia. The tendency of educational development units to report to pro-vice-chancellors in the UK is treated as largely unproblematic despite evidence of pro-vice-chancellors' integration into and key role in 'new managerialism' (Deem and Johnson 2000). Pro-vice-chancellors also typically have much greater power than the average head of HRM so, arguably, units reporting to them are potentially more deeply implicated in 'management'. One attempt to square this apparent circle is the search for professionalism.

Professionalism in staff development

Arguing for a more central role for SD prompts questions about the capacity of the SD community to work at a strategic level. There is, after all, no clear route into the SD role; nor is there formal preparation for it, and most staff developers have no experience of senior management roles. Such concerns have shown themselves in recent discussions within the SD community on professionalism, notably in the journal of the recently formed International Consortium for Educational Development (ICED) representing 15 national associations. The claim to professionalism is most frequently advanced in relation to that subset of SD concerned only with academic staff. Christopher Knapper, head of the Canadian affiliate to ICED, has described 'educational development' as an 'emergent profession'. There is, it is said, increasing agreement on the scope of the field, accepted standards of practice (including codes of ethics discussed in the next section), formal organizations and structure, some conceptual underpinnings and procedures for training and accreditation (Knapper 1998: 1). The creation of a fellowship scheme by the British Staff and Educational Development Association (SEDA) in May 1994 is clearly significant (although that organization is arguably not fully representative of the SD community in the UK). Furthermore, some commentators appear to see potential for an academic discipline in its own right too (Andresen 1996). Recent attempts by some pre-1992 universities in the UK to combine inquiry into their own educational practice with practical academic SD (Oxford, King's and University Colleges London, and Nottingham) suggest movement in this direction in a group of universities not normally associated with SEDA or ICED.

The lack of a clear career path amongst heads of Australian units (Hicks 1997) and divergent and sometimes diametrically opposed views in the Australian SD community (Fraser 2001) indicate that there is some way to go. Indeed, this professionalizing route has apparently been discussed and rejected in Australia (Hicks 1998) and is not available to many emerging SD communities, for example in South Africa (Collett and Davidson 1997). As we noted earlier, Gosling's survey suggested a tendency for academic SD to become more distributed within HEIs, and this also works against the notion of a cohesive 'profession'. Staff developers concerned mainly with support staff do not fit readily into the situation. They tend to be more mobile between employment sectors and may be more attracted to membership of economy-wide bodies (like the Chartered Institute of Personnel and Development in the UK) rather than HE-only organizations.

Although staff developers' claims to professional status may interest few out-side their community, there are some significant issues about standards, preparation and training which underlie the issues of capacity and capability mentioned earlier. Developments in the quality agenda may yet bring these issues to the fore. The harmonization of quality assurance across the EU, signalled by the Bologna declaration, suggests the possibility of SD partially reinventing itself around a quality assurance and enhancement role in Europe. In the UK, the quality system is in flux at the time of writing, with the possibility that a new quality enhancement organization, bringing the Learning and Teaching Support Network (Chapter 6), the Institute for Learning and Teaching in Higher Education (Chapter 7) and the Higher Education Staff Development Agency more closely together, may be created from 2004. If these developments precipitate increased interest in, for example, accrediting academic teachers (see Chapters 2 and 7), which they might, it is likely that the credentials of those who undertake the development will come under increased public scrutiny, casting the UK debate about professionalism in a new light.

Ethics

There has been some interest in codes of ethics, including as protection against the more malign influences of managerialism (Cranton 1998; Hicks 1998; Knight and Wilcox 1998; Weimer 1998). The SEDA accreditation scheme has an underpinning set of values (Baume and Baume 1996), if undertheorized, and others have been proposed (D'Andrea and Gosling 2001). Second, Land's (2001) study of the orientations to change of SD specialists reveals a startling range of perspectives, many of which appear strongly value-based, for example the cluster around 'person-centred' working with individuals. This raises interesting questions about whether such ethical stances may thrive in organizationally aligned functions and, from the point of view of the organization, whether they can make contributions to its effectiveness. Two strategies are of particular interest, 'the deviant innovator', which addresses the concerns of those worried about managerialism, and 'tempered radicalism', which addresses the needs of person-centred practitioners.

The 'deviant innovator' contrasts with the conventional 'conformist innovator', who seeks to earn success through accepting organizational ends and policy. The deviant innovator seeks to put their work on a more independent professional footing, change some organizational ends and the criteria for evaluation of their activities (Legge 1978). It is thus predominantly an organizationally focused perspective, which offers much in times of change, or when innovation is required for example to challenge a non-learning culture, or dysfunctional community of practice. It accords with the need for double loop learning, too. However, the deviant innovator strategy is only really available to heads of SD functions, requires 'boom' conditions and in reality practitioners are observed to oscillate between it and conformist innovation (Legge and Exley 1975). Tempered radicalism appears to have a wider relevance as it is more individualistic in orientation. It embodies a 'dualist strategy of ambivalence'. 'Tempered radicals are individuals who identify with and are committed to their organizations and are also committed to a cause, community or ideology that is fundamentally different from, and possibly at odds with the dominant culture of their organisation' (Meyerson and Scully 1995). This dualism is acknowledged to face many challenges (notably perceptions of hypocrisy; the danger of isolation; pressures for co-option; and emotional/ psychological stress) but strategies for change do exist, including an opportunistic small-wins strategy and using the language of both constituencies to uncover unexpected allies. From an organizational point of view, tempered radicals may be a source of vibrancy and change. Taking the 'outsiders within' perspective, they may more easily engage in 'double' and especially 'triple loop' learning. Such questioning of established principles and practice may have organizational benefits at times when 'step-changes' are required because of their natural ability to 'think outside the box' or in particular policy areas. Second, tempered radicals may be both critics of the status quo and of 'untempered' radical critique, identifying the risks of being too radical. In some ways, it is claimed, their stance may be seen to be more balanced and credible than that of the traditional change agent who is always in favour of change regardless of its implications (Meyerson and Scully 1995). In this way staff developers who perhaps choose a radical person-centred approach may prosper within an SD function that has a more organizational focus. Such approaches seem most likely to flourish in a relaxed institutional funding regime, when the SD function has independent access to external project funding, or as a minor part of a more organizationally focused activity.

A situational ethic is implied, however, for those required or choosing to work at multiple levels and with multiple constituencies, including with top-down change. Buchannan and Badham, focusing on the politics of change, have commented that universal ethical principles are difficult to apply to political behaviour in organizations. Decisions need to be based on 'informed judgements of what is possible, of what is acceptable, of what is justifiable and of what is defensible in the situation' (Buchanan and Badham 1999: 206). In the HE SD context, Hicks (1998: 111–12) argues that

> the ethical position . . . should be a complex and shifting position taking into account a broad array of influences [including faculty members, university administration, government, students, parents, employers and members of the community]. . . . it is a balancing act that I perform not formula driven, but also not totally inconsistent and not indefensible . . . A simple and enduring solution will not be found to the complex ethical dilemmas . . . and I believe this is the way it should be.

Conclusion

It is an exciting time for staff development. There is a growing recognition of both the importance of SD to particular agendas, such as the quality agenda, and to broader organizational needs for a flexible, learning culture. The SD function will continue to have multiple foci and constituencies, whose relative interest and influence in SD will inevitably wax and wane over time. The review of organizational learning theories and the debate on professionalizing SD suggest that the balance of input needs to continue to shift from emphasis on individual academic members of staff towards greater organizational alignment at both the institutional and departmental level. However, in a complex and ambiguous world even this conclusion is less clear than it might seem. Elsewhere in this volume, authors argue for the importance of the subject dimension and bringing it into dialogue, at least, with institutional SD (see Chapters 5 and 6). Moreover, in Chapter 15 a scheme focused on the non-vocational 'wants' of individuals is shown to have had considerable organizational benefit too. Indeed, that study warns against a narrow, dirigiste focus on job-related training, especially for support staff. The analytical distinction between individually focused and organisationally focused development is in practice blurred and the relative 'gain' from learning is often shared in somewhat unpredictable proportions. It is therefore a matter of balance and interpretation, and that is likely to vary from one context to another.

Key learning points

Senior staff

- Staff development can make an important contribution to organizational development and learning at a variety of levels, notably the institution (responding to and shaping corporate agendas), department (by supporting communities of practice) and individual level (through structured serendipity). In practice, the focus and impact of learning activities are more ambiguous than this neat categorization implies. SD approaches not primarily focused on the organization may produce organizational gain and can be valuable in stimulating double and triple loop learning.
- SD functions that demonstrate effectiveness at lower strategic levels should be enabled and encouraged to participate in more demanding strategic tasks, such as environment scanning, to identify future needs and help form policy agendas.
- Structures appear to be largely contingent on historical, policy and micropolitical factors. Reporting lines and the way in which the function is supported and operates are probably more important than its location *per se*.

Heads of department

- The community-of-practice literature emphasizes situated, informal learning embedded in daily life. This places prime responsibility for SD in the department itself. Heads have a special responsibility for creating learning opportunities and bringing together tacit and distributed learning (see Chapter 10).
- The SD function is primarily a consultant and supporter of developing learning opportunities locally in this context. It may play a role in creating new, inclusive communities and offer a range of useful tools and services to existing communities.
- The SD function may also play a key role in working horizontally across communities, enabling them to network learning, and ensuring learning does not become stuck within the 'single loop'.

Professional staff developers

- The literature on strategic human resource development and, to a lesser extent, on the learning organization in higher education suggests that alignment with institutional goals and values especially and, more problematically, policy implementation is a precondition of strategic influence. It is unlikely to be simply given. The focus of some SD is in practice ambiguous, and greater organizational alignment does not mean that other foci can or should be completely squeezed out.
- SD units need to work at multiple levels with multiple approaches. There is a need to work from the top down, from the middle in, and from the bottom up. Departments and other communities have been relatively neglected and require facilitative consultancy approaches. There may be capacity and capability issues to address, whatever one's stance on professionalism.
- The SD community displays many value orientations and is unlikely to achieve consensus on professional standards and ethics easily. A situational ethic is implied for those working as change agents at senior levels (head of unit), and this includes the possibility of utilizing a 'deviant innovator' approach. There may be space for others to adopt move radical approaches and strategies, which can bring organizational gain, depending on circumstances.

2

Academic roles and relationships

Paul Blackmore and Richard Blackwell

Introduction

Many writers on higher education assert that universities are in the midst of great change. Globalization, the neo-liberal policies of national governments and information technology may sweep away universities as they currently exist. The collegial academic, undertaking teaching, research and administration or management, is a relic of the past. Few of these claims are based on empirical research: most are highly speculative. Fundamental changes may be taking place, but there is apparent continuity too. Ironically, despite their traditions of liberalism, universities tend to be conservative in approaching their own change (Altbach and Finkelstein 1997: viii). At the level of the teacher and researcher, practices show remarkable consistency over time, to the frustration, at times, of staff developers. Despite the immense claims made for information technology, the vast majority of teaching occurs face-to-face, although information technology is often a valuable assistant. The job of funding, undertaking and publishing research is consistent at its core. Change is, in the main, incremental.

This chapter considers to what extent academic work, and the work that supports it, is changing. Empirical evidence from the United Kingdom, Australia and the United States is summarized. The nature of role and of professionalism forms a basis for discussion of the adequacy of the traditional role of the academic. Finally, some implications for staff development are explored.

Empirical evidence

Among the relatively limited number of major empirical studies of academic role are surveys of Australian academic staff in 1993 (McInnis 1996) and 1999 (McInnis 2000, b,c, 2001), of US faculty in 1993 (Finkelstein *et al.* 1998) and of UK academic staff (National Committee of Inquiry into Higher Education (NCIHE) 1997).

McInnis surveyed 2609 academics in 15 Australian universities in 1999, replicating a 1993 study. He found a continuing high level of motivation, arising from the nature of the work rather than salary levels. However, working hours had increased from 47.7 to 49.2 hours, with administration growing from 6.4 to 8.4 hours. Job satisfaction and security had fallen significantly and work stress had risen. Significantly, a main source of satisfaction, the opportunity to pursue one's own interests, had declined from 66 per cent of academics to 53 per cent. Some diversity was reported. Women were more likely to be stressed and less likely to be satisfied with opportunities to pursue their interests, but more likely to say their job satisfaction had improved. Late-career academics were most likely to be negative about job satisfaction and outlooks and mid-career academics to be most stressed and overworked. The proportion of part-time and casual staff had increased significantly; for many this was a deliberate choice.

Finkelstein used data from a 1993 survey of 25,000 faculty members to compare new entrants and established staff in USA. The average age of faculty members was high, but there was also a substantial proportion of new staff, a 'new generation', particularly in private research universities. The majority of new staff were in vocational fields. The proportion of women had increased to over 40 per cent, there was more diversity in race and ethnicity and a substantially increased number of non-US-born faculty, particularly in research institutions. The proportion in tenured posts had dropped significantly. Many more staff were in interim postdoctoral positions. There were many more part-time appointees, the majority of whom preferred this. More staff had previous work experience. Satisfaction levels for new staff remained high, but with concerns over job security and advancement opportunities. Both new and established staff were less satisfied with salary and time for scholarship, and women tend to be less satisfied on all scales. New and established staff had similar teaching approaches. New staff were more research-orientated. In research universities the numbers of new staff favouring research as the main promotion determinant and favouring teaching were equal; in other institutions teaching was the preferred factor.

The NCIHE (1997) report included the results of a survey of 809 UK academics. It found teaching concerns about student calibre and poor staff–student ratios, and signs of greater use of learning technologies and interaction with students. Seven in eight staff undertook research. Those who did it spent on average a fifth of their work time on it, and a great deal of their own time too, working mainly for enjoyment and self-improvement. Here, as elsewhere, there were significant differences between pre- and post-1992 institution staff. Half of the sample spent more than 15 per cent of their time on administration, with professorial staff particularly concerned about the burden. Almost all the researchers surveyed were on fixed-term contracts (see Chapter 13), as were more than a quarter of academics, including two-thirds of those aged under 35. Only one in ten academics had worked for more than three months outside the sector, although one in six had worked in a foreign university. Stress, poor pay and job insecurity were concerns, and more than a quarter expected to leave higher education before their retirement age. A little over half of academics had received training in teaching methods, most of them only at the start of their careers. Only half spent more than 1 per cent of their time on self-improvement, although this has probably changed significantly in the last five years (see Chapters 6 and 7) and raises questions about what counts.

It is hard to draw general conclusions from these surveys, although there is remarkable similarity in UK and Australian academics' perceptions of their working situations, in terms of increasing administration and declining job satisfaction and security. Certainly there appears overall to be a more varied profile for academic staff. Partly this reflects, as the US survey shows, a widening of the university through the development of vocational provision. Partly it shows an increase in the number of women in academic life, although heavily skewed to non-promoted posts. Alongside the increasing variety, and related to it, is casualization, which appears to affect all the systems surveyed. All of this has implications for the support of staff, and suggests that the mix of academic staff is changing over time and that varied provision is needed if it is to be appropriate to the widening range.

Role and professionalism

All higher education systems categorize staff, using terms that have considerable historical, social and cultural significance, particularly 'academic' or 'member of faculty'. Occupational groupings of this kind may be beneficial. They provide a context to which staff can relate and a group of peers for support, comparison and self-regulation. They make for convenient, sometimes logical, divisions that assist in description and analysis. Increasingly work roles are set out as lists of functions, in job descriptions and in systems of occupational analysis (Blackmore 1999).

However, role – referring to rights, responsibilities and relationships to other groupings – is more complex than this. Groups are defined by difference from other groups, and relationships between them may be problematic. One group may, through self-interest or a belief in the centrality of its work, seek a dominant position. There may be substantial differences between formal and informal roles. This may occur at a system level, if a formal description does not capture the reality of the job, or at an individual level, where the characteristics of the role holder may make a major difference to the way a role is enacted. Centrally, role boundaries and descriptions are never politically neutral since, whether formally or informally, they have to do with human interrelationships and, usually, access to resources.

Roles fluctuate over time, for a number of reasons. Most powerfully, external conditions, particularly in relation to funding, may affect roles substantially. Work may change in form, requiring groups to interrelate in different ways or calling into question traditional boundaries. A perceived need for equity and efficiency may prompt formal review. For example, equal opportunities concerns require institutions to have defensible practices in the reward of staff.

Many occupations are increasingly professionalized. The benefits have often been stated – classically in Parsons (1954). In complex areas of expertise requiring sophisticated judgement, a profession may protect its members' necessary autonomy and ensure high standards through self-regulation. An equally long tradition asserts that professions may be conspiracies against the public interest and a means of gaining advantage over other occupational groups (Perkin 1989). In an increasingly bureaucratized workplace, professionalization may allow a group to reassert influence over its work (Freidson 1973). The professional status of occupational groups in higher education is therefore a very significant aspect of their roles.

Current issues in academic role

The academic role in flux

The traditional notion of an academic role supposes that a core of staff, who are members of the university rather than simply employees, engage in the academic pursuits of teaching, research and administration. The model still holds in chartered universities in the UK, is enshrined in the tenure system in many US universities, and was to some extent adopted in Australia. There has never been quite such a rigid distinction in the non-chartered UK institutions, although even here there are contractual distinctions between academic and support staff. The argument made for such a relatively privileged arrangement is that universities can be strong, self-governing, self-regulating communities, able to ensure that properly academic decisions are made by those with academic expertise. The counter-argument is that it may stifle competition, encourage complacency and lack of productivity and inhibit the necessary actions of management.

However, the traditional conception of an all-round individualist academic is under heavy pressure. As universities grow, academic numbers remain roughly the same (DeBats and Ward 1998: 103). A great deal of teaching and research is undertaken by staff other than tenured academic staff, so that staffing categories in the UK, USA and Australia now contain major anomalies. For example, over half the undergraduate teaching in Australia is undertaken by part-time and contract staff (Coaldrake and Stedman 1998: 115) and the proportion is similar in many UK courses. In the US system, the proportion of part-time staff exceeds 40 per cent.

New roles outside the academic structure have been established to support academic work. A university cannot now function without substantial information technology support, whilst quality assurance and enhancement, learning resources, research exploitation, international recruitment, press and public relations and many other areas have grown substantially. Very few of these new posts have academic status, even though many of them include academic activity.

An increase in managerialism, evident internationally (Halsey 1992: 303; Trow 1994: 11), has affected many roles and relationships profoundly. Certainly the decline in power, influence and social standing of academic staff on the whole is the most striking aspect of changes in recent years (Halsey 1992), although this has to be seen in the context of an attack on professions in general (Hodkinson and Issitt 1995). Some have concluded that academic staff are becoming a proletariat (Barnett, 1994: 34; Hyland 1996: 168), although differences between senior and junior staff must be noted. Both the UK and Australia have seen a growth in professionalized, and increasingly specialized, university administration. Relationships with academic staff are often productive, but may also be adversarial (DeBats and Ward 1998: 169).

It could be argued that there is now a poor fit between the nature of the work of institutions and the way they are managed, if a higher education institution is viewed as a knowledge-based organization, characterized by 'non-standardisation; creativity; high dependence on individuals; and complex problem solving' (Sveiby 1992). Yet the trend towards managerialism continues, particularly in the highly centralized UK and Australian systems, and staff dissatisfaction with aspects of their work has now reached a high level (Martin 1999). This is particularly significant when academics report that a main motivator keeping them in a poorly paid job is the freedom to pursue their own interests (McInnis 2001: 49).

Academics therefore find themselves with new roles – as consultants, as entrepreneurs, as business managers – but are increasingly bound to departmental and institutional missions. Meanwhile traditionally academic jobs have become in some cases more technical and are increasingly performed by non-academic staff. Some fundamental structural questions arise about the nature of academic role, its continued relevance, its relationship to other roles and its title to professionalism.

Conceptualizing academic expertise

In an era of credentialism, when universities are training and accrediting many professions, higher education has difficulty in coming to terms with its own professionalism, and there is a 'crisis of professional identity' (Nixon 1996: 5). The academic community has a weak claim to being a profession. It has no control over entry or exit or requirement for registration. The most common preparation route, the PhD, is geared towards research but not to other duties. It can be argued that the academic community's grip on its own standards of practice is loose, and amateur in the worst sense. No professional code exists. Standards, of either an ethical or an academic kind, are largely implicit rather than codified. There is no requirement for professional updating in any area of expertise, other than those of external professional bodies, although again that may be about to change (see Chapter 7). Pay levels set against comparable groups (in the UK) indicate that academics do not have full professional status.

Nevertheless there remains a significant although decreasing degree of autonomy and, in many universities, a tradition of collegiality. The notion of peer review is well established, particularly in research, but also through the external examining system in the UK. Many academics have professional ties elsewhere, through subject discipline or vocational links.

There are particular difficulties in conceptualizing academic expertise, for high-status professionalism usually requires the possession of a body of 'hard knowledge' (Schon 1983: 23), but the main constituents of academic work are of different, often uncertain, status. This has particular force in a university, for academic staff are often the creators and are always the custodians of hard academic knowledge (Blackmore 2000: 57). 'Soft knowledge' disciplines have in the main come late to the university, and have a lower academic status. Universities therefore find difficulty in valuing much of the expertise of their own staff, or basing claims to professionalism on it.

Teaching expertise is a particular area of difficulty, compounded perhaps by the underdevelopment of research into learning in higher education, and little engagement with its outcomes by university teachers, so that to many there does not appear to be a substantial knowledge base beyond 'craft knowledge'. Attitudes towards management – a word that still has to be used with care in many contexts – are similarly equivocal, and there is relatively little preparation for management roles. Therefore many academics prefer to base their claim to professionalism on the surer and more accepted foundation of membership of their own disciplinary community. In the U.K., such disciplinary identity may have been re-enforced by successive Research Assessment Exercises (Henkel 2000: 258).

These attitudes underlie and help to produce the research and teaching tension that is such a marked feature of academic life. Most academics see themselves as undertaking both activities (Harvey and Knight 1996: 158). If they are not managed well together, each can damage the other and individuals may have considerable difficulty in dealing with the tension. The balance of prestige between them has certainly shifted over time and is now heavily towards research (Elton 1992: 252). Competitive research funding allocation encourages universities to prioritize research at the expense of teaching, and promotions structures have mirrored this (Luby 1997: 57). It is generally held to be easier to evaluate research excellence than teaching excellence (Swinnerton-Dyer 1991: 208) and most institutions reward research excellence far more than teaching excellence (Hounsell 1994: 98). Some institutions have tried to redress the imbalance (Magin 1998) but it remains a problem that may be increasing. McInnis (2000a: 144) showed that young staff prefer to spend time on research – this may be in part because they are aware of its importance for reward. Given that research opportunities cannot expand to meet all aspirations, there may be tensions that can be resolved by making teaching more attractive and by seeking to lessen the gap between the two activities (see Chapter 11).

Towards an academic profession

Higher education institutions need a core of staff to provide academic identity, continuity and coherence. Academic life has to be sufficiently attractive to retain key staff and to ensure that there will be a next generation of academics. However, the surveys cited show a growth in part-time and casual working, and a growing dissatisfaction with control over work. Academic staff are subject to major tensions in their working lives, which institutional systems often do little to resolve. In many disciplines recruitment is often very difficult.

Professionalization – or perhaps reprofessionalization – of the academic role offers a number of opportunities: to protect the legitimate role of academic judgement; to develop the knowledge base that informs it; to develop capacity for self-evaluation and thus safeguard standards; to counteract fragmentation in academic roles; to give due weight to preparation and updating; and to raise the morale and self-esteem of staff. Probably the most complex aspect of the task is that professionalization has to face in several directions. It has to support the integration of the various components of the academic role at an individual level, whilst taking note of increasing specialization. There is also a danger that professionalization may exclude and disadvantage other groups that are not in the profession. It is particularly important, for reasons explored above, to recognize that academic work is done by many who are not academics, and that teamwork is necessary in the increasingly complex work of teaching and research.

It might be argued that professionalisation is indeed occurring, but that it is fragmented as an inevitable consequence of complexity and specialisation. Professional status, one might conclude, comes in an increasing number of forms through membership of a wide range of disciplinary and professional bodies. This is certainly happening; there are more professional bodies and many staff are members of more than one of them. However, there are obvious disadvantages when individuals' professional affiliations do not cover their full range of roles. Some work areas may be neglected, leading to real or perceived low standards, and thus to managerialist intervention. Some links between roles may not be recognised and supported. Finally, fragmented professionalism divides and weakens the academic community, with results that have already been explored here.

Professionalization is a major project, and one that is unlikely to happen quickly. There is as yet no national body, either in the UK, Australia or the USA, to support the professionalization proposed. Indeed, the UK's Institute for Learning and Teachng has, as its name suggests, the aim of raising the status of teaching, as a counterweight to research. Whilst some staff have welcomed the attention thus paid to teaching, others have not found it an attractive professional model. There remains a vacant space for a professional body for academic practice, and the current review of UK enhancement bodies, whose outcome is unclear at the time of writing (September 2002), may yet produce movement towards that goal. However, development is in any case possible at an institutional level, through probationary and continuing professional development arrangements, performance review and promotions procedures.

The prescriptions that follow are practical and achievable. They may appear restricted, and indeed they are, since institutions have limited power to facilitate professionalisation. Some are simply good development practice, and some are already taking place. However, ownership is a key difference. For all professional groups there is a difficult balance between accountability and autonomy. At present, a growing managerialism, encouraged by the academic community's failure to define academic work on a professional basis, is moving universities away from achieving such a balance. Real professionalisation will not be achieved by further extension of management-determined standards and structures. As far as possible, they should be produced and safeguarded by those who are undertaking academic work. In that respect, the Institute for Learning and Teaching in Higher Education's focus as a membership organization is praiseworthy.

The implications for staff development

Universities neglect their stock of human capital (Keep *et al.* 1996). Ironically, institutions that provide professional development for others do little of it for themselves. Yet staff expertise is the most important asset in a university; without it literally nothing can be achieved. Its development should be a vital and central function. Staff development should here be understood broadly, referring to the structures, processes and provision that enable an institution to recruit and retain staff appropriately skilled to undertake its mission. It has to do with roles and relationships, resources, incentives and rewards. It ensures that all staff are fully prepared for their work, that staff are able to develop to their full potential, and that they work efficiently and effectively, both individually and collaboratively. Therefore staff development includes induction, probation and continuing professional development. It extends far beyond the limited set of functions that are commonly labelled as 'staff development'.

No single prescription can be offered for all institutions, since there are substantial differences among them, not least in the relative size of research and teaching activities. These differences are currently masked in the UK and Australia by centralized university organization and funding. In addition, institutions in all three main systems under consideration here have converged on a single, research-led model, resulting in distortion of their missions and practices. However, the differences are substantial and there may be greater diversity to come if pressure groups lobbying for differential fees in the UK and Australia are successful, and where more entrepreneurial approaches produce alternative sources of income for universities. If this happens, institutions may wish to develop more varied staffing profiles, and there may be less movement of staff between the layers of a stratified system (Altbach 1995: 11).

Staffing structures and categories

In many institutions, staffing structures are out of alignment with operational reality. The issue is a complex one, where there are obvious national constraints and institutional sensitivities, but at institutional level changes can be made.

Categorization of staff is highly contentious. The notion of a body of academic staff has an enduring appeal – certainly to academic staff themselves – and there are strong arguments for a degree of autonomy and control over academic matters. The question is whether to leave the situation as it is, so that with time the academic body in a university becomes less representative and less relevant, although with a capacity to obstruct, or whether to work towards its reform in a professional and inclusive way.

In practical terms, this probably means increasing the number of academic staff, by giving academic status to those who undertake either teaching or research only. Some would resist this fiercely, and there are certainly strong arguments for retaining a unified role so that one activity can inform the other. However, there is no good argument for relegating to a second-class status all those who are employed to undertake only teaching or only research, as happens at present. Oddly, those who are employed both to teach and to research but who do little or nothing of the former are frequently held in the highest esteem of all. Recent discussion on scholarship provides a means of looking beyond the two terms to a unifying factor, and is discussed below.

The position of professional administrative staff may also benefit from review. McInnis (1998) found that they differed from academic staff in their views, that they were in general more positive about their work and their institution and impatient with academic staff attitudes towards administrators. Parity of esteem between them and academic staff is hard to achieve but is important if an organization is to gain the best from all staff. The division is, at the level of work done, increasingly blurred. Teaching and, to some extent, research have become part of the work of many staff in information services, in staff and educational development units and in some departmentally based support roles. Many administrative staff have PhDs and some are qualified to teach. Furthermore, many academic staff are not research active, many have no teaching qualification and some spend a great deal of time on tasks that are administrative. Yet it is extremely uncommon for support staff to be redesignated as academic staff or vice versa. If staff are to continue to be categorized in this way, it should be obvious why a member of staff is qualified to be an academic in all aspects of the role, and it should be possible for staff to cross the divide, in either direction, with no alteration in status.

Part-time and short-term contract staff present another structural challenge. In both the UK and Australia, an increasing proportion of academic work is undertaken by such staff, although less so than in the US system (DeBats and Ward 1998: 103). This is not always exploitative: many staff prefer to work part-time, and many disciplines benefit from part-time work by practising professionals. However, some staff may find themselves in insecure and poorly paid employment, on the periphery of the institution for which they work. Increasing the proportion of part-time and short-term staff may worsen the workload for permanent staff, in that the major tasks of a department, including communicating with and supporting part-time staff, may fall on relatively fewer shoulders. Whilst the financial attractiveness of decreasing the proportion of full-time permanent staff is obvious, therefore, there are hidden costs, and the trend is undesirable. For staff development, there is a major task in ensuring that part-time and casual staff receive equal and appropriate support.

Defining academic expertise

Traditionally, many professions have had no explicit code of practice or set of functions, but this is not now tenable, and most professions have adopted a social market approach (Elliott 1993) and have become more specific about the components of their work. Professionalization requires that some statements be made about the nature of the role. A broad ethical code would probably not be too hard to achieve at any level within an education system, provided there was a forum for discussion and decision acceptable to those involved. Certainly an Australian study found a surprisingly high level of agreement among academic staff about their shared values (McInnis 1992: 10) and a U.K. study noted continuing stability in academic values (Henkel 2000: 257). Acceptability of such a code would no doubt increase with its generality. Specific statements of expertise in any areas of academic role can be highly contentious, as the furore over a draft set of competences for the UK's Institute for Learning and Teaching in Higher Education (1999) showed. There are difficult areas to do with simplistic representation of complex skills, with allowance for local context, and so on. However, some statements about what constitutes proficiency and perhaps excellence are possible, initially locally agreed. Indeed, for teaching at least, they have commonly been agreed within institutions and, in the UK, nationally. Again, very general statements are likeliest to win wide support, certainly at the outset.

Continuing professional development

An ethical code and statements of expertise provide a vocabulary and a means of measurement for inclusion in systems of probation and continuing professional development.

In many institutions research capability is monitored carefully during probation. Confirmation of appointment may require completion of a PhD, for example. With the exception of the UK, most systems have a very low entry requirement for teaching expertise, and this has to be raised if teaching performance is to be universally of a professional standard.

Continuing professional development requires a systematic career-long approach to performance review and development. Appraisal has a substantial history in UK higher education, having been introduced in 1988 as a central government initiative. Current practice is extremely patchy (Hughes 1999), and recent proposals to introduce performance-related pay as part of institutional human resource strategies will lead to review. Australian review arrangements are currently dealt with under enterprise bargaining arrangements at institutional level. Formal review is often not a popular activity, either with reviewers or with those being reviewed, and it is necessary to ensure that staff feel – and have – some ownership of the professional standards. Crucially, they need to feel that something happens as a result of the process taking place.

Common standards can coexist with an acceptance that careers take many shapes. It is not helpful to measure all academic careers against the idealized profile of a research scientist (McInnis 1992: 11). Staff have very different strengths, and teaching, research, administration and other academic activities all have to be valued. Further, the balance of activities may change substantially over a working life. Indeed, a varied career may be a great deal more stimulating (Baldwin and Blackburn 1981: 62). Review can support those changes.

Increased emphasis on continuing professional development is likely to lead to a need for more staff development provision. However, McInnis's survey shows that a relatively small number of established staff undertake formal staff development activity. Most of those who do are not enthusiastic about the quality of what is provided. The message for staff developers is an obvious one, if continuing professional development is to capture academics' attention and gain their respect.

Balancing aspects of academic role

Rewards significantly affect the relative importance that staff attach to aspects of their work although, interestingly, studies of academic staff show stronger intrinsic than extrinsic motivation. Money is not the only criterion (McInnis 2001: 53). The weighting given to academic activities should presumably be in keeping with the institution's mission, so one can expect variation, but where an activity occurs in an institution, those who undertake it should surely expect to be valued and rewarded appropriately.

Of course some institutions are predominantly either teaching- or research-focused, and some staff may in practice be engaged solely in one or the other activity. Clearly the notion that all academic staff should both teach and research does not always hold good. The two activities could be separated altogether, as frequently happens at present, so that staff are either teachers or researchers. Attention then has to be paid to incentives, rewards and progression if one of the paths is not to be a poor relation.

However, there are obvious difficulties in such a separation. Research activity can beneficially inform teaching and vice versa, as is argued in Chapter 11. Separation makes this less likely. It might be more fruitful to look beyond the terms and note that both activities require capabilities in common. Elton (1992: 256) laments 'the dichotomy of research and teaching' and argues for scholarship, which he defines as 'deep understanding of knowledge' informing both research and teaching. Boyer's (1990) four-part model of the scholarships of discovery, integration, application and teaching is widely cited as a means by which the fragmenting conception of the academic can be brought together.

Surveys of academic staff, such as those cited earlier, generally show support for parity of esteem for teaching and research, as well as a belief that there is no parity at present, and this is in keeping with many staff developers' experiences of difficulties with institutions' reward systems, particularly in relation to teaching development. The reward of teaching is significantly inhibited by the belief that teaching performance cannot reliably be measured. Institutions can and do devise relatively streamlined qualitative processes, supported sometimes by more quantitative indicators. Criteria can be expressed at a number of different performance levels, against which judgements can be made. One challenge may be to assist in the adoption of such approaches and in the briefing and preparation of promotions committees that use them.

The role of management remains an equivocal one, discussed in more depth in Chapter 9. Whilst some institutions have fairly extensive management development programmes, this is by no means the norm. Many staff therefore find themselves in quite significant management roles without a great deal of preparation. The previously noted trend for a separation between departmental and cross-institutional management may to an extent be inevitable, but may not be healthy.

Leadership and management development is probably the next major growth area for staff development.

Diversity

Being strategic requires that an overview be taken, but without losing sight of differences among those at work. Studies of academic work show that staff often have different views about their role according to their career stage (McInnis 2000b: vii). Their preference for teaching or research, their interest in taking a management role, their willingness to work long hours, may all be affected. There may be a generational divide. One U.K. study found young, academic staff were more 'ambitious, determined and focused', and more accepting of external accountability and of performance evaluation (Henkel 2000: 205). Similarly, gender makes a difference not just to attitudes to work, but to the likelihood of obtaining a post and of gaining promotion.

Credentialled staff development

The growth of credentialism has been noted. This has to be approached with caution. Since academic staff invest many years in achieving a PhD, the idea of further accredited provision will not necessarily seem attractive. However, it is interesting that in the UK, the completion of a certificate course in teaching is now mandatory even in most research-intensive universities (Blackmore 2001). There may also be a case for the strong encouragement of promoted staff to undertake formal management development. Use of the best contemporary approaches to professional development (which universities themselves use for other professional groups) would ensure that such courses were directly helpful and effective. Mentoring, coaching, work shadowing and action learning sets may be much more appropriate ways of developing some forms of expertise than short courses (see Chapter 10). Certification may be desirable, in that it can add coherence and academic credibility.

A possible future

Commentators are largely in agreement that the outlook for universities and for academic staff is not a cheerful one. Government action, budgetary constraints, social and cultural changes all present challenges to universities that are likely to make life no easier than it has been in the past decade. A legacy of highly interventionist government is that universities have become used to responding to external requirements, but have become less confident, with less of a distinct sense of purpose. The capacity for 'genuine self-production' (Marginson and Considine 2000: 6) has been eroded. Staff may feel demoralized and cut off from previous certainties. Compounding this, it is claimed, is the growth of an executive style of management, removed from and suspicious of traditional academic concerns (Marginson and Considine 2000). Nevertheless, there is evidence that many younger staff feel more positive about their work than do older colleagues, and it is important that this attitude is reinforced (McInnis 2001: 50).

Professionalization of academic work offers a means of protecting much that is valuable in a higher education institution and that distinguishes it from any other organization. It also offers a means of bridging the apparent divide between senior managers and the departmentally based academic heartlands, since it is a way of improving working effectiveness that has the potential to gain wide support from the academic community. If Higher Education academic communities were to review and re-define academic work, placing it on a more secure, inclusive professional footing, the prospects for universities and for those who work in them would be a great deal more cheerful.

Key learning points

Senior staff

- Review staffing categorizations for their appropriateness and equity.
- Work with staff to develop an ethical code and broad statements of expertise, to inform development, evaluation, incentives and rewards.
- Ensure that all academic activities are appropriately valued and rewarded, including the adoption of a robust means of evaluating teaching, within a continuing professional development framework.
- Review policy and current situation regarding casualization and devise ways of reducing it or counteracting its negative consequences.

Heads of department

- Maintain a system of supportive developmental review for staff, which may be the institutional appraisal scheme, where that is in place and working effectively.
- Review use of part-time and casual staff and ensure that they are appropriately included and supported.

Professional staff developers

- Review definition of staff development and its forms, with the aim of engaging all staff appropriately throughout their working lives.
- Take an academic practice perspective, taking account of the whole staff role – even where the staff development remit is for teaching.
- Pay particular attention to part-time and casual staff support.

3

The challenge of lifelong learning

Stella Parker

Introduction

Lifelong learning is a term that is relatively new to higher education but already seems to have a ring of familiarity within the UK. This may be due to high-profile publications (National Committee of Inquiry into Higher Education (NCIHE) 1997; National Advisory Group for Continuing Education and Lifelong Learning 1997; Department for Education and Employment 1998) which stress the importance of lifelong learning. In addition, several new posts have recently appeared in higher education, with titles such as professor of lifelong learning or director of lifelong learning, some of them having cross-institutional responsibility for research and development in the field. There is evidence that at least some of these new posts are rebranded versions of precursors located in units of continuing education, but nonetheless it seems that higher education is prepared to signal publicly that lifelong learning is part of its mission.

Even though relatively new to higher education, lifelong learning has been part of the vocabulary of specialist educational circles for the past three decades, although initially referred to as lifelong education (rather than learning). Now it has moved from the preserve of specialist circles towards the centre of higher education, it may be helpful to unpick the meaning of lifelong learning and to explore the challenges it poses. This chapter will attempt to do this and illustrate some of the consequences for staff development in higher education.

The discussion here is too short to cover in any detail the background to the genesis of the ideas that underpin lifelong learning, as their roots lie in the socio-economic changes that are characteristic of the past 40 years or so, particularly in the economically powerful countries. The changes are the result of political, economic and demographic factors (Scott 1995) and have gone hand in hand with changes in the educational aspirations and systems of many countries in the developed world (Schuetze and Slowey 2000). In the UK, for example, there are government plans to raise participation in higher education to 50 per cent by 2010.

Alongside the increase in the proportion of traditional students going on to higher education, there has been a parallel growth in adult enrolments. This has happened without any planning at national level. The majority of these older students study on a part-time basis and, for the purposes of this chapter, they are referred to as adult students. Technically, adult students are those aged 21 years or over when enrolling on a first degree or 25 years or over when enrolling on a postgraduate degree. Overall they represent 53 per cent of undergraduate students and 70 per cent of postgraduates (Universities UK 2001a). Their educational requirements have challenged higher education to become a more comprehensive sector dealing with a wider range of students, who balance the demands of life and work with the demands of study. These demands will be examined in more detail below, but we begin by looking at the origins of the concept of lifelong learning.

The concept of lifelong learning

Lifelong learning's antecedents can be traced back to discussions held in the 1960s by educationalists whose academic interests lay mainly in the education of adults. These educationalists pointed out that, whilst there was almost universal agreement that children had a right to education, there was no universal agreement about the rights of adults. The idea that all adults should have access to state-supported education has taken much longer to develop, and arguably is still in its infancy. This is despite the historical evidence provided by Kelly (1992) and Rose (2001), both showing a latent demand for formal adult learning.

Throughout the 1960s and into the early 1970s, in the UK and elsewhere, there had been an unprecedented demand from adults for learning for job-related reasons, for leisure or for interest. This formal, organized educational provision was the result of an expansion of higher education (Neave and van Vught 1991). The expansion, together with the general explosion in other sources of knowledge (the media, newspapers, magazines, television, film and radio), provided the potential for people to know more about their world than ever before. Inevitably, the consequences of this knowledge explosion became the subject of debate at international level, particularly amongst those who were interested in the effects it could have on society in general.

Arising from these debates, one official outcome was a publication from the United Nations Educational, Scientific and Cultural Organization (UNESCO 1972). This report delineated lifelong education, the aim of which was to enhance the quality of life for individuals. Essentially the concept was based on the idea that education should be made a universal right for adults and that higher education (then the preserve of relatively few) should be made available to all, through policies aimed at widening access.

The ideas contained in UNESCO's report were not then universally adopted but did re-emerge in the 1990s in a publication from the Commission of the European Communities (CEC 1994) which argued for extending educational opportunities to adults on the basis that education and training are the key to economic competitiveness. This paper was later accompanied by others (CEC 1995; Organization for Economic Co-operation and Development 1996, 1998) whose various themes were picked up in the UK by the Labour government soon after it took office in 1997. It inherited the Dearing Report (NCIHE 1997) from its predecessor (the Conservative government) and commissioned other high-profile reports (referred to above) on post-school education. These reports and the government's responses to them are underpinned by a concept of lifelong learning, which is strongly influenced by European ideas. Consequently, the UK government is now committed to an international movement which aims to raise the educational aspirations and achievements of all from 'cradle to grave'.

The stakeholders in lifelong learning

Lifelong learning (as we have seen) is a concept with heterogeneous origins and is now on the agenda of many governments, all of which have different ideas about how to implement it. Belanger (1998) argues that these differences are not surprising because the concept has had insufficient time to develop and thus has not achieved a common and universal understanding. Despite this, there are several related themes running through many governments' policies on lifelong learning in higher education (Gorard *et al.* 1997). The first is premised on social justice and social inclusion. Higher education is the only educational sector to which there is not universal access (in contrast to primary and secondary education), and in the UK it draws its intake from the relatively affluent (NCIHE 1997). Higher education is thus ripe for widening participation, to promote social inclusion and at the same time to accommodate at least some of the rising demands for learning beyond school. The second theme is premised on economic imperatives and the role that higher education plays in raising education and skill levels, so contributing to national economic success. However, these demands are unlikely to be satisfied by a gradual expansion of traditional state-funded education, nor are governments willing to commit to the expenditure that this entails. Other ways of delivering education and training are therefore a focus of government policies, including the formation of partnerships at local and regional level with other providers and with industry, commerce and e-learning. The third theme is the role of higher education in improving the quality of life by providing (*inter alia*) learning for pleasure, for leisure and for personal fulfilment (see Chapter 15 for an initiative based on this theme).

These three themes are not necessarily compatible, and may exist side by side within any one set of policies. But government policies represent the interests of only one set of stakeholders that shape the nature of higher education. There are two other stakeholders, one being the 'market' (students and employers), the other being the staff working in higher education (Clarke 1983; Young 1999). If this analysis is correct, then there are three groups of stakeholders each adhering to their own version of lifelong learning, and they have not yet worked out common grounds (Aspin and Chapman 2000). These three stakeholders will continue to be the main forces that affect the future of lifelong learning in higher education. In this chapter the UK will be used to illustrate how the interaction of these groups of stakeholders can shape the development of lifelong learning, but similar developments arising from the interaction of the three sets of stakeholders are in evidence in other countries too (Schuetze and Slowey 2000).

Governments as stakeholders

Scott (2000) argues that the UK government's agenda for lifelong learning beyond school (i.e. tertiary education) is a continuation of an agenda that began in the 1960s with the aim of making all secondary education comprehensive (secondary schools were then selective, with only a small elite going on to academic study beyond the age of 11 years). Scott's argument implies that lifelong learning, as an overarching theme, can unite and rationalize tertiary education in the UK, which currently consists of higher education (universities and colleges of higher education) and colleges of further education. If this is the case, then we should expect to see government policies aimed at a dissolution of the boundaries between higher education and other forms of tertiary education, together with imperatives designed to widen participation. In the UK there are few government policies with lifelong learning in their title that refer to higher education (Lifelong Learning News 2001), but there are initiatives that pioneer the development of higher education in new educational territory, and others that open higher education to new groups of students. Since the publication of the Dearing Report (NCIHE 1997) there has been a raft of funding incentives aimed at widening participation, particularly for young people. Government targets are for 50 per cent of 18–30-year-olds to be enrolled in higher education by 2010, although some of this may be delivered in colleges of further education. This aim has produced an unprecedented flurry of activities such as funding incentives for institutions of higher education to provide summer schools and Excellence in Cities programmes, together with government grants (channelled through the higher education funding councils) to institutions to encourage student diversity such as the Excellence Challenge (Department for Education and Skills 2000). The numerous publications available on the Higher Education Funding Council for England (HEFCE) website (HEFCE 2001a) provide further evidence of the seriousness with which this issue is being taken at national level. To assist institutions in developing effective activities to widen participation, the funding council has an access consultancy service, the Access Advisory Partnership, which aims to support the transition towards new forms of higher education that are more inclusive and equitable. In June 2001 Universities UK (whose membership is drawn from the heads of all UK universities) issued a statement produced by its strategy group on widening participation and lifelong learning (Universities UK 2001b). The statement announced the strategy group's initiatives, which include the New Opportunities for All Concordat, reports on good practice in widening participation, funding for innovation and for research on barriers to access for students. Furthermore it stated its support for the government's aim of increasing the numbers of 18–30-year-olds in higher education. The universities also announced that, through collaborative efforts, they would narrow the gap in participation between the most affluent and least affluent socio-economic groups; improve retention and progression for certain groups; and narrow performance gaps between subjects and between universities (Universities UK 2001b).

In addition to promoting diversity, there are government initiatives aimed at the promotion of partnerships between higher education and other agencies (HEFCE 2001a). These agencies include further education colleges, employers and the business and industrial communities. The newly launched two-year foundation degrees are an example of such collaboration, the degrees being tailor-made for employees and delivered in collaboration with further education. Another example of partnership arrangements is the eUniversity project 'UK eUniversities Worldwide' with Sun Microsystems, further education colleges and private sector partners (HEFCE 2001b). Yet another example, the University for Industry (UFI) delivers distance learning via information technology. The UFI is a new variant of higher education, with programmes that can be delivered to many different sites. Its future survival depends on its commercial success, unlike other forms of state-subsidized education. A final example is Higher Education Reach-out to Business and the Community (HEROBC), which aims to link higher education with commerce and industry.

The initiatives described above are just a selection of the many that are now in train. They have implications for staff development, as institutions are likely to require the development or enhancement of marketing and publicity strategies to reach previously underrepresented groups; training for admissions tutors when dealing with non-standard applicants; training in advice, learning support and guidance for relevant staff; development of flexible curricula, including exit at points other than at degree level; and enhanced career advice and guidance services.

Each of the above initiatives involves a change in the role of academic staff from autonomous professionals to collaborative partners in the design and delivery of new forms of provision. This role change presents a major shift in traditional academic practice, mainly because it challenges the status of professional knowledge and the authority of 'the teacher'. It requires a move away from didacticism and towards facilitation, and this is more likely to happen if supported by staff development. In fact, staff development will be required for each of the above initiatives if they are to be successfully embedded in higher education.

National policy initiatives have also been established in relation to the quality of teaching. These may also impact on lifelong learning, if they help to improve teaching quality and thus have an effect on retention and later participation rates.

Employers and adult students as stakeholders

The increase in participation by 18–21-year-olds in the UK changed higher education from an elite to a mass system. Adult students played their role in this massification, but they are now moving higher education towards lifelong learning which, in its many different forms, may not even be regarded as higher education by some. The adults who are returning to higher education are but the tip of an iceberg – even greater numbers of adults engage in learning activities at work, in further education colleges, in local education authority provision and in community education (Kennedy 1997). In other words, learning at intervals throughout life is part of the lifestyle of many adults – at least one in four in the UK now does so (Sargant 2000). Participation rates are likely to increase as educational achievement rises and as people live longer.

Adult enrolments, according to the evidence to date, are found mainly in occupational updating programmes. There is every reason to suggest that this will continue (Gorard *et al.* 1997), although learners aged 50 or over tend to engage in a wider range of programmes that enable them to pursue study for its own sake. Whatever their motivation, adults tend to favour programmes that do not conform to the traditional full-time mode. Indeed, the further the mode of provision departs from traditional degree arrangements, the greater the number of adult enrolments (Universities UK 2001a). In addition to non-accredited short courses, there are two other modes of study that enrol adults almost exclusively: these include award-bearing sub-degree programmes and part-time degrees.

In 2000, there were just over 750,000 adult enrolments on non-accredited short updating courses in UK higher education (Ramsden 2001). Generally, such courses are not assessed and may form part of a loosely coupled programme to which other agencies such as professional bodies, independent profit-making organizations and employers may also contribute. Any occupational group could therefore experience a range of *ad hoc* providers contributing over time to their work-based updating. Currently this state of affairs is regarded as acceptable, but consider how we would regard such unregulated diverse provision as a basis for undergraduate curricula or for initial professional training. It would probably be regarded as rather odd (at least) because there are universally accepted views about the structure of undergraduate curricula and/or initial training. Society insists that these forms of initial education and training should be coherent and regulated, with standards that can be maintained. But there is as yet no universally accepted view about the structure of curricula that are lifelong, and most adult education or training curricula have been heavily influenced by models that exist in schooling (institutionally located, teacher-dominated, etc.). Clearly staff development in higher education can have a role in the systematic development of curricula at this level and can rise to the challenge of ensuring that these curricula (where appropriate) lead to credit-bearing awards. We need to bear in mind that if adults wish to keep up to date throughout their working lives, then this implies a period of up to 30 or 40 years of intermittent education and/or training. The UK's national qualifications framework (in common with similar frameworks in other countries) assumes that accredited learning stops at doctoral level and so is not appropriate for accrediting learning over a period of 30 to 40 years – so what is to be done? Herein lies a challenge for staff development in higher education.

For adults, the second most popular type of higher education is classified as 'other undergraduate', and accounted for approximately 155,300 adult enrolments in 2000 (Universities UK 2001a). Essentially, these are programmes that are credit-bearing and can lead to certificates, diplomas or simply to institutional credit. Postgraduate degree programmes are the third most frequently chosen by adult students, with 100,800 enrolled on postgraduate degrees, and undergraduate degrees are fourth, with 90,400 enrolments (Universities UK 2001a). These enrolments are in disciplines and fields that are professionally and vocationally relevant (Watson and Taylor 1997). Many occupationally related programmes involve collaborative provision, with higher education institutions working in partnership with employers, professional bodies or other interest groups to design and deliver them (Langley 2000). In some cases, large employers design their own programmes, importing academics or other specialists into their own corporate universities (Cervero 2001).

Where the ever-growing demand for occupationally relevant programmes encounters the supply of traditional academic values, there is the potential for conflict. This is because the aims and practices of higher education are controlled by those who work there – they are used to setting the learning agenda and deciding what is to be taught and how. If they are required to accommodate the demands of others then, effectively, they are being asked to relinquish their control to a greater or lesser extent. Collaborative provision thus represents a fundamental challenge to higher education and staff development can have a role in preparing staff to grasp this nettle.

Higher education staff as stakeholders

We have seen that higher education institutions in the UK appear to have had considerable success in adapting to the changes that led to their massification. Whilst massification has been embraced more readily by some institutions than by others, the change has been relatively gradual and incremental; it has not been the result of explicit policies aimed at changing higher education from an elite to a mass sector. The national agenda for lifelong learning is, however, different. Essentially higher education is being subjected to reforms similar to those experienced by both primary and secondary education in the last century. These reforms aim to make it less exclusive and more accessible to new learners, drawn both from the traditional 18–21 age group and from older learners. Lifelong learning thus appears to represent a significant challenge for the sector and the challenge can only be met if staff in higher education develop new sets of values, assumptions and norms. The changes will be needed for all staff working in higher education but especially for those at the institutional operating core, which is where the academic staff responsible for teaching and learning are located. They have the main responsibility for delivering the educational programmes of their institutions and, as professionals, they hold well-developed views about their autonomy, their relationship with students, the purpose of higher education, their relationships (if any) with employers and other external agents. They are likely to be resistant to changes that may appear to debase their notions of academic knowledge and of professionalism, but the institutions in which they are employed are unlikely to change unless these staff change too. One way of effecting such changes is through programmes of planned staff development.

Staff development for lifelong learning

At institutional level, change is unlikely to happen unless top management is able to create an acceptable vision for the future and to communicate this effectively.

Daft (1997) and Senge (1993) both describe how this can happen in a 'learning organization' and their views may be useful here. In addition to having a team of top managers with vision, their model of the learning organization has flat structures, and well-informed employees who work closely in teams to identify and solve problems and who pull in the same direction (see Chapter 1). The role of staff development is to mediate this vision, to work towards gaining consent and commitment and to neutralize opposition.

This model of an idealized learning organization may not reflect the reality of organizations in higher education, but it does imply that staff development is central to organizational change strategies. Although there are many definitions of staff development, it is normally considered to include the institutional policies and programmes that support staff, both personally and professionally, in achieving their own and their institutional needs. In higher education, this generally centres on the enhancement of teaching and learning, and in reality refers to the continuing professional development of staff involved in this core activity. Whether or not staff development in higher education is regarded as pivotal in organizational change is open to question, and there is little clarity about the role that staff development has played overall in the change from an elite to a mass system. Furthermore, there appears to be no universal model for delivering staff development for all institutions of higher education in the UK. A recent national survey indicates that staff development in institutions of higher education is delivered from several different outlets within any one institution (Universities' and Colleges' Staff Development Agency (UCoSDA, 2000). These outlets include central staff and educational development units, subject-based units (for example, education departments) and administrative units such as computing services. In general, staff development units (wherever located) deliver to all categories of staff, who may number up to several thousand in any one institution. The UCoSDA survey indicates the relatively small size of the central units (4–12 staff), and inevitably there are questions as to whether or not such units have the potency to contribute significantly towards organizational change.

There are many topics that could form the basis of a lifelong learning programme for staff who are engaged in delivering lifelong learning. An agenda for action has been covered in the earlier part of this chapter and includes development for: promoting diversity; promoting partnerships in learning; the development of distance learning and the use of e-learning; quality assurance procedures for these forms of learning; enhancing the quality of teaching; leadership and management.

If this provides some ideas on the content of staff development for lifelong learning, what about the models for its delivery? According to Boud and MacDonald (1981) there are three delivery models to be found in higher education. The first is the professional service model, where development focuses on the acquisition by teaching staff of technical skills such as audio-visual aids or multimedia. The second is a counselling model where teaching staff work with staff developers to overcome classroom-based problems and seek solutions. The third is a collegial model where developers and teaching staff work together to improve practice. All three have their strengths and weaknesses, so Boud and MacDonald suggest that all three models be drawn upon, depending on the uniqueness of each situation.

As individuals and occupational groups attempt to maintain the advantages of being in employment and to keep abreast of socio-economic changes, their demands for lifelong learning are likely to increase. Over time, the current unsophisticated notions of continuing professional development are likely to become more coherent, with higher education playing an important role as a producer for other occupational groups. The same changes are likely to take place in relation to the professional development of higher education staff, as is suggested by Cervero's (2001) study of the trends in the continuing professional development of a range of occupational groups. The trends are described below, and there is some evidence to indicate that they are beginning to be manifest in staff development in higher education.

The first trend is that many in employment increasingly expect work-based education and training, and the provision of such education and training is becoming more coherently organized and less *ad hoc* and reactive. In higher education, funding council grants for coherent staff development plans are reinforcing this trend, and grants are available through a teaching quality enhancement fund to enhance teaching and learning (HEFCE 2000). There is evidence that significant amounts of staff development resources are being devoted to initial teacher training and membership of the Institute for Learning and Teaching in Higher Education (UCoSDA 2000, Chapter 7).

The second trend is that employers and employees increasingly expect employment-related study to be credit-bearing and lead to recognized awards. In higher education, this is now manifest in credit-bearing initial teacher training programmes for new teaching staff. The third trend concerns the regulation of professional practice. Will those working in higher education be expected to 'renew their licence to practise' through participation in continuing professional development programmes? This is a trend which is established in many professional groups in the USA (Cervero 2001), and whilst all occupational groups in the UK do not insist on regulating their members in this way, there is evidence that many professional groups are moving in this direction (Parker 1998).

A fourth trend is the growing importance of partnership in the design and delivery of occupationally relevant programmes. One innovative example is a higher education partnership between institutions from different member states of the European Union. The outcome is a staff-training programme that draws upon the particular strengths of each institution, with each being responsible for delivering a part of the whole (Dale 2000). Other more established examples in higher education include partnerships with consultants and with privately run training organizations such as the Office for Public Management that exists to provide such services.

The fifth trend is an increase in the use of web-based distance learning for many forms of occupationally related training. In higher education, the HEFCE has set up 24 subject centres that aim to encourage the development of good practice in teaching and learning (Learning and Teaching Support Network 2001, see Chapter 6 below). The centres communicate with teaching staff mainly through electronic means, aiming to draw together good practice in learning and teaching. A sixth trend involves the role of corporate higher education. Cervero (2001) considers the development of corporate higher education still to be in its early stages of development, but cites as an example the Argosy Education Group Inc. which awards (*inter alia*) higher degrees in education.

Conclusion

The lifelong learning agenda represents just one of several external factors that are likely to have an impact on the internal environment of higher education institutions over the near future. If institutions are to respond to these external factors in a co-ordinated and coherent way, what are the challenges for staff development? This is probably for institutions to decide for themselves, but questions arise at several different levels within any institution.

Firstly, at senior strategic level, where (arguably) the responsibility for scanning the institution's external environment is located, should those with overall responsibility for staff development be part of the institution's strategic management team?

A second and related question at strategic level is concerned with the role of staff development in organizational change. Should staff development be reactive and responsive by equipping staff with the skills needed to cope in response to foreseen and planned change? Alternatively, should it be geared towards helping staff to be proactive and anticipate the changes heralded by lifelong learning? How can these questions be best resolved?

At departmental level, there are issues concerned with equal opportunities and access to staff development. Occupationally related education and training tend to be the preserve of the well educated and affluent (Sargant 2000). For those employed in higher education, the better qualified tend to be better paid, but this generalization is crude – for example, male academic staff tend to earn more than women despite both being equally qualified. There are contractual differences, too – for example, between full-time and part-time workers. If higher education has a commitment to the equity principles underpinning lifelong learning, then how can this be demonstrated through its staff development policies?

Also at departmental level, managers are likely to work with individuals to identify their staff development needs through (say) appraisal. Although staff development can be viewed as a vehicle solely for improving work-related performance, it can be seen as an opportunity for personal development, too. Should departmental managers ensure that the personal development needs of their staff are met through staff development, and if so, how can this best be done?

For those involved in delivering staff development there are two questions, the first of which is whether there are lessons to be learned from the trends identified by Cervero. The second question focuses on the major challenge of identifying suitable models for the delivery of occupational education and training as staff development tends to be based on episodes of theoretical input supposedly followed by practical application. According to Cervero (2001), this is the least successful way to develop anything other than the most basic of skills. Is it possible to develop other more integrated forms of learning which rely less on models borrowed from schooling (the education of children) and more on models based on how adults can continue to learn throughout their lives?

Key learning points

Senior staff

1. Staff development needs to be part of the agenda for the senior management team as the lifelong learning agenda has fundamental implications for the academic role and the shape of institutions. There is a case for including the functional head of SD on the senior team to ensure pro-active shaping SD rather than just responsive actions (see Chapter 1).
2. The lifelong learning agenda has major implications for the way in which institutions treat their own staff, raising issues of equity in career development across and within staff groups including in SD provision for personal development.
3. SD needs arising from the lifelong learning agenda are substantial at both operational level (for example basic skills training) and strategic levels (for example in facilitating organizational change and defusing resistance). SD has a key part to play in enabling a shift in the academic role from autonomous professionals to collaborators in learning. It is doubtful whether existing SD units have the size and capacity to address the agenda adequately without additional resource.

Heads of department

1. Departments have a major role to play in ensuring implementation of the lifelong learning agenda for actual and potential students (for example in relation to curriculum development and delivery) and for staff. Staff development needs to be a high priority and actively organized at this level, drawing on appropriate resources within and outside the university or college. Part of such work may involve facilitating changes in attitudes and orientations (see Chapter 10).
2. One strand of lifelong learning emphasizes personal growth and development which some argue is integral to achieving learning organizations too (see Chapter 1). To what extent do departments commit resources to all staff to encourage personal development?

Professional staff developers

1. Lifelong learning presents an opportunity to create a pro-active shaping SD function that is central to organizational change and life. Embrace it.
2. The breadth of needs is enormous and SD functions will need to operate at a variety of levels and across staff groups. Alliances with other providers will be necessary, prioritization and more resources.
3. The lifelong learning agenda is likely to stimulate demand from staff for more coherent and accredited provision rather than ad hoc, menu-style provision. There is a need for many SD functions to re-orient their efforts and enhance their own skills.

4

Promoting entrepreneurship in higher education

Martin Binks and Edward Lumsdaine

Introduction

The increasing emphasis upon entrepreneurship in higher education has implications for staff development strategies. To understand them it is necessary to consider the sources of this relatively recent phenomenon in education policy. This chapter will identify the key manifestations of this trend in terms of curriculum innovation and technology transfer and will consider its implications for staff development. A case study using examples from the USA will provide additional information, and strategies to encourage entrepreneurship in universities will be outlined.

The chapter focuses on the issues and problems that arise when universities attempt to increase the entrepreneurial emphasis within their own teaching and intellectual property management activities.

Problem exploration

In the context of higher education, entrepreneurship can be considered from two main viewpoints. The first refers to entrepreneurial skills development in both students and staff, and the second to the commercialization of research outcomes. Both areas, together with the concerns of those with vested interests in each, need to be addressed if entrepreneurship is to flourish in higher education in general. Individual universities will vary in their requirements. All can benefit from curriculum innovations involving entrepreneurial skills development and the student interest this will generate. Only research-intensive universities may have a strong incentive to consider commercialization and intellectual property issues.

Entrepreneurial skills development

Entrepreneurial skills and traits refer primarily to generic attributes such as creativity, lateral thinking and problem-solving. Added to these are the frequently quoted generic management capabilities such as those cited in the mid-1980s by Timmons *et al.* (1985) when examining entrepreneurship through an analysis of a large number of research studies:

- total commitment, determination and perseverance;
- the drive to achieve and grow;
- opportunity and goal orientation;
- taking initiative and personal responsibility;
- persistent problem-solving;
- realism and a sense of humour;
- seeking and using feedback;
- internal focus of control;
- calculated risk-taking and risk-seeking.

As labour mobility increases and the traditional view of a career path more closely resembles 'crazy paving', these skills become more important in enabling individuals to adjust to changing conditions and patterns of demand within the labour market. The explicit emphasis upon the acquisition of these skills by students in higher education reflects the recruitment strategies of employers, particularly larger firms, and their recognition of the importance of such skills in their workforce.

Issues around the encouragement of entrepreneurship in higher education are by no means new or restricted to the UK. More general evidence on the relationship between entrepreneurial activity and economic development has served to encourage developments in many economies, although the case of the USA is probably the most frequently quoted as an example of the integration of entrepreneurship and higher education. A recent study exemplifies well the underlying rationale for encouraging a more entrepreneurial approach (Reynolds *et al.* 1999). The Global Entrepreneurship Monitor project examined the relationship between entrepreneurial activity and economic growth internationally. The results strongly indicate that a 'higher rate of entrepreneurial activity appears to be positively related to economic growth (Bednarzik 2000: 14).

This global study documented entrepreneurial activity in ten different countries, as shown in Figure 4.1. Those countries with high entrepreneurial activity (the United States, Canada, Israel) also had high economic growth. The study points out six factors considered to be the most important in fostering entrepreneurial activities:

- entrepreneurial opportunity;
- entrepreneurial capacity;
- infrastructure;
- demographics (age structure, female entrepreneurs, and population growth);
- education;
- culture.

Thus the larger, societal context represents a strong motive for encouraging and teaching entrepreneurial skills in higher education.

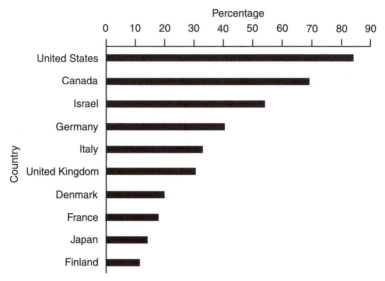

Figure 4.1   Proportion of adults participating in entrepreneurial activity in selected countries, winter 1999
Note: Entrepreneurial activity in this particular survey is defined as any attempt to start a new business or expand an existing one.
Source: Reynolds *et al*. (1999).

It is helpful to consider the acquisition of entrepreneurial skills by university staff and the issues of commercialization of research outcomes within the same argument. Although it is clear that students are more likely to recognize the importance of entrepreneurial skills if these are manifested in staff behaviour, the most significant relevance for staff-based entrepreneurial skills lies in the commercialization of inventions that occur in universities.

This new emphasis is by no means universally welcome in higher education. Many would argue that generic skills associated with successful entrepreneurship, such as initiative and problem-solving, can be acquired without referring to commercial activity, whilst the more specific skills of business and management can be acquired elsewhere. Supporters of the emphasis upon entrepreneurship in higher education highlight the demand for associated skills by students and industry, and the benefits to the acquisition of discipline-based skills, which occur through the inclusion of an entrepreneurial element in curriculum delivery.

Commercialization of research

Policy is also clear in its focus upon the need for greater integration between universities, industry and entrepreneurship and a more systematic approach to the commercialization of research outcomes. This is clearly demonstrated in the design of UK government initiatives such as Science Enterprise Challenge and University

Challenge and is well evidenced in the White Paper on science and innovation (Department of Trade and Industry 2000).

In economic terms, university research reflects a high level of investment at the forefront of knowledge, resulting in a significant level of discovery and invention. In a sense this represents the conversion of investment capital into knowledge and understanding. The actual return on this investment is indicated by the potential stream of income that these discoveries and inventions represent. In the UK, for example, where significant volumes of university research are paid for out of public funds, it can be argued that an important part of the return on this investment refers to the income generation potential that the commercialization of intellectual property could yield, where appropriate.

Some would, of course, argue that research should not be influenced by the commercial potential associated with likely outcomes. Indeed, the primary objectives for the vast majority of academics are the publication and wider dissemination of discoveries. In the majority of cases no conflict exists between this process and the realization of any potential income streams that may arise through commercialization. The vast majority of discoveries and inventions do not represent viable commercial possibilities. In a significant minority of cases, however, there is the possibility that intellectual property rights will be lost through the publication and dissemination process, and the economic returns from successful commercialization may be realized elsewhere or not at all. Failure to recognize and protect intellectual property generated within universities which has commercial potential may be criticized. Therefore, the second motive for encouraging a more entrepreneurial approach in higher education is to avoid lost returns on investment.

Integrating entrepreneurship and higher education

The encouragement of entrepreneurship in higher education may be justified in terms of arguments based on contemporary labour market conditions and on the economic and social responsibility to ensure that returns on investment are properly protected and realized, but the reality in terms of acceptance within higher education is complex.

Innovations within the curriculum that attempt to integrate entrepreneurial skills generation with discipline-specific knowledge and understanding will naturally be met with some resistance by subject specialists who do not regard this kind of skills development as part of their responsibilities or understanding. Indeed, for most academics the pursuit of entrepreneurial experience should always lie outside discipline-specific curricula. This creates a tension in terms of curriculum development because entrepreneurial skills may be most appropriately acquired as an integral part of subject-specific curricula rather than a completely separate area of activity. Indeed, some scientists would argue that an appreciation of the implications of commercializing science is very valuable to students in perceiving their subject area from a completely different viewpoint.

As with curriculum innovation to encourage entrepreneurial skills acquisition, the commercialization of inventions and discoveries from research also raises significant issues as far as staff reactions and development are concerned. In order to realize fully the potential commercial returns from investment in research in higher education, it is necessary to change the way in which the research outcomes are assessed. In addition to evaluating their contribution to knowledge and understanding, it is necessary to apply a 'commercial lens' in order to assess these developments in terms of commercial potential. As indicated above, this will be largely irrelevant as an exercise in the majority of cases. Potential conflicts of interest and behaviour arise, however, when the commercialization of research outcomes becomes the norm rather than the exception in an academic discipline. This is not to say that the majority of research outcomes are commercialized but rather that the assessment of potential in this context is routine and accepted. Under these conditions it will be more common in the sciences and engineering for individual academics to receive significant levels of remuneration as a result of their applied research.

A further potential source of tension arising from the encouragement of technology transfer through commercialization emerges from the potential or anticipated impact on the balance between pure and applied research. At present higher volumes of pure research may generate more opportunities for successful technology transfer through the development of applications. For example, Cambridge and Oxford have the highest levels of pure research, applications and spinout business in the UK universities. However, since the probability of identifying and protecting intellectual property for the purposes of commercialization is likely to be higher in the case of applied research, it might be expected that there will be a tendency for the balance to move towards an emphasis upon applications. Were this the case, the implications of this movement would be twofold. The first is that university research would gradually lose its pre-eminence in 'pure blue skies' research since it is the very absence of a predictable return on investment that has in the past tended to encourage this work more in universities than industry. Secondly, it would tend to erode, in the longer term, the source of research discoveries that, through applied research, generate commercial income potential. In short, a movement away from pure research would, under this scenario, eventually lead to a significant reduction in the capacity for universities to gain from the commercialization of applied research that has sprung from the pure research that preceded it.

To some extent the tensions within curriculum innovation for entrepreneurial skills development will naturally be counteracted, especially in the sciences and engineering, through the recognition by professional accrediting bodies of the importance of such skills. This is certainly recognizable in the UK in engineering, chemistry, physics and in non-scientific areas such as accountancy. The tensions around commercialization of research and the balance between pure and applied work may well be resolved in the medium and long term through a more sophisticated appreciation of the value of intellectual property arising from pure research. Indeed, there is evidence from industry that the value of pure research is now being recognized as a necessary crucial development for long-term competitiveness. In universities this is a strategic management issue. Realizing the potential returns of research and development requires a medium- to long-term view. The 'pipeline' from pure research, through its application, to commercial return will eventually dry up if revenues are not reinvested in the source.

There are many examples of developing 'good practice' in European universities in terms of both entrepreneurial skills development and the commercialization of research outcomes. Many of the science enterprise centres in the UK were founded on existing, well-established models. It is often developments in the USA that have inspired models of operation in Europe, and it is useful to focus on the American case for examples in these areas of activity.

Entrepreneurship education and activity in universities in the USA

Entrepreneurial education

The past 15 years have seen entrepreneurship education grow dramatically in the USA, Europe and Asia (Charney and Libecap 2000). In the USA, entrepreneurship courses have been introduced in some high schools. Approaches to entrepreneurship education vary from a single offering of a course in entrepreneurship development (Ember 2000) to integrated curricula that include invention, finance, competitive analysis, business plan development and marketing.

The number of entrepreneurship courses offered by colleges and universities in the USA increased from 163 in 1980 (Vesper 1985) to over 400 by 1993 (Vesper 1993) and an estimated 1000 by 2001. Over 400 universities and colleges are offering programmes in entrepreneurship (Fenn 2000). A complete listing of world-wide entrepreneurship programmes can be found at www.marshall.usc.edu/ entrepreneur

A number of colleges and universities have offered entrepreneurship courses for decades. The Snider Entrepreneurship Center at the Wharton School of the University of Pennsylvania claims to be the oldest. Most of these programmes in the USA involve introducing one or two entrepreneurship courses to an existing MBA degree programme and are, as in the UK and Europe, taught in business schools. Some colleges, such as Babson College, are well known for their emphasis on entrepreneurship, with the entire MBA programme focused on starting a business.

Advantages and benefits of entrepreneurial education

Charney and Libecap (2000) suggest that entrepreneurship courses are popular for several reasons:

- The development of business plans allows students to integrate accounting, economics, finance, marketing and other disciplines.
- They may promote the founding of new businesses by graduates or enhance their employment prospects.

- They may promote technology transfer from the university to the marketplace through the development of technology-based business plans.
- They forge links between business and the academic community.
- Entrepreneurship education allows for experimentation with the curriculum since it is outside the traditional discipline boundaries.
- In the USA, the fiercely independent culture encourages the population to 'be your own boss'.

In addition, many managers in companies see entrepreneurship education as useful because it is an applied approach to the study of business and economics. There is ample evidence to show that those with entrepreneurship training within companies, especially within small firms, significantly increase sales growth (Charney and Libecap 2000).

A number of studies demonstrate the benefits of entrepreneurial education. An early study, carried out in 1994 by Baylor University (Upton *et al.* 1995), assesses the effectiveness of undergraduate entrepreneurship education for almost a third of its graduates between 1979 and 1994. From the response, about 27 per cent are in family firms, 32 per cent own firms and 32 per cent work for others. About a third of those working for others have owned a business in the past. Intriguingly, the entire group responded with a desire to own a business in the future.

A recent research project compared MBA graduate alumni who graduated from an entrepreneurship programme with those from the traditional business school programmes in the same college (Charney and Libecap 2000). The key findings show that the entrepreneurship graduates were generally more successful and innovative. Of course there is always the possibility that the type of student choosing to attend such courses may simply be more likely to achieve these outcomes.

The engineer-entrepreneur

In the 1990s there was a strong trend towards the introduction of entrepreneurship courses in science and engineering. For example, the world-renowned California Institute of Technology started a course in entrepreneurship development for its undergraduate students (Ember 2000).

Many US colleges of engineering are initiating enterprise programmes to teach technology students how to start and run a business or 'enterprise'. Many of these programmes use the term *technopreneurship* to differentiate them from 'business' entrepreneurship programmes.

In 2001 the American Society for Engineering Education set up an 'Entrepreneurial Division'. This is an important step in recognizing entrepreneurship as a legitimate part of engineering education. The 2001 International Conference in Engineering Education, held in Berlin, featured 'teaching entrepreneurship to engineers' as one of its main themes. These developments are reflected in the UK in initiatives like Science Enterprise Challenge that focus attention on entrepreneurial skills development in science and engineering. There are also examples of direct links between the UK and US experience. These range from formal institutional collaborations, for example between Cambridge University and the Massachusetts Institute of Technology (MIT), to joint academic research such as the conference in Nottingham run by the University of Nottingham Institute for Enterprise and Innovation and the US National Academy of Sciences on promoting entrepreneurship in a knowledge-based economy.

Evidence of change and social enablers

The movement towards a knowledge-based economy requires both technical knowledge and entrepreneurship. A recent survey of business executives and managers revealed that highly successful engineers exhibit entrepreneurial skills in addition to being academically knowledgeable (Arora and Faraone 2001). In the past decade, universities such as MIT have recognized that alumni heading the majority of the successful firms started by their graduates were trained as engineers (BankBoston Economics Department 1997).

A recent study (Hudson Institute 1999: 11) forecasts 'rapidly increasing entrepreneurial activity throughout the global economy' and 'fast-growing employment in small and medium-sized firms and in self-employment in engineering'. If this forecast is borne out, then engineering colleges will be doing a great disservice to their graduates by not equipping them with this very important skill.

Staff expertise in entrepreneurship

Entrepreneurship curricula primarily benefit students. The development of staff expertise has not received as much attention, partly because staff may have very different priorities. The focus of researchers is to seek funding and turn money into knowledge, whereas the focus of an entrepreneur is to seek funding to turn that knowledge into money. This is not to say that discoveries such as DNA, polio vaccine or penicillin should be examined from the standpoint of mere market value, but essentially researchers and entrepreneurs have different mindsets and walk different paths. The entrepreneur has to be opportunistic, examine the market potential of these discoveries, and develop useful and marketable products for society. Magnetic resonance imaging, now being used world-wide as a key medical diagnostic tool, is an excellent example (Mattson and Simon 1996). In general, entrepreneurs are not concerned if they are using frontier knowledge, current knowledge, old knowledge or even ancient knowledge. Their primary concern is whether there is a market for their product or process. Most successful entrepreneurs start without a proprietary idea, without exceptional qualifications, and without significant amounts of capital (Bhidé 2000).

It is perhaps these important differences in the objective functions associated with 'traditional' academic activity and entrepreneurship which help to explain the relatively low level of licensing income generated from commercialization in universities. Consider evidence from the USA. Table 4.1 (Zacks 2000) summarizes

Table 4.1 Licensing income as a proportion of total research spending for the ten US universities with the highest licensing income

Institution	Licensing income ($)	Licences generating income	US patents issued	US patent applications filed	Start-up companies formed	Total research spending ($)	Income/ research (%)
University of California System	73,101,000	696	242	633	19	1,709,929,000	4.3
Columbia	61,649,002	245	35	85	5	260,700,000	23.6
Florida State	46,642,688	10	15	22	2	112,077,647	41.6
Stanford	43,197,379	299	86	234	9	401,049,000	10.8
Yale	33,261,248	84	24	83	6	299,800,000	11.1
Carnegie Mellon	30,065,000	20	14	43	5	169,899,765	17.7
Michigan State	24,336,872	41	61	67	1	193,611,000	12.6
University of Washington Research Foundation	21,299,214	204	48	146	8	432,383,000	4.9
University of Florida	19,144,753	55	51	102	4	240,900,000	7.9
Massachusetts Institute of Technology	18,046,991	267	126	372	19	761,400,000	2.4

Source: Zacks (2000).

the licence income generated from research together with the research expenditures for the top ten research universities in the USA during fiscal year 1998. A review of the data from the top 100 universities (listed in the report posted on the referenced website) shows a positive correlation between research expenditure and licence income, but the ratio of income to expenditure is in most cases quite low.

Staff development strategies to encourage entrepreneurship in universities

The integration of entrepreneurial skills development and activity in higher education could create tensions within universities and pose a potential threat to the balance between pure and applied research. A successful staff development strategy to encourage this integration, while ameliorating the tensions and threats, is challenging and should incorporate several crucial characteristics. These can be portrayed quite clearly by identifying them with the four pillars of successful innovation discussed, albeit in a different context, by Lumsdaine *et al.* (1999).

Awareness raising: providing necessary rationales, background and information

The successful introduction of entrepreneurship in higher education requires that staff and students be informed as to the nature of entrepreneurial activity and offered clear reasons for its importance. Like any other curriculum innovation, such a development is more likely to be successful if it reflects a genuine need, if it produces learning outcomes that are seen to be relevant and appropriate, and if examples of best practice elsewhere can be cited.

The approach to the commercialization of research and innovation must be equally clear, describing the process of opportunity identification, evaluation and innovation. Clear policies on reward structures and intellectual property management are also needed.

This overriding emphasis upon clarity should be accompanied by a policy of opportunity presentation and issues identification rather than any element of compulsion or coercion. Experience suggests that only a minority of academics will become actively engaged in technology transfer. In the case of skills development it is important that staff choose the means most appropriate to their curriculum.

Application: process and structures

The applications aspect concentrates on the processes of curriculum innovation for entrepreneurial skills development and for the successful commercialization of research outcomes. Again, processes and support available should be clear to staff and students. Successful curriculum innovation requires a focal point, responsible for making clear the processes which apply within the institution. In the case of Science Enterprise Challenge in the UK, some centres have been established within business schools while others have been set up on an independent basis. The advantage of being aligned with a mainstream department such as a business school is that there will usually be strong and established links with the many departments across the university with which the entrepreneurial skills developers wish to work. Independence offers advantages in higher levels of budgetary control and, possibly, greater flexibility in terms of the curriculum innovation that is offered.

In encouraging the commercialization of research it is again crucial that there be a strong focal point which makes clear the processes involved and the variety of support available to academics in order to enable them to access the potential gains of commercialization without necessarily accumulating entrepreneurial skills themselves.

Although these two focal points will often be closely interrelated by the bringing together of entrepreneurial skills development and live (real-world) case studies in the form of technology transfer, there may also need to be some separation. Curriculum innovation requires academic input, whereas aspects of commercialization such as intellectual property management and contracting require the services of professional administrators.

One of the most important roles of these centres concerns both inreach and outreach. It is important that those involved monitor developments within the institution with a view to continually improving the effectiveness of the processes involved. It is also crucial that best practice elsewhere is clearly identified and, where appropriate, adopted for the institution concerned.

Climate: engendering enthusiasm for curriculum innovation and technology transfer

An appropriate environment for the successful development of entrepreneurial activities in higher education can be provided most effectively through the 'demonstration effect'. In short, students are more likely to be persuaded of the benefits of entrepreneurship options in the curriculum by the recommendations of other students and their honest assessments of the learning outcomes that they experienced. Similarly, academic and support staff members are more convinced by evidence from other academics in the same discipline areas than by a centrally organized university management marketing campaign. Examples of successful practice need to be disseminated widely to their respective audiences. Experience from the USA in the case of MIT and from the UK in the science enterprise centres, such as the University of Nottingham Institute for Enterprise and Innovation, demonstrates the effectiveness of peer recommendation and dissemination.

Communication: informing the process as well as the staff

The key to enhancing each of the three 'pillars' discussed above – awareness raising, application and climate – is good communication. The clarity referred to in the first should be maintained through the establishment of a two-way communication process which enables those responsible for each aspect of entrepreneurial activity, be it curriculum development or commercialization, to monitor the effectiveness of existing processes and offerings and undertake a continuous process of review, redesign and improvement.

In application, clear and consistent communication between academics and administrators, between researchers and students working on case studies, and between academics and the business community is crucial to developing effective inreach and outreach and must thus be explicitly established and facilitated. Communication is also the foundation in building and sustaining a conducive climate for entrepreneurship and innovation in higher education.

The final and possibly greatest challenge confronting staff development strategies in this area is the need to encourage the integration of curriculum development with technology transfer. Since much entrepreneurial skills development relies heavily on experiential learning rather than a more traditional lecture-based approach, it is important to avoid separating skills development from commercialization of research. The commercialization process is a potentially invaluable source of experiential learning on the basis of 'live case studies' that engage students directly in the entrepreneurial process.

Conclusion

The experiences of institutions such as MIT are instructive because they reveal how entrepreneurial developments in universities can be self-perpetuating and grow rapidly once a certain 'critical mass' has been achieved. In universities where this is unlikely to occur naturally in the foreseeable future, policy initiatives such as Science Enterprise Challenge and University Challenge are needed to accelerate the process. The growing recognition of the role of entrepreneurship in determining relative competitiveness ensures that increasing emphasis will be placed on it in all areas of the economy, with higher education being one of the most important. Universities that seek to encourage entrepreneurship in the curriculum and in their research will need a carefully designed and flexible strategy, however, to ensure that their academic integrity is not compromised and the support and loyalty of their academic staff is sustained.

Key learning points

Senior staff

- Decide on a strategy rather than waiting for one to emerge. Changing the culture in higher education is often problematic. Issues around entrepreneurship both in the curriculum and with respect to research are often sensitive and contentious. When taking a position on these issues it is important that senior management examine carefully all the relevant issues and principles involved and make a clear decision as to the position of their institution on the basis of the evidence and the arguments involved.
- Identify examples of best practice which can be used to inform new initiatives designed to achieve and secure the new strategy.
- Transmit these decisions strongly and with clear explanations to all staff and students affected. Senior management support for those involved in delivering the new strategy will be critical to its success.

Heads of department

- Understand the strategy and decisions transmitted by senior management along with their rationale.

- Assess the implications for each section and member of the department/school.
- Communicate the new strategy and decisions to all members of staff with summary rationale and implications for all concerned. Review progress on a regular basis and provide additional support and resources where required and available.

Professional staff developers

- Identify examples of best practice from other institutions and the extent to which they are transferable to the home university.
- For curriculum innovation, provide a wide range of examples and alternative approaches from which academic staff can choose to suit their particular requirements and disciplines.
- Specify the knowledge, understanding and information required by academics to equip them for undertaking technology transfer activities, and determine how best to deliver these to staff using internal resources, external expertise and case studies as examples of good and effective practice.

Part II

Extra-institutional influences

This part of the book focuses on extra-institutional influences, themes and developments. Chapters 5–7 examine some relatively new initiatives to enhance learning and teaching and their status within higher education, which has been the historical core of much staff development and the continuing focus of units catering for academic staff only (see Chapter 1). Chapters 8 and 9 discuss a major initiative for all staff, Investors in People, and an emerging issue, leadership and management development.

The subject dimension of SD, addressed in Chapters 5 and 6, is an increasingly important theme largely developed outside institutional structures by subject specialists, rather than staff developers *per se*. The two chapters represent different approaches, in particular national contexts. The first focuses on largely voluntary efforts supported by charitable funding, the second on the development of publicly funded project work into a formal network. Some convergence is notable in the growth of project making in the USA and growing UK interest in the scholarship of teaching and learning, including within the Learning and Teaching Support Network (LTSN).

In Chapter 5, Mary Taylor Huber charts the growing interest in and engagement with the scholarship of teaching and learning, a largely voluntary movement that has spread outwards from the work of Boyer in the USA. Huber focuses on disciplinary styles, the application to teaching and learning issues of methods and standards of proof drawn from within the discipline's own research traditions, with a view to enhancement. She notes the importance of 'interdisciplinary trading' across boundaries, especially in the sciences, and presents a vibrant picture of converging national and local support in the USA, the latter involving staff (faculty) developers.

Chapter 6, in contrast, focuses on the long-standing UK public funding of short-term, discipline-based projects. Although much valuable development work is evident, illustrated by four brief case studies, issues of sustainability and embedding have encouraged the emergence of a formal LTSN network of 24 subject centres. The authors assess the opportunities and challenges facing such a publicly funded network and argue for the importance of synergistic collaboration and joint working between subject specialists and institutionally based staff developers.

In Chapter 7, Caroline Bucklow and Paul Clark focus on the issues of professionalism and accreditation raised in Chapter 2, describing the emergence of the Institute for Learning and Teaching in Higher Education in the UK. This publicly sponsored professional body is shown to have grown rapidly, accredited many courses of initial training and attracted considerable international interest. Connecting to themes in the previous two chapters, the authors underscore the importance of continuing professional development and the need for academic staff (and staff developers) to engage with the scholarly literature on learning and teaching.

In Chapter 8, Bob Thackwray discusses Investors in People. Although it was originally conceived as an economy-wide quality standard, he shows that it has been adapted well for higher education and points to the high institutional take-up in the UK and growing engagement in Holland. He argues that it contributes to and is congruent with some conceptions of strategy discussed in Chapter 1 and that the reflection that the process requires can produce organizational and individual benefits.

In the final chapter in Part II, George Gordon provides a comprehensive overview of extra-institutional provision on leadership and management development. He examines the background to the rising interest in this area, emphasizing the importance of context and diversity. He notes, amongst other things, the uncertainty of managerial 'identity' at head-of-department level, relevant to a number of chapters (such as Chapter 10), and changing models of leadership and management. He charts and reviews the growth of extra-institutional provision in the UK and internationally and sees a number of potential challenges for institutional staff developers. These include ensuring that provision is informed by research and scholarship in the area, demonstration of the effectiveness of programmes and adjustment to renewed interest in this area.

At the time of writing (September 2002) the configuration of publicly funded staff development and enhancement bodies is under review in the UK including ILTHE (Chapter 7), LTSN (Chapter 6) and HESDA (Chapters 8 and 9). We feel confident that the themes we have chosen will continue to prove central, whatever changes to institutional arrangements may occur.

5

Disciplines and the development of a scholarship of teaching and learning[1]

Mary Taylor Huber

The scholarship of teaching and learning in higher education belongs to no particular country, has no single professional association, and has no unique campus address. As befits a vigorous, emergent area of intellectual discourse and debate, the scholarship of teaching and learning is springing up in established departments, programmes, and centres, and developing new forums and outlets of its own. Across the academy, interest in teaching and learning in higher education is spreading beyond a few specialists, as more and more 'mainstream' faculty members take up a systematic interest in curriculum, classroom teaching, and the quality of student learning. Professors in disciplines from anthropology to zoology are beginning to consult pedagogical literature, look critically at education in their field, inquire into teaching and learning in their own classroom, and use what they are discovering to improve their teaching practice. Many are making this work public in forums ranging from local teaching circles to national (or even international) conferences, from course portfolios to journal publications, from face-to-face conversation to print media and the web.

These developments are encouraging, but they are not taking shape uniformly across the academy. Campus contexts rightly are receiving much attention, because it is in specific colleges and universities that teaching and learning in higher education take place. National contexts are also important: work flying under the flag of the scholarship of teaching and learning (or of learning and teaching, or teaching, or just learning!) can be found in Hong Kong, Australia, New Zealand, Canada, UK and the United States. In addition, the scholarship of teaching and learning is taking shape within the extraordinary diversity of disciplinary cultures that constitute post-secondary education. This paper will focus on the role of the disciplines in the development of the scholarship of teaching and learning in the United States. However, because disciplinary cultures cross-cut campuses and even countries, this study *should* be of interest internationally as well. I begin with a little historical background about the US context, then look at how the disciplines are influencing the ways in which US faculty members are approaching the scholarship of teaching and learning, consider the nature and role of interdisciplinary exchange in this area, and finally review some of the ways in which campus efforts are supporting the growth of this work.

Setting the stage

The idea of a scholarship of teaching and learning gained prominence and momentum with Boyer (1990), a report from the Carnegie Foundation which presented a vision of academic scholarship that extended habits of thought conventionally associated with academic research to other activities such as interdisciplinary and applied work (or outreach) and to teaching (see also Glassick *et al.* 1997). The idea that these areas might be elevated from 'journeyman activities to creative intellectual activities' (Benson 2001: 3) has been highly suggestive to people looking for ways to engage more fully in teaching, outreach and public scholarship and to be recognized and rewarded for their full range of academic work.

In the years since its publication, Boyer's report has helped shape a lively debate about the work of faculty members in US colleges and universities. For example, the American Association of University Professors (1994) report on the work of faculty directed attention to 'total faculty workload rather than classroom hours' and stated: 'We now approach the question of balance through definitions of teaching, scholarship, and service that emphasize the great variety of activities so embraced'. Individual campuses have been changing tenure and promotion guidelines to embrace a wider view of scholarly work, while a whole array of scholarly societies have drafted statements exploring what a broad vision of scholarship in their fields would look like (see Diamond and Adam 1995; 2000). National associations have chosen one or more of the 'new' scholarships as an annual conference theme, while the American Association for Higher Education, inspired by the Boyer report, has sponsored a series of ten annual conferences on faculty roles and rewards (see Glassick *et al.* 1997: 10–16).

This has been an especially exciting time with regard to teaching and learning. The National Science Foundation has been funding ambitious projects to engage faculty in developing and assessing curricula for science, mathematics, engineering and technology; the explosion of new media has spurred creativity not only in instruction, but also in the production and distribution of new courseware and teaching materials; and there has been a rise in the number of teaching and learning centres on campus and a growing number of forums for people to get together to discuss pedagogical themes. Foundations too have developed new programmes, one of the most visible being the Carnegie Academy for the Scholarship of Teaching and Learning (CASTL), with its national fellowships for individual scholars who wish to investigate and document significant issues and challenges in teaching and learning in their field; its companion programmme for colleges and universities prepared to make a public commitment of their own to fostering teaching as scholarly work; and its partnerships with scholarly societies that wish to pay more attention to these matters.[2]

In the process, of course, the idea of a scholarship of teaching and learning has been enriched, gaining subtlety and depth from many streams of thought and practice, including work that deepens our understanding of teaching knowledge, sharpens our focus on student learning, and widens our view of the audience for teaching to include peers as well as students. I wish to highlight here the contribution of my colleagues at the Carnegie Foundation, Lee Shulman and Pat Hutchings, who have made some very helpful distinctions along the way. All college faculty members have an obligation to be excellent teachers, they argue, well versed in their own fields and able to promote the development of real student learning. When they also make use of what is known about teaching and learning and 'invite peer collaboration and review', they may well be called scholarly teachers. But the scholarship of teaching goes even further. As Hutchings and Shulman (1999: 13) say:

> It requires a kind of 'going meta' in which faculty frame and systematically investigate questions related to student learning – the conditions under which it occurs, what it looks like, how to deepen it, and so forth – and to do so with an eye not only to improving their own classroom but to advancing practice beyond it.

What is most important here is that college and university faculty members start thinking of teaching as serious intellectual work, and find ways to make teaching public and available to peers so that it can be reviewed, built upon, and contribute to the field (see Hutchings 2001). Bass (1999) got the spirit right in his article on how we might think of a teaching 'problem':

> One telling measure of how differently teaching is regarded from traditional scholarship or research . . . is what a difference it makes to have a 'problem' in one versus the other. In . . . research, having a 'problem' is at the heart of the investigative process; it is the compound of the generative questions around which all creative and productive activity revolves. But in one's teaching, a 'problem' is something you don't want to have, and if you have one, you probably want to fix it. Asking a colleague about a *problem* in his or her research is an invitation; asking about a problem in one's teaching would probably seem like an accusation. Changing the status of the *problem* in teaching from terminal remediation to ongoing investigation is precisely what the movement for a scholarship of teaching is all about. How might we make the problematization of teaching a matter of regular communal discourse? How might we think of teaching practice, and the evidence of student learning, as problems to be investigated, analyzed, represented, and debated?

Disciplinary styles

This brings me to my second theme concerning the role of the disciplines, because, like teaching itself (Shulman 1987; Grossman *et al.* 1989), all of these activities that Bass invokes – investigating, analysing, representing and debating – are clearly inflected by the disciplinary cultures that we in higher education know and love. To be sure, there are many issues that cut across fields. But it is important to start with disciplines first, because that is the starting point of most faculty members when they think about teaching and learning and it is where many of their best aspirations for students lie. Biologists, historians and psychologists may all agree that they want to foster 'deep understanding' in their college classrooms, but what they mean by 'deep understanding' is different (Donald 2002; see also Becher and Trowler 2001), and so too is the way they are likely to go about the scholarship of teaching and learning itself.

In our CASTL fellowship programme we have a women's studies scholar doing 'close reading' of student interviews for insight into which materials were helping them move most effectively around the highly charged gender issues discussed in her class. But we also have scientists, like the chemistry professor who told us:

> In order to convince the teachers of organic chemistry that there truly is a place for active and cooperative learning in the chemistry classroom, they will need to see good data that support this theory. Scientists are scientists and they know that the data do not lie.

In fact, each discipline has its own intellectual history of agreement and dispute about subject matter and methods that influence what is taught, to whom, when, where, how and why. Each has a set of common pedagogies, such as lab instruction and problem sets in the sciences, seminars in the humanities, and small-group performances in introductory theatre classes. As the essays in Huber and Morreale (2002) make clear, each field also has its own community of scholars interested in teaching and learning, often with one or more journals, associations, and face-to-face forums for pedagogical exchange. For good or ill, then, scholars of teaching and learning must address field-specific issues if they are going to be heard in their own disciplines, and they must speak in a language that their colleagues understand.

This language, which I call a discipline's 'style', involves, at its core, what Joseph Schwab so elegantly distinguished as substantive and syntactic structures: the 'conceptions that guide enquiry' (1964: 24) and the 'pathways of enquiry [scholars] use, what they mean by verified knowledge and how they go about this verification' (1964: 21). To put it more plainly, our discipline's style influences the problems we choose, the methods we use, and the arguments we find persuasive.

Let us look at problem selection with the help of two scholars who have written about their work in Pat Hutchings's edited collection, *Opening Lines* (2000). First, consider Dennis Jacobs, a chemist at the University of Notre Dame, who took up the problem of student attrition – a problem that has bedevilled introductory science courses and dominated reform efforts in these fields for years (Seymour 2001). He began his work in the scholarship of teaching and learning when he 'began teaching a large general chemistry course with nearly 1000 students divided in four lecture sessions. It was a traditional introductory science course', and Jacobs became concerned when he realized how many students were struggling (Jacobs 2000: 41). Poorly prepared in high school, they were 'caught off guard' by exams that required real problem-solving, and after scoring low marks on one or two exams, they would withdraw. But the problem was that they were not just dropping that one course. Introductory chemistry is a 'gateway to a number of majors', and for many students, dropping it meant the end of their dream of being a scientist, an engineer, a doctor. So, instead of just writing those students off as 'too dumb' for science as, unfortunately, so many others have done (see Tobias 1990), Jacobs created an alternative learning environment where lectures are interspersed with opportunities for students to work together on challenging problems, defend their ideas, and articulate their understandings. He consulted the literature on chemistry education, he assessed the impact of the new approach using a mixture of methods (some quite new to his own repertoire), and he began to participate in campus conversations and national discussions about teaching (see Jacobs 2000).

Equally engaging, but quite different, is the work of Mariolina Salvatori, an English professor at the University of Pittsburgh. Salvatori's scholarship of teaching and learning focuses on the 'role of difficulty in the learning process', because both her own experience as an international student doing graduate study in the USA and her theoretical commitments in reader response theory and hermeneutics (especially to Gadamer) have taught her that 'moments of difficulty often contain the seeds of understanding' (Salvatori 2000: 81). For example, what a student might identify as a difficulty in reading a poem, say a change in tone from beginning to end, may actually be a sign of understanding, which the teacher can help the student to see. Thus, Salvatori began regularly asking students to write 'difficulty papers', to provide them with a way of recognizing their problems with a text and developing strategies to get beyond them. She is examining the effectiveness of this pedagogy by using the methods of her own field: doing close readings of her students' work, looking for signs that indicate movement towards more complicated forms of thinking. And she is recruiting colleagues in English and neighbouring humanities fields to try 'difficulty papers' in their own courses and see if their students make the same kinds of gains.

In fact, disciplinary styles empower inquiry into student learning not only by focusing attention on certain kinds of problems, but also by giving faculty members a ready-made way to imagine projects and present their work – for example, metaphors such as the classroom as laboratory, text, field site or theatre might act as pointer to different methods of inquiry and styles of analysis.

Indeed, in our experience with CASTL, most people inquiring into teaching and learning are drawn to the normal procedures of their field, whether they be humanists leaning towards 'close readings' of student work, or from those corners of the social and natural sciences where numbers are preferred to text. Consider some of the metaphors that scholars in the social sciences use to picture teaching and learning in ways that draw on the intellectual capital of their own particular field. In the management sciences, people talk about 'the classroom as organization' (Bilimoria and Fukami 2002); in communication studies, there is an inclination to look at 'teaching as communication' (Morreale *et al.* 2002); in psychology, it is tempting to see 'teaching as inquiry into learning' (Nummedal *et al.* 2002).

A case in point is psychologist Daniel Bernstein, who has been using the experimental methods of his branch of his field to help him decide which teaching techniques are helping his students gain a better understanding of psychological measurement. Hypothesizing that students might do better with more opportunities to interact with course material, Bernstein gave one section a live lecture on the topic, gave a videotape of his lecture to a second section, and gave interactive courseware on the topic to the rest. When reviewers of the study suggested he needed better control conditions, Bernstein then compared performance among groups hearing a live lecture, groups working on the web, groups reading relevant material, and groups reading irrelevant material. 'This is what you get when you enter into that community,' Bernstein jokes, 'additions of more conditions.' He continues to test and retest new innovations: 'Statistics are fine,' he says, 'but replication is the most important thing you can do' (see Bernstein 2000).

For many instructors, however, pedagogy is still a new topic of inquiry not only for themselves but also for mainstream scholarship in their fields, and even in psychology, as Bernstein would be the first to agree, classroom research does not present ideal conditions for following most methodological protocols. If you are working in a field where quantitative methods predominate, it is often hard to observe the normal scruples about sample size and representativeness, which in that community warrant confidence in research results. Of course, these same scholars often find practitioner research very helpful in focusing attention on student learning and in thinking about what works best in their courses. But some worry that methodological issues may limit their work's reach beyond their own classroom, and that it may not find a receptive audience among their disciplinary peers.[3] Indeed, even when your field emphasizes interpretation over explanation, and welcomes ethnography, contextually rich case studies or close readings, it can be a challenge to develop an approach to the study of teaching and learning that both you and your colleagues find interesting and sound.

So, while it is true that the disciplines provide some powerful and distinctive models of inquiry from which scholars can choose, it is also clear that no discipline has all the answers or even asks all the questions, and there is much to be gained beyond the borders of disciplinary imagination in what I have been calling – taking a cue from Gallison (1997) – the interdisciplinary 'trading zone'.

The interdisciplinary trading zone

In fact, my third theme is precisely to wander a bit in this trading zone to comment on the role of interdisciplinary exchange in advancing the scholarship of teaching and learning. Here are some examples of what I have in mind. In the sciences, people cannot simply transpose the methods and arguments with which they are most familiar to classroom research, and many actually seek out collaborators – for example, Carnegie scholar and mathematician Anita Salem, of Rockhurst University, recruited a colleague in psychology to help her explore student understanding in her calculus class (Salem and Michael 2002). Chemist Dennis Jacobs did his work alone, but received a great deal of help from his teaching and learning centre to design a variety of appropriate assessment tools. Jacobs also borrowed freely from other science education research: for example, he was inspired by physicist Eric Mazur's (1997) discussion of 'concept questions'. Such borrowing is common, but so too is what science studies scholars call 'reconstruction' (Hess 1997: 139) – the effort to reinterpret and remake knowledge as it moves out of one group and into other groups elsewhere. For example, I know of scientists who are intrigued by Mariolina Salvatori's focus on the role of 'difficulty' in the learning process – and I bet that if they borrow the idea, they will drop every reference she makes to Gadamer, phenomenology and reader response theory when they bring it home to their own community.

The historians writing in *Disciplinary Styles* cite an interesting twist on the same plot. Until recently, they note, there was little in the literature on teaching and learning in history to tempt historians to take it seriously. But the field is being energized by some provocative work on how experts and novices approach historical texts – work that is being done by psychologists, but made available to historians in ways that respect that discipline's style. For example, when cognitive psychologist Sam Wineburg presented his work to his own colleagues in the *Journal of Educational Psychology* (1991), he spoke in the technical language of that field. But when he presented the same work in the American Historical Association's *Perspectives* newsletter (1992), he did something completely different.

> When addressing historians . . . Wineburg translated his findings into an argument-driven narrative . . . [dropping the heavy statistics] and mov[ing] forward on the strength of evidence that historians are used to evaluating: quotations from research subjects, summaries of empirical results, revealing anecdotes, and references to other sources within the range of their reading habits.
>
> (Calder *et al.* 2002)

This is a story, I submit, about the strength of disciplinary styles in shaping efforts to improve student learning. But it is also a story about the emergence of a trading zone among disciplines, a place where scholars are busy simplifying, translating, telling and persuading 'foreigners' to hear their stories and try their wares. In this zone, one finds scholars of teaching and learning seeking advice, collaborations, references, methods and colleagues to enrich what their own disciplinary communities have to offer and to fill in for what their own disciplinary communities cannot or will not provide.

Fostering the scholarship of teaching and learning

Scholarship is a deeply communal enterprise. It is, in essence, a conversation in which one participates only by knowing what is now being discussed and what others in the past have said. We talk of successful scholarship as 'contributing to the field'. If a project does not speak to current issues of theory, fact, interpretation or method, it is unlikely that anyone would say that a contribution has been made. This is fairly uncontroversial with respect to established fields of scholarship. The catch with a 'new' or 'emerging' area, like the scholarship of teaching, is that, to quote an old saying, 'you can't jump if there's no place to stand'. One of the major challenges in fostering the scholarship of teaching on campus or in the disciplines, is not only to encourage those individuals who are interested in pursuing such work, but also to help develop the 'field' itself. The scholarship of teaching can flourish only with the development of communities of scholars within and across the disciplines who share, critique and build upon each other's work.

Something like this is the thinking behind the Carnegie Foundation's three CASTL programmes, which are attempting to build leadership and capacity for the scholarship of teaching and learning through work with individual scholars, campuses, and scholarly and professional societies. Even the Carnegie Scholars Program, which provides fellowships to individuals, brings them together as *classes* three times over the course of their fellowship year. The scholars work in interdisciplinary groups to refine their project plans and report their findings, and meet in plenary sessions to discuss matters of common concern. Disciplinary differences over issues for inquiry, method and argument can run deep. But over their fellowship year, virtually all the scholars find colleagues in unlikely fields. For example, when communication professor Tracy Russo's plans to study 'presence' in an online communication course fell through, biology professor Spencer Benson offered his on-line course instead. Opportunities for collaboration continue past the fellowship year, as the programme's alumni organize sessions together at conferences, invite each other as guest speakers to their own campuses and scholarly meetings, and arrange conferences of their own.

CASTL's work with scholarly and professional societies has included very modest grants to help support the growth of a scholarship of teaching and learning in the various fields. For example, the American Historical Association expanded its course portfolio website; the American Sociological Association sponsored an invitational seminar on the scholarship of teaching and learning in sociology; and the Association of American Law Schools sponsored a special conference on the scholarship of learning. Beyond the grants, however, have been opportunities for education officers of these societies to meet together. At one of these meetings, Carla Howery from the American Sociological Association described an interesting service her group provides members: they produce lists of books and articles they have gleaned from the generic literature on teaching and learning and other materials for the teaching of sociology. But, Howery said, her group seldom has the time to scan work coming out of other disciplines on teaching and learning. In general, these scholarly society representatives were surprised to learn about what the others were doing and suggested that, as a first step, they might link to each other's websites.

Campuses, of course, are especially critical sites for the development of the scholarship of teaching and learning. In its first five years, over 200 campuses joined the CASTL Campus Program, coordinated by Carnegie's partner, the American Association for Higher Education (see Cambridge 2001). Participating institutions began with 'campus conversations' to draft definitions of the work to fit their situations, identify conditions that would support or challenge the effort, and decide on a focus for campus-wide work. In a second phase of the programme, campuses began sharing their work with others, and many later completed a full audit of the conditions for the scholarship of teaching and learning.[4] This mapping activity included questions about institutional mission, infrastructure, and integration; the participation of students, faculty and campus leaders; campus support, including money and time; faculty selection and development; faculty evaluation; collaboration across and beyond the campus; and uses of technology. As I write, the campus programme is moving to a next stage, in which clusters of campuses will work together to advance the larger goals of the scholarship of teaching and learning.

This initiative to foster a scholarship of teaching and learning, involving the Carnegie Foundation for the Advancement of Teaching, American Association for Higher Education, other foundations (notably the Pew Charitable Trusts, which helped fund CASTL's first five years), campuses, scholarly societies and individual scholars, is only one of several teaching initiatives under way today in the USA. On any particular campus and in any particular discipline, there are likely to be many other ongoing change efforts as well. Some of these are local, for example the workshops, conferences, retreats, working groups, and consultations orchestrated by faculty and professional development leaders through the teaching and learning centres that are springing up at a growing number of US colleges and universities. Some efforts involve a particular cohort of campuses, for example Indiana University's Faculty Colloquium on Excellence in Teaching (FACET) which draws participants from the several universities within the Indiana state system. And then there are programmes with connections with national associations, such as the Association of American Colleges and Universities, or the League for Innovation in the Community College. In a recent article, Cambridge (2002) examines 15 programmes of national scope aimed at defining student learning outcomes, building an infrastructure of support, and establishing evidence for purposes of accountability.

Many of these initiatives are entirely congruent with the spirit of the scholarship of teaching and learning, offering multiple avenues for campus or individual involvement and – just as important – multiple uses for activities associated with any one effort. As Cambridge (2002: 39) notes:

> Time is the most precious resource for faculty members. If a faculty member decides to dedicate effort to a particular project, then it is important that the results of that project be used in as many ways as possible. For example, if a faculty member adopts student portfolios as a learning and assessing tool, the time invested in development and implementation will be better spent if the portfolios contribute to assessing student progress, representing the university in accreditation, and providing a basis for curriculum change.

Perhaps the most encouraging thing about this convergence of initiatives and efforts, local and national, is that they are providing the opportunity for the development of a broadly based discourse around teaching and learning. The hope, of course, is that as this discourse becomes richer and more attractive, it will raise the level of reflection about teaching and learning and improve practice among instructors, administrators and students alike.

Conclusion

The genres, topics, and methods of the scholarship of teaching and learning are being invented as we speak: Its role in academic careers is being written case by case; new practitioners announce themselves every day; and they are just beginning to seek each other out. We can see that disciplinary styles are rightly influencing the way scholars approach teaching and student learning; but fortunately, disciplinary 'boundaries' in this area are not that well established, facilitating border-crossing and collaboration across fields.

But this is not to say that the disciplines will ultimately prove irrelevant to the scholarship of teaching and learning. The feature of interdisciplinarity that so intrigues most people who take it up is the dawning sense that their own discipline has distinctive contributions to make to a larger project to which other disciplines can contribute as well. There are questions that come more naturally to some disciplines than others, problems that call for different methods, issues that lend themselves to different explanatory strategies, and audiences that respond to different forms of address. There is something to be gained from what happily has been called 'methodological pluralism' (Kirsch 1992). And there is something to be learned by looking at classrooms as organizations, at teaching as communication, or at teaching as a kind of inquiry into learning (to name just a few provocative images), regardless of one's own discipline's favoured metaphors and styles.

Of one thing we can be certain. Whatever the future of the scholarship of teaching and learning, it will no longer be mostly a matter of parallel play. I am convinced that scholars will continue to discover and rediscover that their own fields have much to contribute to a common language for trading ideas, enlarging pedagogical imaginations and strengthening scholarly work. The very distinctiveness of the disciplines, which some find disturbing, can be a source of strength for the scholarship of teaching and learning (see Gallison 1997: 444). What matters in the end is whether, through deft use of our own disciplinary styles and participation in this new trading zone, student understanding is deepened, mind and character are strengthened, and lives and communities are enriched.

Key learning points

Senior staff

- Development may flow from focused peer interactions. Make space to enable colleagues to interact on a disciplinary basis.
- Value and reward scholarship in teaching and learning in its own right.
- Address the imbalance between research and teaching in institutional missions, procedures and reward structures.

Heads of department

- Encourage staff to engage in discussion, teaching projects and publication designed to improve teaching and learning within the department and through external disciplinary networks and connections.
- Create space for reporting developments and successes in routine meetings and events.
- Lead by example – get involved.

Professional staff developers

- Make connections with discipline-based and other bodies developing a scholarship of teaching and learning and promote their activities, where relevant.
- Enable and celebrate discipline-based interactions within higher education institutions and departments by providing project funding, chairing/facilitating meetings, reporting upon successes and so on.
- Create forums for scholars from different disciplines to come together to share experiences and operate within the 'trading zone'.

Notes

1 This chapter is a substantially revised and expanded version of a paper presented at the opening plenary session of the Second Annual Joint UK & USA Conference on the Scholarship of Teaching and Learning, 23–24 May 2002, London, organized by Vaneeta D'Andrea and David Gosling. Educational Development Services, University of East London and the Educational Development Centre, City University cosponsored it. The paper draws on the 'Introduction' (Huber and Morreale) and 'Orienting Essay' (Huber) to Huber and Morreale (2002). An early draft of the paper was used to stimulate electronic debate in the UK through the LTSN Generic Centre website (www.ltsn.ac.uk/genericcentre/scholarship/) too. I am grateful to the editors for working on the key learning points with me.
2 For more on this programme, see: http://www.carnegiefoundation.org/CASTL/highered
3 One Carnegie scholar, citing a recent article about the second-class status that educational researchers accord 'classroom research' by teachers in primary and secondary schools, worried that scholars of teaching and learning in higher education might also have to ask whether there are other kinds of validity they could claim for their work. See also Anderson and Herr (1999) on the problematic status of practitioner research in schools and universities.
4 Documents from the campus programme, including campus inventories ('Mapping Progress Reports') are available from the AAHE WebCenter at http://aahe.ital.utexas. edu – It is necessary to register to access the site.

6

Developing the subject dimension to staff development

Cliff Allan, Richard Blackwell and Graham Gibbs[1]

Introduction

The strong disciplinary identity and focus of academics in higher education, arising from epistemological and social sources, is well documented (Becher 1989; Becher and Trowler 2001; Henkel 2000). Academic staff tend to think about issues relating to learning, teaching and assessment predominantly in terms of their own discipline – their own 'tribe and its territory'. Furthermore, it has been argued that many practitioners seeking development will only respond to peers in the discipline and are often antipathetic to staff development, advice, theory or research which is not discipline-based (Jenkins 1996). These issues have been recognized internationally in, for example, the three-year technology-focused Committee for University Teaching and Staff Development (CUTSD) initiative in Australia (Department of Employment, Education,Training and Youth Affairs 1998; Johnston and Peat 1998; Phillips 2001) and the increasing 'discipline styles' emphasis of the scholarship of teaching and learning debate in the USA (Huber and Morreale 2002; see Chapter 5). In the UK the past decade has witnessed a series of short-term project-based initiatives, notably the Computers in Teaching Initiative, the Teaching and Learning Technology Programme and the Fund for the Development of Teaching and Learning (FDTL) (see Higher Education Funding Council for England (HEFCE) 1998).

This chapter discusses four illustrative case studies from different disciplinary settings. These case studies demonstrate the positive potential of subject-based approaches and raise key issues about sustainability and integration with institutional policy and SD provision. First, the FDTL is briefly described and the four case studies introduced. The case studies then explore SD issues associated with working within a discipline. The cases have been selected to illustrate the potential within disciplines displaying different characteristics (for example on Tony Becher's convergent and divergent dimension of disciplinary communites). Second, we describe the arrival of the Learning and Teaching Support Network (LTSN) which has built on the early successes of the FDTL programme and other previous subject-based support initiatives. It was designed to address issues of sustainability and co-ordination that arose from evaluations of previous initiatives (HEFCE 1998). Third, we consider some issues arising from the subject-based approach, identifying the need for partnerships and collaborative working if the potential for synergistic working with other sources of development support is to be achieved.

The Fund for the Development of Teaching and Learning: discipline-wide staff development through national-scale projects

The FDTL is an initiative of the HEFCE (http://www.hefce.ac.uk/Pubs/hefce/ 2001/01_60.htm). It operates primarily within disciplines, and works across institutions. It arose from the perceived need to disseminate and transfer 'good practices' identified in inspections of departments (subject review) carried out by the UK Quality Assurance Agency. Since 1996 over 130 discipline-based projects have been funded with up to £250,000 each, largely to collate and disseminate existing best teaching, learning and assessment practice within their discipline. Most have been single-discipline projects. A number, however, have functioned in effect as staff and educational development networks for their discipline. The emphasis within these projects has shifted from the technical components of a particular teaching topic to the staff and educational development, and sometimes organizational development, processes involved in working effectively with end users.

Four such projects are outlined here in the form of short case studies, in order to explore and analyse SD issues associated with working within a discipline. Each project is very different. The case studies have been written from the perspective of the project staff, and focus on a particular component of their project that involved an apparently effective SD process. Following the case studies some issues concerning effective national-scale disciplinary SD will be explored.

Case study 1: Chemistry

An FDTL project called 'Project Improve' aimed to develop and disseminate good practice and innovation in teaching and learning in chemistry. The project collated many examples of good practice and ran many SD events within chemistry departments, regionally and nationally. The project developed a substantial website containing materials about the teaching of chemistry (http://science.ntu.ac.uk/ chph/improve/improve.html). However, key to the project's success was a realization that influential staff in departments had to become involved. Directors of study and heads of teaching, who have no forum for discussion, were invited to an initial meeting geared to their needs. Most departments were represented, including many staff who would not normally have attended a teaching event, and feedback was positive, with the opportunity to meet colleagues dealing with similar issues being appreciated. In further meetings the work of the project was included, alongside other topics such as quality assurance, recruitment and professional body relationships. On conclusion of the project the professional body, the Institute for Chemistry, took on the forum. A main benefit was thus to engage a significant group of staff in teaching and learning issues, by giving them something they wanted and valued – a continuing forum for the sharing of experience with colleagues.

Case study 2: Languages

Collaboration was achieved between a cluster of ten FDTL projects concerned with the teaching of languages. Rather than risk projects duplicating each other in their focus and competing with each other with parallel publications and events during their dissemination, the projects agreed to allocate a proportion of their funding to an existing 'neutral' co-ordinating agency: the Centre for Information on Language Teaching and Research. The website of the combined languages projects can be viewed at http://lang.fdtl.ac.uk/ A co-ordinating group met three times a year, organizing newsletters, conferences and seminars. Project staff would compare plans and experiences, and a valuable supportive community developed, which was helpful for those not experienced in managing projects. Thus the process of offering staff development to others provided staff development for the developers. The bottom-up nature of the initiative was key to its strength. When the funding ended, regular meetings ceased. The new LTSN Subject Centre, subsequently created, is making use of the lessons learnt about co-operative networking.

Case study 3: Geography

The Geography Discipline Network collated a large number of examples of good teaching practice and made these available to the entire discipline. Outcomes included a searchable database (see http://www.chelt.ac.uk/gdn), a series of ten publications, and associated workshops that were customized for delivery within all geography departments in England. The project was felt to have worked well because groups of geographers who had previously worked together were assembled, together with educational developers. Backers and advisers were assembled, the project plan was clear, a full-time project manager provided co-ordination and the community was involved from the start. Web material, some of it from overseas, offered something of value. Workshops were run in departments and guides distributed to ensure that target staff were reached. The guides were of high quality and easy to use, offered practical examples drawn from the community and referred also to general principles and research.

Case study 4: History

History 2000 wanted to help historians to promote a supportive and critical 'community of practice' (see Chapter 10) that would encourage development of history teaching. To achieve this, the project used half of its funding to support small-scale 'action research' projects within history departments throughout England (http://www.bathspa.ac.uk/history2000/). Preparation involved a newsletter-guide to good practice, and other materials on practicalities of projects and on their value to the community. Participants were expected to feed back their findings in conferences and publications. Twelve projects were selected, and project teams were supported with workshops on action research and ongoing advice, guidance and materials. Care was taken to raise the status of action research, by a scholarly approach and an emphasis on outcomes developing the discipline and providing publications. Many historians' views of educational development were substantially changed. In many cases, so were staff–student relationships.

This project preferred the word 'participation' to 'dissemination', and this was key to its approach. It encouraged collaboration, including between departments, institutions, staff and educational development units, students and subject associations. Guidance and support were provided, including introduction of relevant educational literature at an appropriate stage, whilst leaving room for project leaders to lead. Activities deliberately included high-quality, prestigious and well-publicized output.

Issues

Of the many issues which could be discussed from these four cases, eight are selected here for comment.

Engaging appropriate end users using appropriate methods
It is crucial to understand who the end users are and to develop appropriate mechanisms to engage them. In the chemistry project 'directors of study' were a key group of end users and their interests were quite particular – for example, concerning professional accreditation. They had previously shown only moderate levels of interest in the main work of the project, but by addressing their management agenda and bringing together a coherent group with this shared agenda, progress was made. Second, appropriate processes were selected too – in this case using meetings that resemble committees rather than experiential workshops. One size does not fit all.

Making dissemination products appropriate and useful
The sheer volume of SD material concerning teaching and learning now being produced is overwhelming and exceeds the desire of most higher education teachers to engage with it. The geography project went to some lengths to make sure their materials were more likely to be used. They:

- involved a large team of geographers in their production;
- had very high standards in terms of content and production;
- emphasized practical examples rather than educational theory;

- offered, at no cost to departments, customized workshops which were designed around exploiting these materials;
- built a searchable web database of examples.

Making the whole more than the sum of the parts
Staff development strategies often comprise a series of separate components. Each may be, on its own, of moderate quality and limited reach, simply as a result of its modest scale and funding, and may operate largely in isolation. End users may experience only one or two of these components, and their perception of the scale and quality of SD overall may therefore be affected. The languages and history projects brought components together and also brought end users together across the components. In such circumstances an informal 'benchmarking' process takes place involving a levelling up of expectations of quality and also a sense that there is a larger shift taking place of which each small corner is just a part.

Building capacity for change
Teachers in higher education do not in the main have any great capacity to run effective teaching improvement projects, though they might be reluctant to admit this. Funding teaching improvement through projects may therefore achieve poor value for money. Within institutions that fund innovation it is becoming more common to provide the kind of support that might result in better value for money but it is not yet common for disciplines to address this issue. The history project went to a great deal of trouble to build this capacity – setting high scholarly standards for outcomes, providing project support, bringing project staff together for SD events focusing on the process of effective action research, and designing projects in a series of stages which gradually brought staff on. History as a discipline was starting from a low base in terms of the scholarship of teaching, and yet some of the outcomes were of a very high standard compared with the outcomes of some other disciplinary projects that had a longer record of teaching improvement efforts.

Undertaking staff development effort within teachers' own contexts
Although the focus of the projects was disciplinary, teaching takes place within particular departmental and institutional contexts, each with its own culture, patterns of practice, regulations and resource constraints. However clever specific examples of 'good practice' may be, they need to be adapted and bent to the needs of particular contexts if they are to be used at all, and this cannot be done by the staff developer. This probably means taking the examples to meetings within departments rather than relying solely on websites or national events for dissemination, and having a 'consultancy' relationship with end users. Decisions about adopting innovations in, say, assessment may require departmental policy agreement and this, too, requires collaboration within departments rather than the private decisions of individual teachers.

Building communities of practice
Although several of the case studies emphasize rigorous management, planning, volume of activity and other such project management issues, they also emphasize

the building of communities. There are differences of values and practices between institutions, divisive rivalries and suspicions, and often little dialogue. While it may be normal to discuss research and disciplinary content outside one's institution, it may be unusual to discuss teaching openly or with rigour. An annual conference or a newsletter about teaching within a discipline is better than nothing. It takes a lot more effort and time to create an active and lively 'community of practice' in which it is normal to discuss teaching and in which differences in practice are seen as interesting and the source of insight, rather than threatening or evidence of inferiority (see Chapter 10). It may be difficult to evaluate achievements in this area and to specify project 'deliverables' in advance, but this should not deter projects and initiatives from emphasizing this vital component of SD.

Dissemination with end users, rather than to end users
The 'participation' point of the history case study is crucial. Staff development is often done to individuals or groups by very different individuals who are paid to do it to them. Teaching development projects become trapped into thinking that they have to tell end users about their deliverables or, even less usefully, about their project. These four case studies highlight the importance of collaborative activity in which dissemination and SD are done together with end users. The agendas of end users become more important than those of the project. The processes they want to use when they meet do not often resemble traditional SD processes in which the 'facilitator' has absolute power. The project may need to change its goals as well as its processes to engage successfully in collaborative activity.

The use of teaching development projects as a staff development activity
It is common to use teaching improvement funding to support development projects. Almost all English higher education institutions now fund such project-led development internally and it is becoming common for subject areas to support projects financially (Gibbs *et al.* 2002). Academics find projects an engaging development process because they resemble the process of research, carry status and prestige associated with the funding and public platform they provide, and involve a more suitable professional development process for experienced staff than does training. However, it is common for the products of such projects to be of limited value and to be adopted by few teachers, especially when the product involves information and communications technology courseware. The most lasting and useful outcomes often involve the learning of those involved, rather than the products. The implications of this for disciplinary project design include the following:

- The project work should be undertaken by teachers themselves, rather than employing research assistants or project officers.
- As many teachers as possible should be directly involved in the project, rather than the project being conducted by one or two people and disseminated to many.

- Teaching experiments involving innovation and risk may lead to more learning (if less success) than following well-trodden paths.
- Much of the learning takes place through talking with other teachers involved in the project, and so frequent meetings throughout the project, developing outcomes in stages through trial and error, can be more effective than isolated individuals attempting to launch a highly polished product on an astonished community.
- Project products usually need extensive adaptation to fit varied educational contexts. Initial development in a wide range of contexts makes transferability more likely (for a fuller analysis see Baume *et al.* 2002).

The emergence of a subject-based support service: the Learning and Teaching Support Network

Project-based funding does not ensure impact beyond the life of the project. Sometimes help is to hand, as in the willingness of the professional body for chemistry to take on the innovation described in case study 1. But who ensures that the emergent 'community of practice' in history is supported, its meetings and activities funded, if no equivalent to chemistry's professional body is to hand? Moreover, these projects tend to create an extensive cottage industry of enthusiasts, innovators, educational and staff developers, project teams and institutional consortia who have developed and implemented a fantastic array of practices in learning and teaching, often within the isolation of their institution or project consortium. Consequently, there has been significant duplication between development activities and programmes, with wheels constantly being reinvented. A related need is to develop a means of disseminating experience in an effective way so that good practice is taken up in many new settings. There was a strong feeling amongst policy-makers and practitioners that new investment in learning and teaching would be wasted if the experience and good practices that already existed in the sector were not harnessed and widely transferred. These and other reasons (HEFCE 1998) led the UK higher education funding councils to invest in the development of a support network, the Learning and Teaching Support Network (LTSN), as an attempt to provide coherence and co-ordination to the range of learning and teaching activities, practices and development opportunities for staff, together with a mechanism to deliver effective dissemination, transfer and transformation of good practices, innovations and developments.

The LTSN principally consists of 24 subject centres/networks and a Generic Centre (see http://www.ltsn.ac.uk for details). The main roles of the subject centres are:

- promoting and sharing good practices in learning, teaching and assessment;
- brokering the transfer and take-up of knowledge and practice between users, experts, developers and innovators;
- setting up, supporting and developing learning and teaching networks.

The subject centres were created in a way that would enable a reasonable mapping of most disciplines into one of the centres. Furthermore, by being part of a wider network the centres were encouraged to develop collaborative activities to ensure that interdisciplinary activity was supported, and to resist the creation of artificial barriers between subject areas. For example, three of the subject centres – for English; Art, Design and Communication; and Sociology, Anthropology and Politics – are collaborating to ensure appropriate coverage of cultural studies. Subject centre activities include the following:

- identifying needs of subject communities (through surveys, etc.);
- provision of resources and materials (especially electronic ones);
- networking and supporting subject teaching communities (through, for example, webs of key contacts in all or most departments);
- oiling the developmental wheels (by, for example, providing competitive small grant funds to promote mini-versions of the kinds of projects reported earlier);
- measuring impact (each centre has its own evaluator and the LTSN as a whole has engaged programme-level formative evaluators).

This broad remit is also underpinned by the need for subject centres to tailor their work to meet the needs of their disciplines, perhaps crucial in these days of regulation where the voice of practitioners seems to have been lost.

Challenges and opportunities for discipline-based staff development

The advantages of developing communities of practice within disciplines, each with its own culture and forms of discourse, are considerable. There is also scope, however, for failure to learn from others' experience, for duplication of effort and for amateurism as everyone attempts to be an educational expert. We now turn to examine some of the most salient criticisms.

Reinventing the wheel

Although the LTSN was set up partly to restrain the constant reinventing of the wheel, with 24 parallel subject centres and several times that many national-scale discipline-specific teaching development projects there is a real danger that disciplines may attempt to learn everything themselves, starting from scratch. Generic literature may be overlooked, as may developments in one discipline by another discipline (for example, advances in problem-based learning in medicine, project-based learning in architecture, practice-based learning in nursing or social work, the use of information and communications technology in learning mathematics).

The extent to which there are real disciplinary differences in teaching has been questioned by some, such as Gibbs (2000), who argue that it is common for disciplines to assume that differences are greater than they really are or that commonalities are more limited than they really are. The way that, for example, peer observation of teaching or student self-assessment operates in practice looks similar in most contexts. Underlying principles and strategies, and even the most successful tactics, may be almost identical.

This points to the need for high levels of co-ordination within project approaches, and the need for continuous dialogue between subject experts and institutionally based, generic SD experts. Within LTSN, this may be facilitated by the LTSN Generic Centre, which has a particular remit to lead projects on sector-wide issues (including projects on assessment and problem-based learning) or derived from policy (such as initiatives on employability); see http://www.ltsn.ac.uk/genericcentre/projects/

Building communities of practice in unpromising conditions

Becher's (1989) classic analysis of 'academic tribes and territories' identified four dimensions along which disciplines varied, relating to cognitive (hard versus soft knowledge and the pure-applied continuum) and social factors (convergent communities being contrasted with divergent ones, and 'rural' research styles being contrasted with 'urban' ones). One implication of this analysis is that some disciplines' boundaries 'are so strongly guarded as to be virtually impenetrable: others are weakly guarded and open to incoming and outgoing traffic' (Becher 1989: 37). Therefore the task of enhancing learning and teaching within disciplines is not the same across the academy, and the pace of change is likely to vary. Hard knowledge areas with a high level of convergence around common norms (such as mathematics and physics) seem to present the greatest challenge in a world dominated by research. The case studies here show what can be done, however, in a largely hard area of knowledge albeit with a rather fragmented community (chemistry) and in developing the discipline in a convergent culture, albeit of soft knowledge (history). Geography, a discipline renowned for its openness, presents a case of a multidisciplinary (divergent) area that might be thought more receptive to external 'soft' knowledge (Becher 1989; Becher and Trowler 2001, Chapter 9).

Some discipline areas have spent many years, even decades, developing a vibrant and sophisticated community of practice around the teaching of their discipline. These networks, with a long history of conferences, journals, meetings and open discussion, working both formally and informally and with or without funding, have made it easier for discipline-based development to work. Some LTSN subject centres have their origins in previous initiatives, notably the Computers in Teaching Initiative (e.g. Economics), and therefore enjoy advantages of continuity too. A major challenge for LTSN's knowledge management and evaluation systems is to assist those disciplines and subjects that might require most help due to the nature of the discipline and/or for historical reasons. Some existing networks have gradually changed values and beliefs (for example, about the extent to which the quality of teaching is solely dependent on the quality of research). Such changed belief systems may be prerequisites for productive SD to improve teaching.

Working with national policy mandates

Until very recently one of the features of project funding has been a lack of focus on policy priorities and, for many, therefore a lack of direct relevance to growing concerns. The LTSN was also set up to promote and enable change amongst practitioners in response to key national policy priorities – for example, in relation to widening participation, student retention, and employability.

Many of these are issues which institutional managers are considering and responding to, and it is the role of the LTSN Generic Centre to focus on these institutional needs, providing intelligence and materials to senior staff and bringing together LTSN subject centres and institutional staff developers. Subject centres can play a key role in providing a focus for debate, exchange of information and practice in relation to their own subject communities too, assisting them to respond to, mediate, manage and enhance the changes brought about by public policy.

However, there will remain a tension in managing top-down and bottom-up interests. The LTSN has been described as 'an experiment in loose–tight coupling' by its evaluators. On the one hand, it is loosely coupled as centres are encouraged to respond to subject-based priorities in ways best suited to the different disciplinary contexts. On the other hand, government, funding bodies and key stakeholders will wish to see the centres and networks also align with their main policy priorities. This is a key part of the role of the LTSN Executive, interfacing with national stakeholders, and aligning subject centre efforts with those of the wider sector. Managing this tension will be crucial to maintaining support from both interests.

An institutional focus?

An obvious challenge for subject-based projects and a subject-based network is interfacing with higher education institutions, demonstrating relevance to institutional leaders and co-ordinating with institutionally based staff developers, most of whom have a predominantly generic role. The creation of the LTSN Generic Centre was partly designed to do this. Rather than subject communities, the SD community and senior managers such as pro-vice-chancellors are among its key constituents. The partial focus on the policy agendas is designed to deliver benefits for institutional leaders and staff developers, through brokerage. One example is the new forms of support and SD created for part-time teachers involving a 'tripartite' model of provision. In this model the institutional SD unit contributes generic input, departments undertake some discipline-specific delivery and support, and the relevant LTSN subject centre supports the department in a variety of ways such as provision of subject specific materials, training and advice (see http: www.ltsn.ac.uk/genericcentre/index.asp?id = 17220).

While every English institution is currently attempting to improve teaching across all disciplines by implementing an institutional learning and teaching strategy, disciplines themselves may be looking outwards to other departments in other institutions, or to professions, for goals, inspiration and solutions. There may be real tensions between what a discipline would like to do for the sake of the development of teaching of the discipline and what institutions would like a particular department to do for the sake of the institution. Even when there is a commonality of broad goals, the form this might take for a discipline and an institution may vary considerably. For example, a professional body's list of generic competencies, or a subject area's favoured list of 'transferable' skills, may differ widely from an institution's common framework for developing employability skills which it expects to be delivered in a common way across all departments.

A number of subject centres have already started to work with institutional staff and educational support units to maximize the local and subject-based support for individual academics and departments. Institutional managers will see subject centres as aids to institutional development if the centres' activities are relevant and useful in institutions' strategic development. The organizational structure of the institution, including the extent of devolved management at departmental level, will also be a factor. However, subject centres could be seen to be unhelpful to institutions if they are perceived to be supporting specific disciplinary interests at the expense of institutional change. Institutions may wish to shape their academic provision in the face of changing student demand and may need to recast their subject mix. The centres' own strategies must be sensitive to such institutional needs and facilitate change rather than simply protect traditional disciplinary interests.

This is already beginning to happen as several centres facilitate discussion on key issues facing their subject communities, providing a focus and means for taking forward developments which follow. Prominent examples include those centres covering subject areas where the future nature and shape of learning and teaching are being hotly debated as changes in student demand and institutional responses to them begin to bite. The LTSN Languages, Linguistics and Area Studies centre has facilitated discussion on and response to the future of language teaching in the face of declining student numbers. A number of other subject centres have begun jointly to look at mathematics provision in higher education in the light of the changing needs of students and subjects requiring mathematics input. There is some scope for linking the change-agent role of subject centres with institution interests, although this will inevitably be enhanced if strong relations of mutual support can be established. A task for institutional staff developers is to reach out to these initiatives, indirectly through the Generic Centre and directly through individual subject centres.

A lack of innovation within departments may be caused by their institutional context, with infrastructure blocks, local regulations and so on, rather than through lack of awareness within the discipline of workable alternatives to current practice. This, of course, points to a role for institutionally based SD. A weakness of the project-based approach is that higher education institutions have often been subordinated to the need to deliver on quantitative targets. Disciplinary communities need to become aware of varied institutional contexts and be more sophisticated agents of organizational change, rather than concentrating only on disciplinary teaching concerns. One LTSN Generic Centre project has developed a set of literature reviews and an overview guide to educational change for heads of department (Trowler *et al.* 2003). However, issues of how to bring about and embed change may be common to most disciplines but may also be institution-specific, so there is considerable scope for collaboration between SD professionals and subject centres. Indeed, an impact on institutional development is unlikely without it.

It is common for institutionally based initial training programmes for new university teachers to involve much discussion between teachers from different disciplines, and this is frequently considered by trainers and new teachers alike to be one of the most enjoyable and illuminating elements of such SD programmes. It helps teachers to recognize and understand why their discipline is taught in the way it is and to see how other disciplines are taught, as well as widening their horizons as to what is possible and increasing their repertoire of teaching tactics. It stops teachers taking their department's teaching practices for granted in a way that project-based initiatives cannot. Discipline-specific SD alone runs the danger of not challenging assumptions and teaching conventions and of simply reproducing the dominant disciplinary culture. Generic courses may be criticized or even rejected for their lack of disciplinary contextualization. For this reason, many institutionally based programmes have blended generic with subject-specific approaches, making use of expertise and case studies from within academic departments. A number of LTSN subject centres have now developed input, and even organized separate workshop sessions, for new staff. Staff development units and LTSN subject centres need to clarify the relationships between their respective provision, to agree credit transfer arrangements and so on, to ensure integrated and accredited programmes.

Conclusion

Project-based case studies have shown the potential of a subject-based approach in a number of different disciplines, including some that might be thought quite difficult to penetrate. Issues of sustainability and knowledge management, stopping the proverbial 'reinvention of the wheel', have moved the debate on in the UK and led to the formation of a network, the LTSN. To address national policy mandates and institutional needs, and to ensure appropriate challenge to disciplinary teaching norms, entails a balance of disciplinary, cross-disciplinary and generic staff development. This requires generic staff developers to become more aware of and able to work with disciplinary contexts and priorities. Disciplinary staff developers need to keep in close touch with the way staff developers in other disciplines go about their business, and to exploit other disciplines, as well as generic institutionally based educational expertise, in their work. Although there will inevitably be some tensions, the benefits of collaboration and the potential for synergy are great.

Notes

1   We are grateful to Tina Overton, Mike Kelly, Mick Healey and Paul Hyland for providing initial case study outlines, on which the chapter draws in a condensed form.

Key learning points

Senior staff

- Subject-based staff development has much potential to appeal to academic identities and provides another route for stimulating flexible learning individuals.
- Aligning subject-based activity with institutional needs suggests proactive liaison by pro-vice-chancellors, rectors and the like with the institutionally focused parts of networks and initiatives and a willingness to contribute to intitiatives focused on areas of priority to institutions.
- Aligning such external input with institutional needs will require encouraging generic, institutional staff development units to collaborate actively with subject-based networks and providers to achieve synergy.

Heads of department

- There are increasing resources and opportunities for discipline-based staff development located outside the institution which may contribute to departmental development. Sometimes direct access and influence may be acquired by nominating departmental links (as with LTSN subject centre 'departmental contacts').
- Aligning subject-based support with institutional culture and requirements may be a significant issue for departments.

Professional staff developers

- Discipline-based staff development has much to offer in terms of perceived relevance and credibility. There is some expertise building up outside the traditional staff development community.
- There is a need to link with those projects and networks developing subject-based approaches for mutual benefit. There is scope to negotiate collaboration based on the generic expertise and institutional knowledge of the staff development professional (see below).
- Subject-based projects and approaches inevitably face challenges when seeking to integrate their concerns with universities' and colleges' needs. Institutionally based staff development professionals can play a key role in informing, mediating and focusing subject influences in appropriate ways. There is potential to exchange this knowledge and access for reciprocal subject-based input to existing and developing generic staff development programmes.

7

A new approach to professionalizing teaching and accrediting training: The Institute for Learning and Teaching in Higher Education

Caroline Bucklow and Paul Clark

Background

The establishment of the Institute for Learning and Teaching in Higher Education (ILTHE) in 1999, as a major outcome of the work of National Committee of Inquiry into Higher Education (NCIHE 1997), chaired by Sir Ron Dearing, marked an important stage in the development of teaching as a professional activity in higher education (HE) in the UK. While the conditions that gave rise to the ILTHE were specific to the UK, many of the issues involved are relevant to other countries and international comparisons are made later in this chapter. The recommendation to establish the ILTHE was inspired by the recognition of the increased importance of effective teaching and learning support for the maintenance of the UK's position in the knowledge-based economy of the twenty-first century. The rapid expansion of student numbers in UK higher education, significant changes in the secondary education system and the application of information and communications technology in many areas of learning and teaching have transformed the student learning environment in ways that demand new forms of teaching and learning support. The Dearing Committee also recognized that, since the mid-1980s, the research agenda has come to dominate even more strongly the professional practice of academics at the expense of teaching and supporting student learning. The Committee saw a pressing need to raise the status of teaching and learning support in UK higher education to meet the changing educational and economic situations described above.

At the same time, the increased focus on accountability and the measurement of standards in all areas of education gave rise to concerns that standards of teaching within UK higher education institutions (HEIs) were uneven and that this was linked to the lack of preparation of academic staff in HE for the evolving teaching role. The lack of preparation for teaching also distinguished HE from other educational sectors, where prior training is mandatory.

The solution to the above problems proposed by the Dearing Report was the creation of a professional body that would take responsibility for the accreditation of staff development programmes run by HEIs, stimulate research into HE pedagogic issues and promote innovation in learning and teaching in HE. This proposition raised the fundamental questions of what it means to be 'a professional' in teaching in HE and which of the traditional functions of a professional body the ILTHE should undertake.

Professionalism and professional body function in HE learning and teaching

There exists a substantial literature concerned with the concepts of professionalism and the structure and function of professional bodies – see Freidson (1994) and references cited. On the empirical side, there exists a range of professional bodies with widely varying structures and activities. Drawing on the literature, one can define a profession as a community of individuals with the following properties. The individuals possess and make use of specialized knowledge; undergo long training and socialization into the activities and ethos of the profession; make substantial use of discretion in the performance of their work; are dedicated to serving a wider community; and adhere to certain standards of performance and codes of behaviour. The community exerts control over the standards of performance of its members, over entrance and 'good standing' requirements for the profession, and over codes of behaviour and disciplinary procedures; and is responsible for reassuring the wider community as to the standard of performance of its members. For the profession of teachers and learning facilitators in HE, the individual characteristics can be broadly recognized, although for the substantial majority of experienced staff the training in the specialized knowledge of teaching has come through experiential learning, rather than organized education. The community of HE practitioners has, as a group, none of the characteristics of a profession set out above.

The planning group of the ILTHE initially specified the requirements for ILTHE membership in terms of a range of teaching outcomes, intended to encapsulate good practice in teaching at HE level. The outcomes-oriented approach was informed by the climate of opinion in the staff development community that preparation for teaching should be measured in terms of what was achieved and not of how many hours of training were delivered. This was felt to be particularly important since the bulk of existing training took place within practice and had to be balanced against the demands of other aspects of the academic role. The way in which the outcomes were specified was driven, in part, by the desire to adopt an approach to standard-setting that was in keeping with developments in other areas of education and in line with the expectations of national training organizations in a range of occupational areas. In response to the results of a consultation process, however, the approach was radically altered, as many experienced practitioners within the HE sector felt that this type of approach would be too restrictive and would result in a culture of compliance rather than in a genuine commitment to improving the status and practice of teaching and the support of learning in higher education. As Nicholls (2001: 32) comments:

> competency-based systems and prescriptive language based on generic norms and values don't bode well with those who essentially come from divers backgrounds and disciplines. That is not to say that academics within these disciplines and diverse backgrounds don't wish to engage in the discourse or dialogues related to teaching and learning in their respective fields. It is more a question of making the demands for membership reflect the diversity of the higher education community.

There are at least three aspects of the creation of the ILTHE that mark it out from the usual history of professional bodies. Firstly, most professional bodies come into being as a result of the gathering together of a group of practitioners who feel that the formalization of their activity and a regulation of its membership are desirable or necessary, in their interests or those of the wider society. The ILTHE was brought into existence by the representative bodies of higher education (Universities UK, the Standing Conference of Principals) the major trade unions (the Association of University Teachers, the National Association of Teachers in Further and Higher Education) and the HE funding councils. Building a basic understanding in the academic and learning support communities of the need for such a professional body and building active support through membership has therefore been a major task for the ILTHE since its inception. Secondly, the ILTHE is focused on only part of the job description of its practitioners, that is, the teaching or learning facilitation role that they carry out – in contrast with, for example, the medical or legal professions. This allows the ILTHE to cater for a wider group than the 'professional academic' but does not cover the full range of activities and concerns of such academics. Lastly, the principal objective of the ILTHE, its *raison d'être*, is to transform the present situation in HE learning and teaching, not to formalize the present situation. It therefore has to build a consensus for the activity that it exists to undertake rather than presume that the consensus exists. All these features pose significant challenges for the ILTHE and put its progress over the first forty months into perspective.

For many teachers in higher education in the UK, recent developments, including the shift from an elite to a mass education system, the increasing emphasis on research as the basis for professional advancement and an increased concern with accountability and external measures of quality, have led to concerns about deprofessionalization and the creation of a new academic proletariat that is neither encouraged nor enabled to exercise professional judgement. Set against this background of what is perceived to be an increasingly managerialist HE system, in which the collegial approach to maintaining standards appears increasingly under threat, the goal of the ILTHE, to establish itself as a professional body governed by its members and reflecting their professional values, appears particularly challenging. However, the principal impact of the ILTHE in this area is to widen the group of colleagues with whom professional values can be shared, from fellow department members to the wider community of academic and learning support staff (including learning technologists and information officers), across a range of disciplines.

The experience of the first three years of operation suggests that there is a significant body of opinion amongst HE teachers and those involved in the support of learning that recognizes the need to embrace a dual professionalism of teacher and subject specialist. The aim of the ILTHE is to develop a concept of professionalism that meets this need and provides a framework and a support system within which individual staff in higher education can manage their own professional development in the face of constantly changing demands and expectations.

The ILTHE model of professionalism

Clark (2000) describes the ILTHE's approach to professionalism as follows:

> The model of professionalism that the ILTHE is seeking to implement on behalf of teachers and learning support staff in higher education has the following objectives:

> * to establish standards of performance in teaching and learning facilitation through a) the recognition of achievement by individuals and b) the accreditation of staff development programmes provided by institutions;
> * to establish standards and implement mechanisms for Continuing Professional Development for teachers and learning facilitators;
> * to provide relevant information, advice, case studies or verified research results to the practitioner/member in support of reflective practice and professional development;
> * to create communities of common interest (both virtual and real) amongst the membership to stimulate innovation and to support CPD;
> * within a reasonable period of time, to pass control over policy formation in the areas of regulation and support to the membership.

Crucial to this model are the two principles of self-regulation and engagement with the scholarship of learning. This is not to say that all those engaged in teaching and learning will necessarily expect to undertake research into teaching. However, the ILTHE recognizes a need to bring together education specialists with practitioners in subject disciplines so that there is a greater interaction along the continuum from educational researchers at one end of the spectrum, through discipline specialists with a particular interest in the pedagogy of their discipline, to practitioners who are not engaged in pedagogical research.

The ILTHE's model of professionalism fully embraces the expectation that ILTHE members reflect purposefully on their practice and adopt a student-centred approach to teaching and supporting learning. This offers a way forward that recognizes the need to support individual staff in their endeavour to enhance the experience of learning for students in an increasingly complex and diverse educational environment. In his discussion of a new model of professionalism for higher education, Nixon (2001: 74) states that

> if the intention is to ensure that academic staff are accountable for reflecting on and improving their teaching and for judging the adequacy of what they

do, then it is essential that whatever approach is adopted should encourage them not only to describe what they do but also to explain and justify, in thoughtful and productive ways, why they do what they do.

He goes on to stress the importance of finding new ways to encourage participation in the exploration of effective professional practice rather than creating additional mechanisms of control. Although Nixon is highly critical of the ILTHE's approach, which he sees as simultaneously highly prescriptive and lacking in clarity, these criticisms were made in the early days of the ILTHE, before its processes had been refined and implemented. The ILTHE's current approach to accreditation and the procedures for individual entry for experienced staff have exactly the reflective focus that Nixon advocates.

Accreditation of staff development and training

Since September 1999 the ILTHE has developed processes of professional recognition both at the individual level, by evaluating applications for membership (and, more recently, associateship), and at the institutional level, by accrediting staff develop-ment programmes and some non-award bearing staff development and teaching excellence schemes, as direct entry routes to ILTHE membership. By July 2002, the ILTHE had accredited 127 programmes and other staff development schemes at 106 universities and colleges in the UK (Figure 7.1) and expected this to rise to 145 by July 2003. This represents a very high degree of penetration within the sector and broadly mirrors the proportions of different types of HEI within the sector. Also by the end of July 2002, the ILTHE had received over 16,000 applications for membership and had accepted over 12,000 as members, the majority of whom had joined through the individual entry route (Figure 7.2). There was a surge in

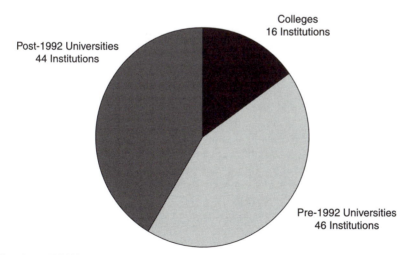

Figure 7.1   ILTHE Accreditation in UK HEIs, July 2002

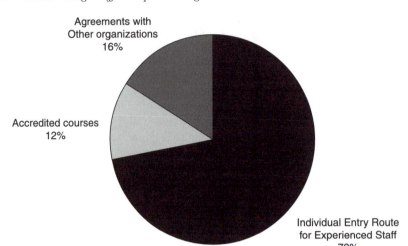

Agreements with
Other organizations
16%

Accredited courses
12%

Individual Entry Route
for Experienced Staff
72%

Figure 7.2   Entry routes for membership of the ILTHE, July 2002

applications during July 2002, as the initial arrangements for individual applications for membership came to an end, and at the time of writing these had not yet been converted into members.

The processes of both individual entry to membership and institutional accreditation focus on five broad areas of professional activity:

1. teaching and/or the support of learning in higher education;
2. contribution to the design and planning of learning activities and/or programmes of study;
3. assessment and/or giving feedback to learners;
4. developing effective learning environments and learner support systems;
5. reflective practice and personal development.

These areas were identified as key elements in the role, through widespread consultation with the HE sector, and are underpinned by the expectation of the command of professional knowledge and the commitment to values, similar to those identified by the Booth Committee and those used by the Staff and Educational Development Association in its Teacher Accreditation Scheme. Within these broadly defined areas, the ILTHE accreditation processes and membership criteria seek to develop a consensus across the HE sector about the appropriate preparation for staff who teach or support student learning in HE.

An aim of the ILTHE is to establish a range of routes to membership and associateship which take account of the varied experience of applicants but which are based on common criteria and are of equivalent status. Currently, the individual entry route for experienced staff recognizes the importance of informal and work-based learning by requiring applicants to discuss the rationale and evidence of effectiveness of their practice in the five areas of activity and by seeking evidence of understanding of how students learn. The accreditation of institutional programmes, which are primarily designed for less experienced practitioners, looks for a more structured approach to learning and seeks evidence that programme participants develop both an understanding of theories of learning and of effective practice in the five areas of professional activity. The ILTHE is also entering into agreements with other professional bodies with a remit to establish standards for HE teaching within specific professional areas, where the standards required can be shown to be equivalent to those expected by the ILTHE.

One aim of the ILTHE approach to accreditation is to encourage diversity within staff development provision, ensuring that all staff have access to appropriate opportunities to develop a professional approach to teaching and supporting learning. It should be noted that one of the challenges in developing the accreditation framework was that the ILTHE was envisaged as an inclusive body, with a membership extending beyond staff on traditional academic teaching contracts to those involved in a number of academic-related areas. The focus on broad areas of activity, rather than the specific outcomes favoured by other accrediting and standard setting bodies, is key to the new approach to professionalism which the ILTHE is seeking to establish. However, there is clear evidence of comparability and compatibility of these broad areas of activity with the areas of activity addressed in the standards for teaching developed by Further Education National Training Organization and by the Teacher Training Agency (TTA) Higher Education Training Organization (THETO 2000b)

Accreditation has proved to be the most controversial element of the mission of the ILTHE, despite the existence of well-established accreditation schemes within the majority of professional and statutory bodies. A number of factors may be influencing opinion in this area. First, there is ambivalence about the status of teaching in HE. The correspondence in the pages of the education press has frequently debated whether there is room for the ILTHE in what is perceived to be an already crowded market for accreditation. To some academic staff the accreditation role is adequately performed by their discipline-based professional body and/or the Quality Assurance Agency, although the cessation of subject review must bring this into question. According to this view, professional bodies such as the engineering institutions already provide professional recognition for academic staff and address issues of teaching within the discipline. A correspondent in *The Independent* newspaper (12 July 2001), for example, commented that

> the problem with the Institute for Learning and Teaching is thus that it is often seen as an additional professional body. Until the role of university lecturer is seen and, dare I say, rewarded in the same way as these other professions, it is difficult to see how there will be any real progress.

As this comment indicates, there is real ambivalence about the nature of the 'dual professionalism' of staff teaching and supporting learning in HE. A substantial number of experienced academic staff still feel that professional credentials and expertise in the subject area should be adequate to ensure teaching competence and that the skills required to teach can either be picked up on the job by trial and error or learned in one or two days' training. Such staff may often be unaware of underpinning research in teaching and learning and tend to characterize the development of professional approaches to teaching and learning support as 'making everybody use OHPs'. For others, the emphasis on the development of professionalism in teaching cannot be divorced from scholarship in the primary discipline area. For this group the main debate focuses on the relationship between 'generic' teaching skills and discipline-based activity. There is, for them, a genuine concern that too great a focus on generic teaching skills may undermine the richness of good practice within teaching in the discipline.

A second area of debate focuses on the relevance and formulation of standards. Early approaches of the ILTHE Planning Group to formulating standards were seen as over-prescriptive and raised fears that the ILTHE had been established to develop a 'national curriculum' for HE teaching practice. In responding to this concern, and in adopting a broader definition of standards, the ILTHE faces significant technical issues as well as political tensions. Pennington describes a number of these in his discussion of the role of the ILTHE in accreditation in higher education. Pennington (1999: 13) comments that 'there is an inevitable tension between institutions' wishes to develop programmes that suit their own particular needs and the ILTHE's need to operate a common national framework which commands wide acceptance among a diverse range of institutions'. As well as commanding acceptance with HEIs, the ILTHE's approach to accreditation must also satisfy the expectations of other stakeholders, including students, employers and government. Pennington identifies as one of the key challenges the need to provide a range of accredited routes to ILTHE membership which allow for the creation of flexible provision to suit staff at different stages of their career and in different institutional roles but which maintain transparent comparability of standards.

In addressing these issues, the ILTHE fosters a climate of co-operation with those responsible for staff development in HEIs. Institutions are encouraged to interpret the ILTHE accreditation criteria flexibly in the light of the specific institutional context and to devise staff development programmes and pathways that meet the needs of teachers and learners in relation to the ILTHE's educational mission. The ILTHE institutional accreditation processes also have a focus on development and dissemination of good practice. The success of this approach can be measured by the comments of staff development course leaders, who frequently report that they find the process thought-provoking and developmental yet rigorous. By encouraging institutions to focus on the development needs of their staff and to find flexible ways to support experienced staff as well as new teachers, the ILTHE can help to create a professionalism that embeds reflective practice in the activities associated with teaching and learning, encourages the use of evidence from pedagogic research as a guide to practice and promotes reflection *in* learning as well as *on* learning.

International comparisons

During the three years in which the ILTHE has been operating, there has been intense interest in its progress from colleagues in other countries. Discussions have taken place with colleagues from Sweden, Australia, Canada, South Africa and New

Zealand about the aims of the ILTHE, its structure, practices and relationship with HEIs and with other stakeholders in higher education in the UK. The aims of the discussions have been mainly to explore the extent to which the ILTHE's approach to supporting and raising the status of learning and teaching in HEIs might be adapted to suit the context of higher education in other countries and the opportunities for co-operation between the ILTHE and similar bodies in other countries. To date it would appear that the ILTHE has a unique position as an independent body owned by its members, providing a national accreditation scheme for those teaching and supporting learning in HE.

The interest shown in the ILTHE may perhaps be attributed to common concerns about appropriate ways to approach the development of professionalism in relation to teaching and the support of learning in a time of great change in HE internationally. As Farnham (1999: 343) notes, 'all the higher education systems appear to be experiencing similar trends such as massification, reductions in public funding, movement to the market, curricula instrumentalism and searching for appropriate methods of managing academic staff in conditions of change'.

In the face of the changes in HE internationally and the trend towards globalization, national initiatives in one country understandably attract interest elsewhere. Moreover, the issue of professional development is becoming increasingly important as a focus of change. Gibbs, in a summary of international approaches to teaching preparation, found that there has been a trend to increase the scale and the funding of programmes and to treat teaching preparation more seriously, sometimes through linking effectiveness in teaching to probation, tenure and promotion decisions. Gibbs (1996a: 44) notes that in Finland and Sweden the government has imposed compulsory initial training, albeit limited in scope, on all university teachers, while in the Netherlands HE teachers in the non-research sector are required to complete extended initial training.

The pace of development, however, varies enormously between different countries. Weeks (2000: 63) notes that in the USA

> the preparation of university teachers is mainly confined to pre-service training for Graduate Teaching Assistants. The format of these programmes appears to vary from university to university. There does, however, seem to be an increasing formalization of these programmes, with some universities offering awards to the Graduate Teaching Assistants on completion.

She contrasts this with the situation in Australia, where there is some provision for in-service staff development for teaching staff in most universities but little evidence of attempts at standardization.

Webb (2001: 8) comments that it is difficult to predict what will happen in Australia in relation to accreditation, since there are concerns within the teaching union and the staff development community about the potential divisiveness of the introduction of a formal accreditation scheme. Similar concerns are raised by the Association of University Staff in New Zealand, whose policy paper on accreditation stresses the need for 'extreme caution' because of the possibility that accreditation might become an instrument of managerial control and could further segregate academic staff into teachers and researchers (Blampied 2001: 37). Blampied also comments on the possibility that the introduction of accreditation in New Zealand might hamper international mobility for academic staff and create problems in recruiting staff from other countries into New Zealand. Blampied (2001: 36) states, however, that interest in teaching quality is on the agenda of the New Zealand government and that the Associate Minister of Education (Tertiary) is thought to be particularly interested in the model of the ILTHE in the UK. Scott (2001), commenting on the situation of staff development in universities in South Africa, stresses the need for effective quality assurance mechanisms in HE and comments that the success of the ILTHE in the UK could help pave the way for similar developments in supporting teaching and learning in South Africa.

Although there are currently no directly equivalent schemes for accrediting university teachers in other countries, the level of international interest in the ILTHE is very encouraging. It is not clear to what extent the concept of an independent professional body that combines the functions of accreditation and the support of development of learning and teaching in HE is appropriate and translatable to other higher education systems. There are features of UK higher education – common salary scales, national bargaining for pay and conditions of service, UK-wide evaluation of research and teaching activity – that can enhance the perception of a UK-wide academic profession. These unifying features do not exist in many other countries, the USA and Canada in particular. It therefore seems likely that if similar organizations develop in other countries they will have to reflect the distinctive structural and political characteristics of their educational context. However, it is to be hoped that in the future the ILTHE will be able to establish mutual recognition agreements with accrediting bodies in other countries. This would provide a firm foundation for international collaboration, would avoid the dangers inherent in exporting an accreditation system designed for the UK to other educational cultures and would facilitate the spread of good practice in teaching and learning on an international level.

In the meantime it is to be hoped that ways may be found to encourage international interest in the work of the ILTHE and to foster international links between ILTHE members and HE practitioners in other countries.

Conclusion: Implications for staff development strategy

The experience of establishing and taking forward the development of a professional body for HE teachers and learning facilitators has led to many constructive discussions with colleagues in the staff development community about the ways in which such a body can support and enhance institutional initiatives. There is considerable support for the view that a national framework for initial and continuing professional development, based around the concept of developing reflective practice, has value as an organizing principle for staff development initiatives both at the institutional and departmental levels and across institutions. This may be particularly valuable where a consortium of institutions, of varying sizes and with strengths in different areas of practice, may wish to collaborate on staff development initiatives. Current work on developing a continuing professional development framework for ILTHE members has attracted great interest from HE as a locus for offering recognition of CPD opportunities provided within the university or college. Some HEIs have also identified the potential to develop or change the culture and ethos of professional development and performance management within the university or college.

The existence of an independent professional body is clearly seen, therefore, to provide a locus for quality enhancement, facilitating national debate about creating evidence-based good practice. This in turn may help HEIs to create well-founded mechanisms for reflecting performance in teaching and supporting learning appropriately within reward and promotion structures. It is perhaps worth noting that anecdotal evidence exists that ILTHE members are already using material generated as part of an application for membership to support claims for promotion on the basis of teaching excellence.

A framework for professional development created collaboratively by members of a professional body that includes people from a wide range of disciplines is likely to command more credibility within the academic community if it is seen to be reflected within reward structures and to align with expectations of other stakeholders such as government agencies and the student body. Moreover, working within a common framework should help to facilitate recognition of staff development undertaken at one institution by other institutions, which will support staff mobility and the free flow of good practice around the HE sector.

Key learning points

Senior staff

- Effective linkage of ILTHE membership with institutions' learning and teaching and human resource strategies.
- Need to create real opportunities for career progression based on teaching excellence.
- Mechanisms to enhance institutional recognition of the dual professionalism expected of higher education teachers

Heads of department

- Key leadership role in stimulating interest in and commitment to the professionalization of learning and teaching.
- Importance of stimulating learning from both generic and discipline-based approaches to learning and teaching
- Encouragement of young academic staff to develop and implement professional standards in both research and teaching.

Professional staff developers

- Proactive engagement with the ILTHE in developing a framework for professionalism in teaching.
- Encouragement of experienced staff to become more aware of the issues and reflect on their teaching practice.
- Promotion of the importance for all staff of familiarity with the literature on the scholarship of teaching.

8

Just another initiative? Investors in People in higher education

Bob Thackwray

Overview

In this chapter I describe the UK Investors in People programme and its interaction with higher education. I outline some of the reasons behind the recent very large increase in participation and examine some of the reasons for not participating. Some relevant literature from higher education staff development, human resource management (HRM), and total quality and change management is cited. Empirical material is drawn in particular from two Higher Education Staff Development Agency (HESDA) projects – on Investors in People in higher education (Box and Thackwray 2001) and on the impact of the building block approach, which allows universities to access and work with the standard in a culturally and methodologically appropriate manner (Box and Thackwray 2002). A section on the Netherlands is drawn from a number of projects with the Association of Dutch Universities (VSNU), notably work with Dutch vice-chancellors and personnel directors, design and delivery of materials in support of Investors in People in higher education and two 'trial' Investors in People audits conducted at Nijmegen University.

The collected experience of almost ten years of higher education engagement with Investors in People suggests that the scheme supports, blends and integrates well with processes of institutional change. It is externally assessed and leads to a national standard yet is evidently flexible enough to be implemented meaningfully in a unique and apparently appropriate way within each institution and/or unit therein. It focuses on the development of people and it leads unit heads at all levels of the institution to clarify and externalize their plans. At its worst, it appears to be, eponymously, just another initiative. At its best, Investors in People appears to offer a self-directed reflective process, or combination of processes, whereby higher education institutions can enhance their position as self-critical communities by developing culturally appropriate systems of institutional self-evaluation.

What is Investors in People?

The Investors in People national standard was one of eight national education and training targets set by the (then Conservative) UK government for organizations to achieve during the 1990s. It was launched in the autumn of 1991, under the auspices of the Training, Enterprise and Education Directorate of the Department of Employment. This was after a pilot group of organizations had worked through, tested and been presented with the first Investors in People recognition awards in October 1991. The then opposition Labour Party's front bench spokesman on employment, Tony Blair, also endorsed the achievement of the Investors in People standard as being one condition for exemption from his party's proposed national training levy (Pickard 1991). By November 1993 over 470 organizations in the UK had achieved the Investors in People standard, while over 4,330 had formally committed to achieving the standard. By August 2001, some 25,000 organizations had been recognized as Investors in People. This equates to 5,573,244 employees or 23.99% of the UK workforce. A further 20,000 organizations are currently committed to achieving the Standard. (Source – Investors in People UK website.)

Early in its development, Peter Critten welcomed the organization-wide and strategic approach of Investors in People, believing its holistic and systemic approach, which aims for transformation and not just improvement, provided the conditions for engendering a learning organization. He predicted that Investors in People would develop the potential to deliver this through organizations offering evidence of a real paradigm shift in the way they view their employees and measure their contribution, provided they do not fall back on using merely a step-by-step, systematic, paper-led approach to meet the Investors in People assessment criteria. Critten (1993: 2) claimed: 'Investors in People provides a mechanism where individuals in an organisation can gain a shared vision of how training and development can contribute to corporate capability rather than only in individual training plans'.

Investors in People appears to have established itself and become embedded in rather stark contrast to other initiatives in this area. Indeed, research suggests that significant improvements have occurred in a variety of ways in a range of types of organization. Research among employees within recognized organizations showed that 94 per cent are satisfied in their jobs, compared to 37 per cent in businesses without the standard (Planet Research 1998). Eighty per cent have increased customer satisfaction and 70 per cent have improved their competitive edge and productivity (CREATE 1999), and the more satisfied employees are with their jobs, the better the company is likely to perform in terms of productivity and profitability (Tamkin and Hillage 1997, 1999).

Although Investors in People is a national standard it is locally delivered, with concomitant impact on consistency of approach, support and funding. It was initially promoted and supported by the training and enterprise councils in England and Wales, and the local enterprise councils in Scotland. The current local 'promoters' of the standard are the learning and skills councils, formally launched in April 2001. The 'delivery' arm for assessment and recognition is now quite separate, with regional Investors in People quality centres operating in

England and Wales and Investors in People Scotland responsible north of the border.

Investors in People is aimed particularly at fulfilling the present and previous UK government's learning and skills priority: that employers must invest in the skills their businesses need by actively pursuing and supporting improved performance from their employees. This is to be achieved through learning and development that is clearly linked to the achievement of organizations' business objectives. In this way it is hoped that employers will be making an effective investment in their human assets. Recognition is only achieved on demonstration that these requirements are currently being met; once recognition is awarded, an organization must be reviewed within three years.

There are four principles underpinning the standard (see Figure 8.1). These are accompanied by 12 indicators, supported by 33 mandatory evidence requirements (for the full national standard, see the Investors in People UK website at http://www.investorsinpeople.co.uk/). These indicators have been designed to be relevant to both small and large organizations, whether in the public or private sectors, and have themselves been subject to continuous review and improvement (Investors in People UK 1993, 1996, 2000). The process must also take into account the variations that there will inevitably be in organizations' approaches to developing their staff (HESDA 2000). Whether requirements are met is decided

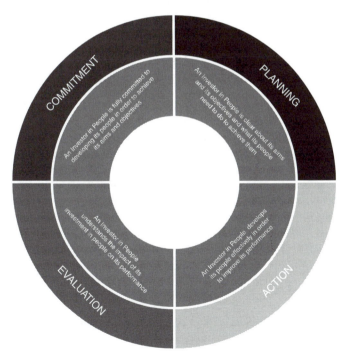

Figure 8.1   The Investors in People national standard
Source: Investors in People UK (2000).

by a 'site visit' by assessors using a variety of agreed methodologies – notably interviews with a cross-section of staff from all levels and across all functions, observation of learning and development activities and attendance at meetings (Taylor and Thackwray 2001a).

Investors in People and the rise of strategic human resources thinking in the UK and the USA

Investors in People aims to encourage good practices within institutions, especially those associated with the development and enhancement of, for example, induction, needs analysis, learning and development and continuous career development, and to ensure that these are integrated with strategic planning. This integration of discrete human resource practices as part of corporate strategy first came to prominence in the US literature of the 1980s (for example, Tichy *et al.* 1982, Beer *et al.* 1984). These in a sense represented the foundations of the concept of strategic human resource management (SHRM). Within this Devanna *et al.* (1984) had developed the 'human resource cycle' which comprised the central generic processes within every organization of selection, performance, appraisal, development and rewards, and Beer *et al.* (1985) further depicted the HRM territory as a conceptual map. This came to be alternatively known as the Harvard framework of HRM and identified the main human resource policy areas, the desired policy outcomes and their importance for overall organizational effectiveness. The rise of SHRM in the USA at this time was heavily influenced by other contemporary American writing which emphasized the importance of managerial strategy and the search for competitive advantage (see Mintzberg 1978; Porter 1980, 1981, 1985).

The concept of SHRM began to appear and be critically discussed in the British literature from the end of the 1980s onwards. Early examples include Guest (1987, 1989, 1992a), Storey (1989, 1992), Blyton and Turnbull (1992), Salaman *et al.* (1992), Brewster (1993) and Brewster and Hegewisch (1994). The key tenets of Investors in People – strategic learning and development at the individual, team and organizational levels – have been viewed as essential elements in any assessment of the effectiveness of HRM strategies within this type of UK literature (for example, Sisson 1989: 34). Guest (1992b) explicitly argued that total quality management (TQM) was inextricably linked to HRM through the vehicle of training because of the need for committed employees, because the credibility of any initiative such as Investors in People would in part be governed by management's treatment of the workforce and because quality implies a high-trust organization if involvement and flexibility are to be integral to quality. Investors in People appears to offer a tangible way for organizations to take a more strategic, integrated approach to development.

TQM has been more talked of than practised. Discussing the US higher education sector, Marchese (1991) noted that

> the number of individuals devoted to the topic of TQM runs well up in the
> hundreds, the number of institutions trying TQM in particular offices might

be near one hundred, the number of those that have committed to TQM on an institution wide basis stands at two dozen, of which the number with deeper experience constitutes a mere handful.

A similar pattern of engagement would be found among UK universities. International experience based on TQM programmes has been summed up by Piper (1993: 88):

> Advocates of TQM have usually decided to ignore the President [Vice-chancellor], the faculty and other offices at least at the outset, to try TQM in their own units and attract attention through results. The 'whole college' approach at Oregon State University that is using full presidential support and a high level (in this case vice-president) champion, has been rare.

Corporate commitment within UK higher education is at least equally rare. Using a study of total internal customer satisfaction, Chaston (1994) demonstrated that British universities were not yet ready to adopt TQM as a unifying managerial principle and institutional philosophy.

The influence of TQM in UK higher education has declined as the impact of Investors in People and, more recently, the European Foundation for Quality Management (EFQM) has grown. Unlike TQM, it appears that Investors in People can be linked successfully to managing and achieving systemic organization-wide change. It may, therefore, be a more recognizable and acceptable mechanism than other initiatives. A significant tenet of Investors in People is its direct link with institutional and unit objectives. The development and explanation of clear objectives for all staff – academic or porter, librarian or cook – is intended to engender an essential sense of ownership, via an understanding of what needs to be achieved and what every individual's contribution is (Thackwray 1994; Taylor and Thackwray 2001a, b). Investors in People cannot be achieved without clear evidence of commitment at the highest level. The vice-chancellor of an institution aiming for Investors in People, or the head of any smaller unit that wants to apply, will be interviewed by the external assessor and the response will be set against further interviews and other forms of evidence gathering. For many, the zenith of this rise in strategic thinking has been the development of the EFQM model in Europe and the Malcolm Baldrige National Quality Award in the USA. The latter award uses clearly defined criteria for identifying organizations with exceptional process excellence. Forty-one organizations have received the award since 1988 in the manufacturing, service, small business, education and health care sectors.

Investors in People is, perhaps glibly, often referred to as a 'quality standard'. This is a hostage to fortune in a sector where around 40 per cent of the working population are trained to question and challenge! Harvey (1994) has commented on the different meanings the word 'quality' can convey within higher education, such as 'high standards' or 'fitness for purpose' or 'value for money'. He recommends that quality needs to be viewed as essentially a 'transformative' rather than a perfectionist process, about transforming the life experiences of students, by enhancing or empowering them. Alternative definitions such as 'zero defects' or 'getting things right first time', which emanate from the ideas of the quality gurus, he considers are not entirely appropriate to the 'business' of education, a view strongly held in many parts of the sector. 'Learning and the development of knowledge is fundamentally a process of critique and reconceptualisation, which is the opposite of a defect-free, right first-time, mechanistic approach to problem-solving' (Harvey 1994: 51). Harvey views the ultimate quality goal for higher education to pursue as 'the need to invest in continuous improvement of the quality of the student experience, through staff development, innovation in teaching and learning, research and scholarship' (1994: 58). He is sceptical about the ability of the essentially accountability-led, 'value for money' quality assurance and monitoring mechanisms, which have been introduced to the UK university sector, to effectively deliver this desired continuous quality improvement or 'process of transformation'.

Harvey argues that what is needed is a shift in emphasis from the external scrutiny of quality to the setting up of internal quality mechanisms within each educational institution so that it owns, controls and drives its own quality improvement processes from the staff–student interface in both a bottom-up and a top-down manner. It is in this shift from external to internal scrutiny that Investors in People appears to be playing a significant role in many institutions, offering the potential for reduction in bureaucracy and repetition of effort. In this regard a valuable agreement had been reached with the Quality Assurance Agency (QAA) to reduce duplication. Since, broadly, the QAA reviews the student experience of an institution and the Investors in People process examines the staff experience, the same questions may be asked by different people for slightly different reasons. However, at the time of writing this arrangement appears to be in question, as the position of the QAA is itself under review.

Higher education experiences of the Investors in People process

Over 70 per cent of higher education institutions have some involvement in Investors in People (Higher Education Training Organization (THETO) 1999). This overall percentage is somewhat deceptive because, in some institutions, a small number of relatively autonomous units such as conference centres might have achieved the standard, with little impact elsewhere, whereas in others there has been considerable activity throughout, so that about 35 whole institutions have sought and achieved it. In addition, there are several hundred recognized units and an increasing number of institutions (about 35 at the time of writing) pursuing the 'building block' route to recognition, which enables units within an institution to progress towards recognition in a culturally appropriate way and within a time-scale that suits them. The unit will also agree assessment methodology with the assessor prior to commencement.

There are clear differences between pre- and post-1992 institutions and between academic and support units, although these are gradually disappearing since the revision of the standard, the broadening of the methodology and, critically, the removal of the authority and autonomy criteria by Investors in People UK. The criteria were originally designed to prevent subsections of an organization achieving the standard if they had no real independence from the parent body. Therefore issues such as power to hire and fire, financial responsibility, and focus of loyalty for staff were examined prior to agreement to proceed. These criteria, now defunct, had the unfortunate side effect of ruling out many departments within universities, especially pre-1992 ones. The demise of these criteria and the advent of the building block approach in the late 1990s saw the start of a significant rise in the numbers and distribution of higher education institutions engaged with the standard. Partly as a consequence, the difference in uptake between 'old' and 'new' seems to be disappearing. Although of the 28 recognized whole institutions only one is a pre-1992 research-based institution (Strathclyde), many more are now able to participate following the introduction of the building block approach. Universities such as Manchester, Bristol, Bradford, Loughborough, Glasgow and the London School of Economics are moving ahead, largely via the building block approach, and parts of Oxford University and Imperial College London are recognized.

Staff responses to Investors in People

The comments of higher education staff, drawn from two sets of interviews for HESDA projects (Box and Thackwray 2001, 2002) illustrate the rewards and the difficulties of introducing Investors in People (Table 8.1).

Criticism from here and elsewhere offers evidence that Investors in People does not appear sufficiently to address ways in which individuals are rewarded for their own investment in learning and development. It was a concern of staff from many institutions that although there exists a very indirect link between appraisal systems and the formal promotion procedures, the higher education sector in general does not seem to possess the flexibility or freedom to reward staff financially and/or non-financially, based on their contribution and not status, in ways which tangibly reinforce learning and personal career development. The lack of readily adaptable structures and the inability to move easily between the different categories of university staffs also form part of this limiting culture, as Partington (1994) and others have already noted. In terms of the 'human resource cycle', Investors in People in higher education may need to deliver more in respect of the horizontal integration of development, performance and rewards (Devanna *et al.* 1984).

Towards a learning organization

Partington (1994: 11) has tellingly remarked that

> as organisations whose central purpose is the development of learning, it is paradoxical that universities have at present little claim to be regarded as 'learning organisations'. It is an irony that universities have within themselves arguably the richest resource of professional development expertise compared

Table 8.1 Higher education staff comments on Investors in People

Comments from interviews & discussions, criticisms and concerns	Responses
We're already assessed – overly so.	It isn't really an assessment – it's a reflective exercise.
It's just another initiative	It isn't just another initiative; it's a tool you can use to improve what you do, whatever it is.
It doesn't 'suit' higher education	It certainly didn't overtly suit higher education in previous forms. The language was very business oriented, the publicity and information was largely 'high gloss, low content'. We had to work hard to get to the good stuff.
Inconsistent advice and guidance	There were many examples of this throughout the UK in the early years of the standard. Advisers with experience of only working with small to medium monocultural mono-product organizations often found it difficult working with large multi-site multi-cultural organizations.
Assessors don't understand the culture. Inconsistent assessment practices and differing levels of perceived competence of assessors. Most of them are used to small to medium sized companies and are out of their depth in higher education.	The National Assessment Centre offers a service to all large multi-site organizations. All its assessors are therefore experienced in working with large organizations and it has a number of higher education experienced assessors on its books.
We're already the best in the world, why would we want to do this?	You have to work very hard to remain in pole position.
They're only doing it for the badge.	Certainly there are many reasons why we're doing it. The [Vice-Chancellor] wants it and the Marketing people need it. It's good business for the Staff Development people. It (Investors in People) will not directly bring us more or better students or help us keep the ones we've got, nor will it bring us more or better staff or help us keep them either. But if what we do doesn't directly address how to bring these things about we are wasting our time.
It's only really for support areas.	It puts us on a par with the academic units – we can show what we can do as well. It was good to achieve recognition as a faculty – I think it acts as a useful counterpoint to the natural cynicism of the academic. We really are doing well!
Don't hype up Investors in People.	The title can be misleading. It is a business improvement instrument, not a 'guarantee of happiness'. Don't do things just for Investors in People, do them because you need to and because they are good practice.

with any other organisations, yet they harness it only rarely and sporadically for their own most valuable asset – their staff.

In her early assessment of the value of the Investors in People award, Pickard (1991: 19) stated

> that it is not a uniformity of approach which matters but evidence of having arrived at the same destination – having become a *'learning organisation'* in which training is embedded, applies to all employees, is linked to business needs and is regularly evaluated. (Emphasis in original)

There have also been links made between Investors in People and the concept of a learning organization. Mills and Friesen (1992) describe a learning organization as follows: 'We conceive of a learning organization as one able to sustain consistent innovation or "learning", with the immediate goals of improving quality, enhancing customer or supplier relationships, more effectively executing business strategy, and the ultimate objective of sustaining profitability'.

The potential Investors in People displays is rooted, as already noted, in its learning and development orientation. Universities themselves are engaged in the provision of education and training and professional development of existing and future employees for other organizations, many of which may well have acquired a quality assurance standard such as EFQM, ISO 9000 or the Investors in People standard. It might well be perceived as advantageous by their present and potential 'customers' if universities themselves therefore similarly achieved Investors in People recognition.

Progression towards Investors in People within organizations displays many visible features which are characteristic of 'learning organizations' (Burgoyne 1992), as predicted by Critten (1993) and described by Taylor and Thackwray (2001a). This was evident in 'participative policy making', whereby local consultation and involvement in the implementation of the Investors in People plans and processes were actively practised and encouraged throughout, leading to a sense of ownership. 'Open information systems' could be seen in the communication of Investors in People's 'steering groups' or 'champions' contributions, which were held to be very important and were made available to all staff, on a frequent basis, and also in the promotion of a learning culture and climate through which institutions and units developed their own distinctive and culturally appropriate Investors in People approaches. This process invariably required overt top management support. There is evidence that on occasion there was public consensus and private disruption (Thackwray 1997), where lip-service was paid to an idea in the public domain which was not supported at the local level. This caused a number of higher education institutions and units to fall at their first assessment.

What has worked well

The way change and development are largely managed in higher education institutions displays a change strategy somewhere between 'participative evolution' and 'charismatic transformation' (Stace and Dunphy 1991) and underlines the importance of both consultation and collaboration for the Investors in People actions to be understood and taken on board smoothly.

In an early evaluation of some recognized organizations in the private sector (Rix *et al.* 1994), it was found that it is the *processes* of Investors in People which prove as useful to these employers as the actual award itself, and that most of these organizations had also conceived of Investors in People as being part (but not the totality) of a total quality initiative. This first Department of Employment evaluation also identified that a change 'champion' had been essential to the success of the Investors in People programme in all the achieving organizations. A common feature of the Investors in People approaches within institutions and units had been the key role of the 'change team' (called variously the internal audit team, Investors in People continuation group, quality enhancement group, Investors in People steering group, etc.) to diagnose, design and take action (where required) against the Investors in People assessment indicators (HESDA 2001). Each team had been led by an internal 'project champion' or 'change agent' acting as the focal point, as promulgated by the programmatic change advocates (French and Bell 1983; Beckhard 1989), with external consultant(s) being used either very early on or in an advisory capacity only. Indeed, the view expressed by many (such as Daniel 2001) is that rigorous institutional self-evaluation is the right and proper course of action for a higher education institution and Investors in People provides an apposite vehicle for this.

Many quality enhancement programmes have not been very successful or have foundered completely because they are excessively top-down and have little or nothing to do with the everyday experience of the vast majority of staff (Binney 1992; Wilkinson *et al.* 1993). In contrast, it was very evident from the experiences of higher education institutions of all types that the Investors in People 'tentacles' had penetrated in all directions – bottom-up, top-down and, critically, laterally – and had involved every staff member, not just the top management layers (HESDA 2000, 2001). The evidence of this actual involvement and practice of the espoused Investors in People principles among all groups and levels of staff as part of both the working towards and the final awarding of recognition all testified to this (HESDA, 2000, 2001). Therefore Investors in People was endorsed as a very apposite vehicle for developing the internal mechanisms and 'continuous quality improvement' processes of a transforming nature, which Harvey (1994) has advocated as being the appropriate approach for higher education institutions to pursue. It is this necessary inclusion of all staff in order to meet the Investors in People standard that differentiates it from other continuous improvement programmes, with the notable exception of the EFQM.

On reflecting on the various experiences of higher education institutions (HESDA 2001), it is clear that Investors in People has engendered much greater integration of formerly fragmented practices and initiatives with the overall institutional and unit objectives within organizations as advocated by SHRM (Beer *et al.* 1985). For many institutions, Investors in People also served demonstrably to link component parts of the planning cycle at all levels much more closely than before, notably induction, appraisal, development and evaluation, in addition to the vertical integration of these activities with institutional objectives.

The value of Investors in People

The contention of the author that the very processes institutions and/or constituent units use to gain and retain Investors in People are in the main much more important for that organization than achieving the Investors in People goal itself (Taylor and Thackwray 2001c) is borne out by a range of case studies of various higher education institutions (HESDA 2001). Respondents note that the tide began to turn when 'people understood the process' and realized that it wasn't really an external assessment but 'a reflective exercise' that was undertaken 'voluntarily'.

Investors in People in higher education in the Netherlands

Investors in People Nederland was formally launched in January 2000. Before then there had been a number of pilot assessments, and several international companies had sought to acquire the standard for branches in other countries such as the Netherlands. Higher education had, in the form of the VSNU, sought to investigate and test this in a variety of ways. There were presentations and discussions with senior staff from Dutch universities and several projects designed to build 'toolkits' for higher education staff to work with. Most relevant here, however, are the two pilot audits conducted at Nijmegen University in October 1999.

The first audit was of the Institute for Applied Social Sciences, a research-based academic unit, and the second was of the University Facility Business unit. Findings were strikingly similar to audits conducted within UK institutions and focused on two issues. For strategic leadership, in addition to a range of specific recommendations, it was agreed that there was a clear need for further development of the senior management team with a view to reviewing their current role and responsibilities (Kouwenberg and Thackwray 1999). With regard to planning and objective setting, there was a need to link the overall objectives to departmental ones, and then to agree and clarify those at individual level (Van den Elsen and Anderson 1999) via an enhanced appraisal/developmental review. Indeed, the findings with regard to appraisal were rather redolent of the inept and contentious manner in which appraisal was introduced across the sector in the UK, which has made it often unworkable, unpopular and patchy, duplicating existing systems (Hughes 1999; HESDA 2001).

Other issues in common with UK higher education institutions included induction, staff retention, communication, recognition of contribution and evaluation. Of those, the last is a problem shared by most higher education institutions everywhere and is the part of the standard that causes organizations in general the most concern (Thackwray 1997). Further information on the development of Investors in People in other countries can be found at http://www.investorsinpeople.co.uk/IIP/Internet/International/default.htm

Conclusion

The contention that Investors in People is potentially a useful vehicle for supporting and managing change, in a manner recognizable to all categories of employee, has been supported by the experiences of higher education institutions as they progressed in their different ways towards recognition (Balderson 1997; Adams 1997; Gordon 2000; HESDA 2001; Williams and Triller 2000). It was the ways in which they progressed towards achieving the award and the actual *processes* involved which scored highly with the management and individual staff, reflecting several 'best practice' approaches such as employee involvement and empowerment, and demonstrating many of the significant features of a learning organization.

Investors in People is not only about staff development *per se* but about practically adding value to the institution's existing and future human assets. It must be more than merely a paper exercise or a bureaucratic straitjacket for each institution, also offering a positive process in support of change management that is essentially qualitative. The higher education sector has always tended to be more comfortable with the qualitative aspects of human resource management rather than the quantitative, and the evaluation integral to Investors in People, based on both the harder cost–benefit criteria and also the 'softer' human resource dimensions, can accommodate this.

In essence, Investors in People is a self-managed, externally benchmarked, reflective development exercise. It is not a requirement, unlike, for example, the QAA's systems of institutional audit, so should engender a clearer sense of ownership. The development of the building block approach, with its direct higher education antecedents in the Internal Quality Award (Thackwray 1998; Wilson and Morley 2001; HESDA 2001), has led to a greater and more appropriate sense of ownership. Investors in People facilitates external benchmarking and internal quality improvement with the clear potential of learning to be a learning organization. Needless to say, pursuing Investors in People does not directly produce more or better students, or more or better teaching and research. However, if the outcomes do not include an enhancement of the quality of the student learning experience and appropriate 'gains' in the various mandatory reviews, assessments and inspections it will have been something of a waste of time. If the empirical material contained within the various works cited in this chapter were to be coalesced into a single soundbite it would be: Investors in People must work for us, not us for it.

Key learning points

Senior staff

- Be visibly committed to staff development in both formal and informal discussions with staff, tackling those middle managers who are not committed.
- Plan and agree policies at an organizational level that consider the broad developmental needs required to achieve the business objectives.

- Ensure that there are adequate resources in terms of time, people and money to meet those development needs that have been identified.

Heads of department

- Review existing staff skills and knowledge and identify the additional skills and knowledge that they need in order to do their jobs.
- Make information about development opportunities available, including access to qualifications as appropriate (also applies to staff developers).
- Agree desired outcomes ('learning objectives') and support their attainment appropriately, such as through coaching and feedback.
- Check that the action has been successful and that the new skills and knowledge can be and are supplied to achieve the desired results.

Professional staff developers

- Ensure that SD unit is appropriately placed organizationally and sufficiently skilled to meet the needs that Investors processes identify.
- Be alert to development needs associated with and arising from the process of implementation.
- Ensure all new employees are inducted into their job. (Also applies to all managers.)

9

Leadership and management development: an overview

George Gordon

Introduction

This chapter deals with issues in the development of leaders and managers in higher education institutions. It explores the nature of universities and the changes they face, offers some definitions of terms in leadership and management, and considers attitudes to leadership and context. Survey evidence of UK provision and examples of development activities precede a discussion of the major issues to be considered in the development of provision.

The nature of universities

Many writers have stressed that universities should not be seen as businesses. Indeed, most writers depict them as very distinctive organizations where the underlying purposes and values are both complex and paramount.

Sporn (1999) identified five distinguishing characteristics: goal ambiguity; client service; task complexity; professional and administrative values; and economic vulnerability. The issue, for the present purposes, is not necessarily the items highlighted in any listing but rather the implications for the nature and style of leadership and management.

Of course, modern universities take many forms, at least partially due to differences in size, academic positioning, governance, style of management, and degree of autonomy. Currently national governments tend to be inclined towards public encouragement of institutional diversity, whilst apparently simultaneously espousing policies for accountability which may foster broadly convergent responses from institutions.

Pressures upon higher education for change

Knight and Trowler (2001: 28–31) emphasize several major sources of change impacting upon higher education systems, including globalization, deregulation, mass participation, decline in state funding, quality concerns and vocationalism. They note changing relationships with other stakeholders, notably employers, and the partly associated complex shifts in the production and application of knowledge which characterize the Mode 1/Mode 2 thesis of Gibbons *et al.* (1994).

At the macro level, analysis may rest on the changes in the balance of relationships between the authority of the state, the authority of the academy and the influence of the market (Kogan and Hanney 2000; Sporn 1999). In any system at a particular point in time, these are also subject to specific national agendas and policies, which lead contemporaneously to the coexistence of convergent and divergent trends.

Whilst such macro-forces may appear distant from the daily life of academic practitioners, they do influence the agendas of academic leaders, and hence managers, and in time practising academics. Relevant high-level developmental issues include support for environmental analysis, scenario planning, agenda setting, visioning and communication.

Definitions

Leadership, effecting or coping with change, may be differentiated from management, the handling of organizational complexity (Kotter 1990). Thus management would involve activities such as planning, controlling, co-ordinating, monitoring and evaluating, in order to enable the organization or department to function efficiently and effectively, whereas leadership entails motivational and strategic capacities. However, in higher education and elsewhere, the distinctions often blur, with many leaders also playing management roles and vice versa. Leaders may major on strategy and managers on operation, but the division is at best imprecise. Equally, suggestions that leaders need followers and that managers require consent have considerable validity, but at the risk of over-simplification.

Moreover, the span and scope of roles varies greatly, sometimes even between apparently similar roles. Thus not only does the role of head of department differ from that of a pro-vice-chancellor or the director of finance, but it can differ in significant ways from the same function in another institution. Nowadays all leaders and managers must be at least fairly effective communicators and, given the pace of change and growing complexity, it is highly desirable that they have, or develop, sound skills of sense-making.

Acknowledging the overlapping nature of leadership, management and administration, Yorke (2001: 6) associates leadership with envisioning and inspiring, management with establishing systems and administration with day-to-day operations. Ramsden (1998) takes a slightly broader view of academic leadership to also encompass enabling, recognizing and developing colleagues to achieve goals. Both definitions provide useful guides to developmental needs.

Roles

At various levels within higher education, numerous explicit roles entail clear expectations of leadership and/or management. Whilst universities are perceived as having relatively flat management structures, there has been a tendency towards greater articulation of hierarchies and management structures. Not only are there often several pro-vice-chancellors, each with a distinct portfolio, but where faculties or schools exist, there are corresponding sets of senior officers/managers, which can also be mirrored in departments or course teams. Additionally most universities now have numerous specialist units and research centres, each with fairly clearly identified managerial structures and with distinct duties allocated to particular individuals, normally on a formal, contractual or semi-contractual basis. For posts at the level of head of department or above, I believe that there are nine key roles: symbolic; representational; strategic and agenda-setting; operational; stewardship; networking; developmental; communicational; and sense-making.

In some posts, even very senior ones, the span of responsibility may be relatively narrow, whilst in others it can be quite broad, again with the caveat that inter-institutional variation is commonplace.

Much attention is paid in management literature to styles of management, which may be directive, supportive, coaching or delegative. Individuals may, and doubtless do, favour particular styles or sets of approaches. However, the continuing dominant ethos in universities expects negotiation and consent. In some universities there is a gradually emerging tone, an expectation, about the style of management, particularly of professional staff. It combines elements of support and development, of coaching and delegation, but these are muted in comparison with the strong ethos of peer accountability.

Attitudes to leadership and management

Reporting on part of an extensive study on managerialism and university managers, Deem and Johnson (2000: 81) encapsulated the situation neatly, stating that they had 'examined a number of threats to the notion of universities as cohesive communities of scholars'. Their data suggested that informal cadres of senior managers, with implicit shared values, were emerging but that these did not extend to the level of heads of department. The latter continued primarily to see themselves as academics, often with some degree of hesitation or even reluctance to undertake the managerial role of head of department. Deem and Johnson add that:

> The concern for control, discipline and regulation of the workforce appeared more important than subject discipline at senior management level, but below that, new conditions of work, resource allocation models and competition for students seemed to have made manager-academics from different disciplines see themselves as potential rivals rather than as complementary to each other.

Attitudes to management and leadership are closely connected to academic traditions, mores and beliefs, including those which inform academic identities. Henkel (2000), reporting on in-depth research into academic identities, stressed two aspects, research and teaching identities. She also explored whether a third was emerging, that of academic manager, as a consequence of 'the deep systems and institutional changes experienced by universities' (2000: 235). Teaching and research identities develop over time, and are closely associated with discipline and with the lengthy socialization and acculturation of each individual. That said, the extent and precise nature varies between individuals depending upon factors such as success, experiences and personality traits.

If an all-encompassing definition is adopted for management and leadership, then most academics assume some relevant responsibilities from an early juncture in their career, for example in managing research and teaching. However most would see these duties as part of the historic mix of teaching, research and administration. For many, the term 'academic management' is reserved for specific posts or roles which command responsibility for a larger bundle of resources. Thus Henkel (2000) found that most participants in the study felt that becoming head of department or dean signalled a move, possibly temporarily, into the sphere of management. Many were uncomfortable with the terminology, preferring leader or administrator, prefaced by academic. This author can recollect a head of department stating that the attraction of the role was the joy in leading highly motivated colleagues, a view which captured an array of beliefs, values and predispositions that are not always perfectly matched by realities.

Henkel (2000), echoing other studies, reported that many academic managers, at least initially, experienced some conflict, even loss, of identity and/or varying degrees of unease in adjusting to a new and, for some, an alien role. The findings for universities closely match other professional areas where it is considered essential for managers to come from and share the values of the profession, and to retain as high a level as possible of professional credibility, sensitivity and allegiance. There are, of course, examples of vice-chancellors, rectors and presidents who have been appointed from other spheres of activity, but they are very much the exception and continue to represent decisions about the attributes of particular individuals rather than any broader and more systemic trends.

The picture for the appointment of senior professional administrators is more complex. Recruitment from outside the university sector is increasingly common for certain specialist posts, and there may be a broader emergent tendency in this segment of managerial appointments. If so it would be likely to introduce some interesting dynamics, and possibly tensions, into the deliberations of senior management teams.

Models of leadership and management in higher education

Various models exist of leadership and management in higher education. A historic, although not entirely extinct, one is that of *primus inter pares*. Rotational election of rectors from within the academy by academics is still a characteristic, for example, of some European countries. Such collegial models have been challenged in recent years by external pressures and trends, leading either to the introduction of stronger managerial models and traits or to refinements of more traditional and collegial approaches. Illustrations of the latter would be processes of consultation rather than direct election, for example of heads of department.

McNay (1993) used a tight–loose dynamic based upon twin axes of policy definition and operational control to generate four types: collegium; bureaucracy; corporation; and enterprise. The collegium embodied the loose–loose definition and control, and the corporation the tight–tight situation. As McNay points out, all four situations coexist within higher education, and to some degree in all institutions. What matters, for leadership and management, is the relative importance and strength of each dimension.

In a similar vein Bergquist (1992) outlined four dominant cultures of the academy: collegial; managerial; negotiating; and developmental. His thesis was that leaders and managers need to be comfortable switching from one culture to another as circumstances dictate; they will have to operate in all of them at some juncture, often frequently, but the relative strength will be determined by the complex chemistry of personal preference and prevailing institutional culture, tempered by external forces and influences. A crucial developmental challenge is that of cultivating such sensitivity, of enabling leaders and managers to become experienced and confident practitioners in the use of each of Bergquist's cultures.

Exploring autonomy, bureaucracy and competition as controls in higher education, Thorne and Cuthbert (1996) argued that there had been a movement in the UK between the early 1980s and late 1990s from the former binary division to a fourfold typology. In their view, in the early 1980s professors and teachers exercised significant influence, with management holding the middle ground between the institution, its clients and external influences. By the late 1990s things had changed. They identified four types of situation, which they labelled: autonomous professional; managerial market; professional market; and market bureaucracy. In each type the power of management is shown as having increased compared to the situation in the early 1980s. This is especially true of the professional market and market bureaucracy situations. The influence of students is depicted as increasing in the latter, with the influence of professors being strongest in the autonomous professional and professional market modes.

Sporn (1999) explores the relevance for the context of higher education of several specific theories of organizational adaptation, largely based upon an open systems perspective, and stressing components such as task and contextual environments, and the relationships between these environments and subsystems. It is not necessary to go into further detail here, other than to note that more attention is being paid to these concepts as it is openly acknowledged that most universities are complex, often large, organizations operating in increasingly complex task and contextual environments. The explicit incorporation of such understanding and experience into developmental frameworks and provision is a growing challenge.

Leadership and management development: survey evidence of provision in the UK

Surveys considered here include the 1994 one by the Universities' and Colleges' Staff Development Agency (UCoSDA), work on national occupational standards and the recent Good Management Practice Initiative of the Higher Education Funding Council for England (HEFCE).

A UCoSDA (1994) Green Paper suggested possible steps towards a national framework for management and leadership preparation and development. Amongst the 12 recommendations were:

- proposals for initial induction as well as regular career-long programmes for enhancement and updating of management skills and capabilities, including those at senior levels;
- recognition of the connections between the quality of management and the quality of provision in higher education;
- an inclusive (all staff) approach to management development;
- more attention to appropriate management models and structures and the connection to tasks and capabilities;
- funding of relevant research and development projects to inform policy and practice;
- the effective marriage of generic and task-related training and development;
- effective use of appraisal to inform development planning;
- adequate allocation of time and resources;
- inter-institutional, regional and cross-sector sharing of experiences, materials and expertise;
- exploration and evaluation of the benefits of adopting appropriate qualifications such as National or Scottish Vocational Qualifications.

The report made a call for national funding to further the agenda and several of the recommendations.

One possible strand of development, national occupational standards for higher education managers and administrators, was the subject of a study by the Higher Educational Training Organisation (THETO 2000a), funded by the Qualifications and Curriculum Authority and the Scottish Qualifications Authority. Although senior managers in higher education acknowledged the topics listed in the highest level (level 5) they tended to view these as inadequately capturing the nature of their roles or their organizations, which may account, at least in part, for the responses which Middlehurst and Garrett (2001) received in their survey.

Research on leadership and management development undertaken by Middlehurst in studies on the late 1980s and early 1990s was incorporated into her seminal volume on *Leading Academics* (Middlehurst 1993) and also summarized in a report (Middlehurst 1991). Since then various surveys have been undertaken, including one by Middlehurst and Garrett (2001) to inform the Higher Education Staff Development Agency (HESDA) Project on Senior Management Development in UK Higher Education, funded by the HEFCE Good Management

Practice Initiative. They found that most institutions made some formal developmental provision for senior managers although the volume, nature and degree of formality varied considerably. Additionally, at least some of the provision was not exclusively for senior managers. Appraisal often triggered actions. Provision included courses or programmes (often external to the institution), work shadowing, external visits and promoting experience through nomination to external bodies, committees, or task forces.

Most responses fitted into a non-formal, person-by-person, approach to the development of senior managers. Management development was portrayed as more relevant to junior and middle staff. In a minority of institutions a somewhat different situation was reported, with formal linkages between management development and institutional strategy. Programmes, often mandatory, included activities such as mentoring, case studies and psychometric testing. A very small number of institutions were moving towards more individually tailored provision.

The study encountered difficulties over data availability and an absence of baseline comparators. If one extended the survey to international comparison, that would be an even greater problem.

Two conflicting, but not irreconcilable, interpretations can be made of the Middlehurst and Garrett (2001) survey. Firstly, quite a lot has happened since Middlehurst's earlier surveys, when many vice-chancellors stated that they had not received any formal leadership and management development. It might also be claimed that informal development was and is often taking place. Senior postholders then and since have reported that particular experiences, such as serving on research councils, major external committees or other bodies, or spending time in other systems or sectors, had been particularly powerful influences upon their learning for leadership and management. The other interpretation is less positive. One might expect greater progress, commitment and strategic integration to have occurred, both as a consequence of substantial pressures and the promotion by many key stakeholders of a positive climate of opportunities.

Examples of development activities

A number of examples in this section illustrate the range of existing provision, including the UK's Top Management Programme, provision in Scotland, the 1994 Group programme and HESDA case studies.

In the UK the major cross-sector initiative is the Top Management Programme for higher education which operates under the aegis of HESDA and is based upon a renowned UK Cabinet Office programme. Each cohort of 24 follows an extended programme of intensive workshops, action learning projects and visits. Participants also have an opportunity to work with a personal mentor. The programme includes senior-level briefings by UK government ministries and European Union equivalents. Five themes were addressed in the 2001/02 programme: the context and future scenarios for higher education; strategic leadership; governance and management; managing change; and strategic financial management.

The programme aims to prepare people for senior office, enable them to broaden their perspectives, address leadership and change agendas, and network. Each objective is important. The author has encountered evidence of the value of the network to fellows, and strategic applications and benefit is doubtless accruing to institutions, all of which are now required to produce an array of strategic and operational planning documents for their respective funding council.

The most significant limitation of the programme is a simple one of supply and demand. Fortunately, there has been a phase in the UK when many vice-chancellors/heads of institution have favoured stability in their senior team. Nonetheless it would take several years at minimum to ensure that every senior manager had undertaken the HESDA programme, or a suitable European, international or commercial equivalent. Another dimension is added by the recent, and apparently continuing, relatively high rate of turnover amongst vice-chancellors in the UK. Often this is followed, in a short space of time, by some restructuring of the senior management team.

In Scotland, higher education institutions collaborate over the provision of two management development programmes, one for heads of department (and equivalent) and one for administrative middle managers. For the past several years the latter three-day residential annual event has been centred upon team-building. Typically around 36 participants attend, primarily, although not exclusively, from Scottish institutions.

The programme for heads of department involves two residential courses each of three days' duration, both with a mix of case studies, expert inputs and sharing of experiences. In total the programme deals with strategic issues, managing change, current challenges facing higher education institutions, and human and financial resource management. Such 'regional events' offer a number of advantages. They reduce the risk of parochialism and, for small institutions, may be a cost-effective way of delivering development. However, institutional programmes may be geared to a specific context.

Sixteen English research universities, known as the 1994 Group, have collaborated to devise a programme called Best Practice for Senior Managers. The aims are to develop the leadership and managerial potential of senior colleagues in these institutions through a set of activities designed to broaden their horizons and widen their experience and to promote the sharing of best management practice. The format involves two intensive three-day modules, using expert inputs, case studies and action learning sets. The events have recruited successfully and been well reviewed by participants during the two years to date.

HESDA (formerly UCoSDA) has commissioned a series of up-to-date case studies on management development (HESDA 2002) as part of the work associated with the HEFCE Good Management Practice Senior Managers' Project. The cases include institutional, inter-institutional and regional examples, including the 1994 Group initiative outlined above.

Most of the case studies describe institutional initiatives. Whilst these generally display strong structural similarities to regional or inter-institutional programmes, the overriding thrust is directed towards capacity building for leadership and management, which specifically connects to institutional priorities, addresses issues, and creates, reinforces or reinterprets institutional culture. In most cases the target group is some (or occasionally all) senior and/or middle managers. One programme has sought to refine the focus, by targeting tranches of participants, who must be nominated by senior managers, to undertake a sustained Leaders for Tomorrow programme. It was reported at the 2001 European Association for Institutional Research conference (Gordon *et al.* 2001) alongside a broadly similar, if problematic, Swedish case study (Askling and Stensaker 2001) which focused on leadership for quality.

International developments

For many years the European Rectors Conference has organized an intensive development programme for rectors/vice-rectors (or their equivalent). Equivalent programmes are run in many countries, for example in Australia, under the aegis of the Australian Vice-Chancellors' Committee, and in Sweden. In the USA there are many programmes and conferences for chairs and for deans, and strong networks, both comprehensive and selective, exist for provosts and presidents. Similar active networks occur, at several levels, in virtually every country and, increasingly, they have a discernible development component. In the USA one route into senior administrative roles is through completing a doctoral qualification in higher education management. A small number of these qualifications are available in other countries but, to date, enrolments are small – understandably so, given the centrality of academic values in leaderships and management in higher education. The valued formal qualifications continue to be academic, not managerial.

One of the widest international networks is that associated with the Institutional Management in Higher Education (IMHE) programme of the Organization for Economic Co-operation and Development. A biennial conference is held in Paris. A number of major thematic conferences are arranged in various locations. Often these thematic events are the product of sustained IMHE programmes of research, for example Universities and Regional Development in the Knowledge Society, or Institutional Responses to Changing Student Expectations.

Finally, development opportunities flow from planned international tours to visit other institutions, to attend courses run, for example by the Association of Commonwealth Universities, the Association of African Universities, the British Council or the growing number of macro-regional groupings.

Concluding remarks

Progress is being made in the range, quality and scale of developmental provision for leaders and managers in higher education. Moreover, some exciting innovations are occurring. Yet challenges remain at every level. Perhaps the greatest occur at the level of heads of department/centre/unit. Knight and Trowler (2001) have written an extensive analysis of the topic of departmental leadership in higher education. They also offer suggestions for developmental strategies, including ways of developing seven forms of leadership and management knowledge: control; people; educational practice; conceptual; process; institutional; and tacit (2001: 168). Developmental practice is informed and enriched by such research and analyses.

Reflections on leadership and management suggests that there are some stunningly simple questions which need to be addressed:

- What are the functions and roles of leadership and management?
- Who is involved (who are the leaders and managers)?
- What knowledge and skills do they have, which need to be extended and what new knowledge or skills do they require?
- How are these developmental needs assessed and benchmarked?
- When should the development occur (for example, induction, continuing development, as required)?
- How should the development occur (for example, action learning, briefings, courses and seminars, mentoring, shadowing, projects, placements, structured reflection)?
- Who should provide the development (internal/external, devolved/central, specialized/generic)?
- How does leadership and management relate to organizational structure, strategies and culture?

Complications occur because some of these issues are contested, unresolved or at various stages of evolution.

Davies (1996) undertook a study for UNESCO aimed at identifying quality indicators for use in the training and development of senior managers in higher education. He drew evidence from several co-operative programmes and a wide range of other sources to develop sets of indicators for design criteria, process criteria and outcome criteria. Design issues include: the context of the programme; the needs of the participants; and the connection between these and the programme design and objectives.

Process issues spanned recruitment, selection and preparation, effective group dynamics, securing 'internationalism' or multi-environmentalism, facilitating transfer/application of learning to the workplace, programme evaluation and monitoring, programme organization, delivery and staffing.

Achieving change is challenging, so the output/outcome criteria merit particular attention. Davies highlighted:

- evidencing gains in the knowledge and competencies of participants;
- identifying attitudinal/behavioural changes;
- demonstrating career development;
- showing related organizational change;
- noting related enhanced networking and collaboration;
- checking the 'after-sales service' of the programme (active alumni network, newsletters, follow-up events).

Gordon (1999) reported the following key messages from a UCoSDA management survey:

- Actively involve experienced managers in the design and delivery of activities and programmes.
- Make use of the experiences of participants.
- Choose external presenters carefully.
- Commitment from and involvement of senior managers is crucial.
- Use a variety of approaches and methods.
- Have fairly clear stated objectives (a minority of respondents favoured pre-agreement on a set of outcomes stated in behavioural terms).

One key indicator, albeit tricky to define and measure precisely, is whether, how, and in what ways, development programmes lead to better leadership and management. This is an area requiring further urgent evaluative research.

The preceding discussion has traced many of the challenges and debates and illustrated progress and developmental outcomes. Considerable diversity characterizes national systems, and there has probably been even greater inter-system variation. There are dangers in oversimplifying trends but there are strong indications that greater attention is being paid, in every country and institution, to the topic of leadership and management development. Different traditions, preferences and balances of power affect both the starting point and the apparent pace of change.

Another complication comes from the extent to which institutions are being pressed to look outside the academy and consider developmental approaches which are in use in other sectors. Whilst resistance can occur when the comparator is perceived as too different, even alien, many approaches to leadership and management development in higher education do borrow, or seek to learn from, the experience of others. Mostly that involves expert inputs but it can include case studies, and occasionally mentoring or placements. In some systems, such as the UK, there are suggestions that higher education should develop something akin to the large-scale leadership and management development programmes that are now in place for senior managers in schools, the National Health Service and local government. There are also the longer-standing examples of the staff colleges of the fire service and the police, as well as the armed forces. The principal arguments in favour of such approaches surround standards and quality of development provision. Against these are ranged the autonomy of institutions and the distinctive diversity within many systems.

It is likely that elements of all of the various scenarios will be translated into action. That would mean substantial upscaling of institutional provision and greater attention to priorities, purposes and integration with strategy and culture. It would also involve further moves towards flexible yet comprehensive provision within institutions. Inter-institutional, national and international strands could usefully facilitate sharing of experiences, the development of high-quality resources, articulation of standards, research, evaluation and benchmarking. The provision of high-quality 'programmes' for a large proportion of senior staff, especially for institutions which could not embark upon that task alone and for individuals whose next step will be to a senior post elsewhere, would also provide useful foci for strands of staff development.

Key learning points

Senior staff

- Ensure that you undertake explicit ongoing personal development, including skills enhancement.
- Ensure that explicit provision is made for the development of middle managers, that it is tailored to utilize personal experiences and strengths and to cohere with institutional strategies, orientation and planned change.

Heads of department

- Accept that leadership and management will, at least for the term of your office, be part of your identity.
- Build upon your experiences and strengths but be willing to analyse and address lacunae.
- Take active steps to network, to share experiences, to learn and to socialize into the role.

Professional staff developers

- Pay close attention to the different needs and experiences of your clients, recognizing the importance of culture and language.
- Maintain and develop both your personal credibility and, even more crucially, that of the provision which you oversee, co-ordinate or manage.
- Undertake regular evaluation, benchmarking and environmental scanning to ensure that your provision remains on the cutting edge of national and international thinking. Ensure appropriate links with and utilization of external provision.

Part III

Intra-institutional matters

The next four chapters focus on organizational matters that are normally addressed at or within institutions, although inevitably the boundary between this part and Part II is thin and could have been drawn differently. A connecting theme is the concern of the authors to analyse behaviour and the views of staff within institutions, and to discuss any necessary or desirable internal action.

In Chapter 10, Richard Blackwell addresses staff development within departments. Returning to a theme in Chapter 1, he emphasizes the importance of social learning and of embedding learning in normal working practices and routines. He examines the roles that the key players may adopt (the head of department, departmental staff development representative and the staff development unit). He asks whether staff development units are necessary in systems emphasizing local social learning and argues that they do have a valuable facilitative role, supporting departments, and working across them and their communities.

Paul Blackmore and Moira Fraser review the connections between teaching and disciplinary research in Chapter 11. They focus on developing research-based curricula and, drawing on staff interviews, identify four types of link (outcomes, process, tools and context) which they argue can benefit students. A range of ways in which institutions can facilitate links are discussed, and they are sensitive to the danger of simply stimulating compliance behaviour. They conclude that benefits may accrue to students, staff and institutions.

Chapter 12, by Martin Oliver and Jacqueline Dempster, focuses on ways in which e-learning may become embedded in academic practices. They note structural issues, including the tendency to locate responsibility in separate units and the dangers of isolation and technically (rather than pedagogically) driven provision that may arise. They review four approaches to engaging academic staff – accredited courses (see Chapter 7), workshops, secondments and informal learning (as discussed in Chapter 10) – identifying the circumstances in which they are most likely to work and the challenges to which they give rise. Managing the tension between developing individuals and divorcing them from their colleagues' shared practices emerges as a key task.

Finally, Marie Garnett and Ruth Goodall (Chapter 13) examine career development for research staff, so often the poor relations of staff development despite the high status of research within higher education. They chart a range of national initiatives in the UK, before focusing on detailed feedback from researchers in four universities and their implications for staff and career development. Proper integration into institutional life is a key issue, including into communities of practice (see Chapters 1 and 10), and may be facilitated by legislative change arising from the European Union harmonization process.

10

Developing departments

Richard Blackwell

Introduction

The department is the main 'activity system' for most staff (Knight and Trowler 2000). For many staff the beliefs and norms of behaviour that dominate their department may well be what they understand as the 'university' or 'college'. Indeed, departmental cultures are so strong that 'if there is a mismatch between the messages coming from mentoring and courses and those embedded in departmental cultures, then it is the mentoring and course messages that will be derogated' (Knight and Trowler 1999: 32). Effective development at departmental level therefore needs to be embedded in departmental cultures. This chapter refers briefly to recent literature, and discusses the nature of departmental learning before focusing upon the roles of key players (the head of department, staff development representative and SD unit). It seeks to strike a balance between breadth and depth of analysis, as well as between literature review and provision of practical examples.

Literature

Despite the importance of the topic, the literature on departmental SD is relatively limited but growing. Gibbs (1996) identified international examples of departmentally focused work in Australia, the UK and the USA, and Hicks (1999) added an overview of Australian experience. Blackmore *et al.* (1999) gathered examples of good practice within departments in the UK, Australia, USA and Hong Kong.

Departmental leadership and management have received most international attention, including in the UK (see Chapter 9; Knight and Trowler 2001) Australia (Moses and Roe 1990; Ramsden 1998) and the USA (Gmelch and Miskin 1995). According to one author, 'simply put, research activity and productivity and the quality of teaching and learning are influenced for better or for worse by the way in which the department is managed or led' (Ramsden 1998: xii). The role of the head of department therefore merits special attention and will be considered separately below.

Departmental learning and internal support

A number of related publications have argued for the importance of socially located, 'situated learning' – tacit knowledge that arises from daily discourse and social practices (Wenger 1998; Knight and Trowler 1999). In many cases it may just be a case of nudging things forward, incrementally developing an existing 'community of practice', encouraging *bricolage* or tinkering (Knight 2002a) without much external or formal involvement. The position taken in this chapter is that maintaining or creating such healthy 'communities of practice' is the main function of SD at departmental level. Although the notion of a 'community of practice' can be criticized for implicit exclusivity and assuming that the mere assertion of its existence is sufficient to demonstrate that learning occurs (as discussed in Chapter 1) no such assumptions are made here. The preceding word 'healthy' denotes inclusive intentions and real functioning in actuality. This stance places emphasis on the department to create mainly informal learning opportunities, and to capitalize on distributed implicit knowledge.

The above supposes that learning is taking place in a period of stability. However, radical departmental-level organizational change arising from mergers of academic units has become increasingly common. These mergers frequently bring together smaller groups who previously competed, for example for students, and who had developed different patterns of organization. The need to establish new and productive working relationships, procedures and policies as quickly as possible creates an important challenge and opportunity for collective SD. Indeed, some would argue that it is an essential part of securing 'ownership' of change by those affected (Slowey 1995; Blackwell *et al.* 2001). Establishing or revising a mission statement, strategies and priorities in key areas by dialogue and discussion may form an important focus for this development through awaydays and the like. Second, there is the question of the relationship between different groups of staff. In most science and engineering departments, academic staff will form probably less than a third of the overall staff complement. Pressure for increased productivity without increasing head count is putting an emphasis on optimum teamworking across staff boundaries and in part lies behind the moves in the UK to establish a common pay spine for all staff. The ability (and willingness) of academic staff to delegate as much of their administrative responsibilities as possible to other staff in departments depends critically on their trust and confidence in their colleagues. A growing feature of SD activity is to develop such trust at department or subgroup level (for example, the research or programme team).

External support

A central SD unit can play a number of roles. It can act as consultant and supporter to the in-department work. There may be a need for 'capacity building', ensuring that the processes that bring about informal learning are understood and facilitated. More formal interventions may help ensure departments do not become stuck in static 'single loop learning', reinforcing existing practice only, and that they instead embrace 'double loop learning' that challenges existing norms and is characteristic of learning organizations (see Chapter 1).

External SD provision needs to be sensitive to dominant patterns of organization and the values and attitudes that go with and support them. Four organizational patterns have been found to characterize university departments – hierarchical, collegial, anarchical and political patterns, the first two of which are articulated in the public domain (Becher 1989; Sawbridge 1996). The first is characteristic of central administrations and large, complex departments with mixed staff undertaking a range of activities some of which are potentially hazardous to staff and students (for example, engineering). The collegial and person-centred anarchical patterns are more typical of academic departments, especially arts and humanities departments, which may involve consensus decision-making and strict rotation of roles and key activities (for example, study leave entitlement). Many change initiatives are contested because they implicitly involve shifting or modifying dominant patterns, threatening established interests, the political patterns of behaviour that lie below the surface of organizations.

When reorganization is taking place, arguably a strategically engaged institutional SD function would have influence over decisions about mergers and their implementation at institutional level. Whether such influence exists or not, where the department lacks the internal skills or requires a 'neutral' consultant-facilitator to achieve consensual change, the SD unit, if it has appropriate expertise and is not tainted by close association with the specific change or local management, may play the role of internal consultant.

Effectiveness of external provision

External provision refers to SD outside the department – including within the institution, offered by a central SD unit, and outside the institution, offered by professional or subject associations or national bodies. The most common forms of provision are probably formal short courses and discipline-based conferences. Within the institution, extra departmental provision will normally consist of short courses for all staff and professional, possibly award-bearing, courses for new academic staff offered by the central SD unit. Induction into the organization or into new roles is commonly shared between the centre and the department.

Opinions vary on the effectiveness of provision external to the immediate workplace. Recent research has tended to be sceptical about the value of external provision unconnected to local practice, presenting a substantial challenge to traditional provision by SD units. Scholars working in the cognitive tradition on transfer of learning from off-the-job-training have emphasized the importance of the 'transfer environment' locally. Four aspects stand out:

- the scope of opportunities to use the new knowledge and skills;
- the extent to which local 'management' positively welcome and support the activity in principle and practice rather than deprecate it;
- the extent to which peers are positively supportive, both in principle and practice;
- whether positive personal outcomes, including career advancement, are associated with the training (Baldwin and Ford 1998; Tennant 1999).

The impact of external courses is therefore problematic, and some studies suggest even excellent provision has limited impact on practice (Weimer and Lenze 1991). Following research into the transfer of learning (for example, De Corte 2000), it can be predicted that the likelihood of transfer of learning from an external course will be related to the complexity of the innovation and of the setting to which it is to be applied. The more complex the innovation and the setting, the less transferability is likely. Rust (1998) followed up participants on workshops run at Oxford Brookes University on teaching and learning issues and found that a high proportion of those who had expressed an intention to change in end-of-course evaluations reported that they had in fact made a change. It is notable that participants were self-selecting volunteers, many of whom had travelled and paid to attend the courses, and might be regarded as particularly highly motivated to change. For such individuals (a minority), one may hypothesize that traditions of academic autonomy and relatively high control and discretion over work provide some space to make limited changes despite the general 'transfer environment', for example in one's own classes. Despite these reservations, there are additional grounds for arguing that important intangible benefits, not evident in change to formal work practices, may flow from external courses for some staff. Maintaining morale and motivation in a hostile or unreceptive departmental environment may be a significant function (and unrecorded gain) for the minority of people attracted to voluntary courses. Looking for sustenance from fellow innovators ('the most important thing was knowing I am not alone') emerged as important informal feedback in sessions on, for example, 'active learning' at the University of Nottingham in the 1990s. Manual, technical and secretarial staff are unlikely to have the job autonomy to counteract the 'transfer environment' although external short courses may play a similar role in maintaining morale and motivation for such groups of staff with limited career prospects (see also Chapter 15). At the University of Nottingham, the secretarial and clerical staff have for 10 years consistently recorded the highest levels of participation in and enthusiasm for events and consultations of any staff group. Similar effects have been informally reported at other UK universities (such as Birmingham).

Role of the head of department

Leadership by the head of department is critical in setting the context and tone for local SD. Indeed, for those taking a social constructionist view, establishing the appropriate culture is arguably more important than specific SD actions: 'get the department right and the learning will follow' (Knight and Trowler 2001: 154). Getting the 'department right' and creating a positive, learning climate may require a focus on SD, although when one is inherited from a predecessor it may be more about maintaining momentum and building upon established practice. Creating a culture in which professional learning routinely happens may involve the head in relatively little formal SD whatever approach is taken to leadership (see Ramsden 1998; Knight and Trowler 1999, 2001). Ensuring 'space' for reflective discussion in regular departmental meetings, encouraging and supporting innovation and modelling learning behaviour are among the things suggested by 'community of practice' approaches (Knight 2002a, b).

The annual planning process that most higher education institutions require nowadays provides opportunities for ensuring a strategic focus to SD and developing a learning culture. The former involves alignment with agreed departmental strategies involving staff in discussion in meetings, at awaydays and the like. In any case, arrangements for bottom-up input from staff are essential, probably via the SD representative. A further area of interest for most heads is the future leadership of the unit itself. This includes the development of its collective leadership or management group, if it has one, and succession planning for the headship where the office rotates or is appointed from among departmental staff for short terms. In many instances these matters will be too politically sensitive to be passed to others and, in some cases, will not be amenable to discussion or planning. An apparent drift away from rotation towards appointment by the institution, in recent years either permanently or for a fixed term, may be reducing this role. Together with growing provision of external training (see Chapter 9), this trend denotes increasing institutional interest in and control over appointments and preparation, even if heads' integration into a managerial community of practice remains tenuous (Deem and Johnson 2000). Delegation, shadowing and other informal processes provide ways of ensuring that appropriate individuals receive development opportunities.

Role of the local staff development representative

At a practical level, the growing size and complexity of units means that only in exceptional cases, such as in small arts departments, or exceptional times will heads be able to play a 'hands-on' role in SD. In most cases heads will need to delegate day-to-day responsibility to 'line managers' and/or a SD representative, the mix depending on the size, complexity and staffing profile of the department.

The role of the representative is likely to vary with context and according to the power resources, capability and attitude of the person in the role. Key

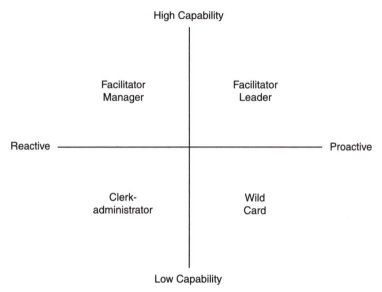

Figure 10.1   Role of the departmental staff development representative

formal features are set out in Figure 10.1. An important aspect of the context is the basis on which the SD representative is appointed and funded, which may affect whom they are perceived to be 'working for' by departmental staff. Although the next section will discuss other options, this section assumes that the representative reports to the departmental head or committee and carries out their role as part of their normal departmental duties, with or without specific time allowance.

Staff development capability refers to the person's understanding and process skills. The categories are not intended to be pejorative. For example, a competent clerk of the works may be appropriate where the head of department plays a leading hands-on role or a learning culture is already well established, a proactive leader appropriate when a learning community is being created. Other factors include geographical dispersal, the range of staff groups, the extent of intra-organizational consensus on SD matters, and the actual and intended role of 'line managers'.

Four sets of relationships appear important: the relationship with the head of department; the relationship with the central SD unit; the relationship with staff in the unit; and the relationship with other departmental SD representatives. The extent to which the person appointed has or can acquire power resources of various kinds, including through delegation by the head and maintaining the trust and confidence of staff, will be critical to the real authority of the role. With this in mind, some commentators have recommended that the person should be an established, senior member of staff (Blackmore *et al.* 1999: 6). The representative's activities may include some or all of the following:

- Gathering information from staff on their 'wants', through formal feedback mechanisms (such as appraisal) and from informal contact and discussion.
- Environmental scanning to identify forthcoming issues and longer-run SD 'needs' related to changes in the environment, departmental policy and so on; and to identify sources of external support or funding for innovation in the discipline or subject (for example, from the Learning and Teaching Support Network featured in Chapter 6). Engaging in development projects and innovations can be a useful source of development for individuals as well as providing departmental benefits.
- Co-ordinating the development, review and implementation of SD policy for the department and ensuring it is aligned with and influences other policies (see Blackmore *et al.* 1999: 40–8 for examples). Liaising with any other colleagues with a SD responsibility (such as line managers in technical areas; leaders of research groups and course teams). Generally 'championing' SD, if able (see Figure 10.1).
- Formal provision, including arranging and actually designing and delivering formal local events.
- Creating and supporting the head in creating, learning opportunities around routine practice. Promoting *bricolage*, or continuous piecemeal improvement as a normal part of 'working here'.
- Ensuring the department does not become stuck in conservative 'single loop learning' by encouraging questioning of accepted wisdom (to enable 'double loop learning'). Introducing local peer processes, such as observation of teaching, teaching circles or discussion groups and mentoring that encourage reflection and linkage between formal and tacit learning (Blackwell and McLean 1996 a, b; Blackwell *et al.* 2001). In the USA, such processes have come together with portfolios and peer review of courses in full 'peer review of teaching' (Hutchings 1996; D'Andrea 2001).
- Monitoring engagement with SD (for instance conference participation, course attendance) and the evaluation of the impact of formal and informal processes, including oversight of record-keeping for institutional quality assurance procedures or external inspection purposes. Other administrative jobs might include reviewing and approving applications for study leave, external courses, etc.
- Engaging external help when required to assist with policy formation, controversial activities (to avoid becoming embroiled into intra-organizational politics), specialist training, etc.
- Self-development: contact and networking with other SD representatives to build a 'community of practice'.
- Liaising with the institutional SD unit, which may be viewed as an external resource within the institution, available to help run and set up events and to broker other inputs from outside bodies. Where no such unit exists the environmental scanning role will assume greater importance.

Role of the staff development unit

The role of the SD unit is typically twofold: to build local capacity to undertake SD on the one hand, and to provide services directly to the departments on the other. Hicks's analysis of Australian experience is instructive. Based on two dimensions, local/central provision and generic/discipline-specific dimension, Hicks identifies four models:

- Central models relying on a strong central unit. This appears still to be the dominant pattern in Australia, the UK and USA.
- Dispersed models in which devolution of resources and local activity is encouraged as a matter of policy, sometimes with the suspicion that it is a strategy designed to obviate the need for a central unit. Variants of this approach have been tried in the UK and are sometimes attractive to finance departments wishing to create an internal market and minimize cost.
- Mixed models in which both local discipline-specific and generic central provision coexist. These models often appear to contain largely unrelated initiatives.
- The integrated model in which the elements in the mixed model are interrelated through collaborative processes to encourage 'holistic approaches'. The latter is thought to be the most difficult to achieve, if most desirable, and few examples appear to exist (Hicks 1999).

Localized models are, not surprisingly, thought to do better on ownership and impact, centrally oriented approaches on access and corporate policy implementation. Discipline-based pedagogical research is thought most likely to develop where partnerships between centrally based staff developers and academic teachers can be forged. Hicks suggests a trend from the (still dominant) generic provision by a central unit towards discipline-based and local provision. Although much of the local and discipline-specific provision appears to be centrally driven in Australia, faculty-based initiatives were noted in the tutor methods training at the University of Queensland and in the decision of one faculty at the University of Melbourne to establish its own teaching and learning unit (Hicks 1999). Similar trends can be identified in the UK, although the establishment of separate units at faculty or departmental level is relatively unusual. These trends appear less advanced in the USA, where the central generic model of faculty development has appeared to remain dominant, at least until the mid-1990s (Lewis 1996), albeit complemented by an increasingly discipline-based debate on the scholarship of teaching and learning (Chapter 5; Huber and Morreale 2002).

In the UK, project-based funding, competitively allocated, has been widely used following the Enterprise in Higher Education initiative in the early 1990s and the Higher Education Funding Council for England's more recent Teaching Quality Enhancement Fund initiative (Gibbs and Habeshaw 2002: 15), especially for teaching and learning enhancement purposes. In some cases such funding has become focused on institutional priorities, and part of institutional reward strategies, for example at University of East London (Laycock 1997; Gibbs and Habeshaw 2002: 15). Sophisticated evaluation and embedding strategies have also been promoted to stimulate organizational learning through a 'good practice' guide (Gibbs *et al.* 2002). Many of these developments, however, appear to have been piecemeal, without explicit underpinning models. Mixed approaches of largely unrelated initiatives are the norm. Trends towards funding focused on corporate priorities indicate growing attention to integration, albeit largely on the terms of the centre, although the strength of departmental cultures and the availability of project funds from extra-institutional sources continue to make corporate control problematic. The recent emergence of the subject-based Learning and Teaching Support Network, working directly with departments (see Chapter 6), provides one potential counterweight to central control within HEIs. This discipline-based pull and local focus suggests movement towards more local discipline-specific development in the UK. It might provide yet further impetus for uncoordinated mixed provision unless SD units are proactive in seeking collaborative working and integration of institutional and subject-based initiatives, such as the LTSN in the UK (Chapter 6) or the scholarship of teaching and learning movement in the USA (Chapter 5).

These developments require a change in the balance of roles fulfilled by staff developers, in particular a shift away from central trainer towards provision of support and resources for locally based activity, including through internal consultancy. Negotiated partnerships, capacity building through, for example, the sponsorship of networks of departmental SD representatives and provision of consultancy services are emerging as priorities (on developing consultancy practice, see Boud and Macdonald 1981; Kubr 1986).

It seems increasingly likely that higher education institutions and their SD units will need to review their own structures, operations and the deployment of resources to meet the needs of their departments. Among the issues that arise are those of staffing, funding, co-ordination and evaluation.

Staffing options include allocating a person from within the central SD unit as a first point of contact for departments or groupings of departments (faculties) or jointly appointing people within departments. Other options include physically locating someone in academic areas funded by the centre, or simply encouraging and supporting the emergence of departmental representatives who have the role as part of their normal brief. These options are not mutually exclusive and choices are constrained by resources. Locally based joint appointments and nominated central contacts have both proved problematic in Australia (Hicks 1999: 50). 'Buying out' some time for representatives is an approach tried by various institutions in the UK (such as Nottingham Trent University) although locally appointed members of staff with the SD role as part of their normal departmental duties remains more usual.

Dedicating parts of the institutional budget to support local initiatives through projects and other activities has already been discussed. One alternative outlined by Gibbs, based on the experience of Oxford Brookes University in the UK, involves a central unit calculating their person-days of capacity for the year, top-slicing that required for central corporate activities and then allocating the rest *pro rata* to departments as free consultancy days (Gibbs 1996). Charge-back models have also been used (for example, at Cardiff University). However, they carry the danger of disconnecting central units from institutional policy and of focusing provision and access on safe, traditional activities favoured by the powerful (such as conference participation). In a patchily developed or immature learning culture, stasis may result.

To achieve an integrated approach, time and effort will need to be deployed by the SD unit into establishing partnerships with departments, co-ordinating activities and disseminating the outcomes of projects and other innovations from particular contexts across the institution. Partnership models that bring together and integrate top-down and bottom-up impulses have long been advocated (Smith 1992; Elton 1995). However, the focus on departments suggests the addition of a 'middle out' dimension (Trowler *et al.* 2003), supporting changes initiated at departmental level.

Monitoring and evaluation of departmental performance arises from the need of institutions to have confidence that they are receiving value for money in the more decentralized approaches, especially where resources are substantially allocated to departments. Quantitative indicators will need to be combined with more subtle qualitative indicators focused on informal tacit learning that arises from practice, which is very difficult to measure in a non-intrusive way. Information of the second type will inevitably rest strongly on feedback from departments, possibly via departmental SD representatives. There is a tension, however, between this monitoring role and the kind of developmental partnerships signalled by Hicks's discussion of the integrated model. In an ideal world these summative and formative roles would be separated.

Conclusion

It is arguable that when a mature learning culture has been successfully established within departments, a central unit is otiose – the function has abolished itself and dispersion is the best organizational strategy. This chapter has made a case for an institutional unit supporting departments in a variety of ways – brokering external resources and input, providing consultancy support, etc. It has noted some intangible benefits of short external courses and questioned the wisdom of decentralization in an immature SD culture. As argued in Chapter 1, there are other important strategic organizational roles (among them environmental scanning, and pursuit of sensitive and important 'corporate' SD in culturally appropriate ways, such as management development for heads of department) which suggest that without a central unit a strategic focus would be difficult to achieve. Difficult to achieve but not impossible – witness the case of the University of the West of England, a well-regarded UK institution. Extant SD units would be wise to ensure that, as well as provision seen as directly relevant to organizational goals by institutional leaders, they provide demonstrably good and valued services to their departments.

Trends in the development of universities suggest that academic units will need to make more systematic efforts to develop their own SD capacity in future. Although there is evidence of much informal, small-scale good practice, both in individual professional development and some peer processes (such as mentoring), there is an increasing need to spread and transfer such practices into all areas. Heads of department and other leaders have themselves increasingly experienced awaydays and residential courses and become aware of the potential for agreed developments in mission and strategy and the kind of team-building activities common outside higher education. Departmental SD representatives are likely to grow in importance and require greater support than hitherto. For SD units this presents a challenge and an opportunity. The emerging agenda suggests an orientation towards local 'capacity building', sometimes in collaboration with external subject-based experts, together with selected direct services, including brokering external inputs and provision of internal consultancy. Such a change requires a focus by SD units on the strategic needs of their departments and their staff. It may entail both a more decentralized structure and further development of capacity, including for internal consultancy.

Key learning points

Senior staff

- Departmental cultures and 'transfer environments' have a major impact on the effectiveness of external staff development. To be effective, external staff development messages need to be congruent with local working practices and culture and the assumptions that they embody.
- Departmentally focused and based staff development has a greater chance of impact on practice and will be increasingly necessary as devolution deepens. Developing healthy 'communities of practice' which embed learning into their normal work routines is likely to be most effective at this level.
- A central unit should normally be retained unless and until a mature 'learning' or staff development culture has been established in departments throughout the organization. It may need to be supported in reorienting its activities towards the needs of departments. An institutional function is also important to deliver culturally sensitive, organizationally focused strategic staff development.

Heads of department

- Strategic staff development involves creating a local learning culture, a community of practice in which learning is embedded in working routines. More pragmatically departmentally based staff development can play a central role in achieving departmental plans, especially by encouraging staff 'ownership' of change, and needs to be integral to strategy and planning processes. Nonetheless external short courses can play a role in maintaining the morale of innovators and some groups of support staff, for example secretaries.

- Staff development should be conceived of very broadly to include a range of activities that go beyond formal courses and involve informal or tacit learning arising from practice. Opportunities need to be made for reflection and discussion in normal meetings, awaydays organized, *bricolage* encouraged. Staff development units may offer or broker useful external input.
- A departmental staff development representative is required in most circumstances who can take delegated responsibility for the area, champion the staff development mentioned in the previous point and adopt a role that fits local patterns of organization and needs. A senior member of staff or someone with other sources of authority/power is preferable in most circumstances.

Professional staff developers

- Tacit and informal learning, arising from everyday interactions and practices, are powerful processes that probably have more influence on attitudes and behaviour than formal, external courses designed for individual members of staff.
- Although a good start has been made in some areas, trends towards devolution and developments in social learning theory suggest staff development functions will need to give even greater priority to delivering services to and building local capacity for SD in departments. There is more chance of real impact on practice at this level, and successful promotion of staff development may create a better transfer environment for other external courses run by the unit.
- Staff development functions may wish to consider whether they are appropriately structured and whether they have the appropriate staff expertise to meet the challenges of a greater departmental focus. If not, 'physician heal thyself'.

11

Research and teaching: making the link

Paul Blackmore and Moira Fraser

Teaching and research, two activities which are fundamental to academic life, have something of a love–hate relationship. On the one hand many academics argue that they are mutually reinforcing, and that participating in research enables a member of staff to have more enthusiasm and a greater depth of expert, up-to-the-minute knowledge of a subject. On the other, the two activities often appear to have conflicting goals and reward systems, and to compete for academics' time and energy. Teaching can become the poor relation, seen to be draining time and resources from staff who are under pressure to produce publications to boost departmental research profiles.

Some have argued that teaching and research are fundamentally incompatible. Newman claimed that

> to discover and to teach are two distinct functions; they are also distinct gifts, and are not commonly found united in the same person. He, too, who spends his day in dispensing his existing knowledge to all comers is unlikely to have either leisure or energy to acquire new.
>
> (1853, p.10)

This view persists in some quarters, and it might be argued that teaching-only or research-only institutions might be free of such tensions and be more cost-effective. Perhaps undergraduates should be taught in environments where staff time was devoted solely to teaching, thus freeing research-active staff to focus their efforts in posts in research-only institutions. Certainly the growing number of research-only and teaching-only posts indicates that this may be happening within institutions. Few academics, however, would argue for such a separation.

In a cost-conscious era of increasing casualization and fragmentation of role (see Chapter 2), research–teaching links are likely to be eroded. It is important therefore to clarify what those links might be, to explore their possible benefits to both staff and students and further to develop them, seeking ways in which they can become easier bedfellows. Research–teaching links are not of interest only to research-led institutions. Opportunities exist in teaching-led institutions to make productive links, and ways of doing so are explored here.

The issue is strategically significant for universities. There are clear signs that unsupported assertions by institutions that research informs their teaching sound less convincing and may well be unwise. The research–teaching link has at last become newsworthy. In the United States, the Boyer Commission (1998) severely criticized research universities, which 'have too often failed, and continue to fail, their undergraduate populations. . . . thousands of students graduate without seeing the world-famous professors or tasting genuine research'. A follow-up report (Boyer Commission 2001) found many improvements. However, the impact of both reports indicates a substantial breadth of interest in the issue.

In the UK, the higher education funding councils periodically examine their policies in allocating research and teaching funding. Many would argue that the presence of research and its effective link with teaching offers a means of nurturing the culture of critical thought that is a fundamental aspect of a university (Barnett 1997). There is no doubt that teaching costs more in an institution with significant research activity. It is that link which 'sustains higher education's claim to distinctive, and distinctively better, treatment in terms of resourcing than other sectors of education' (Brown 2002). The level of research funding is therefore a live political issue, and universities would be wise to ensure that the claims they make about the value of research to teaching have substance. Distribution is equally significant. Given the major expansion in research activity in recent years, prompted in part by successive rounds of the national research assessment exercise, it has become apparent that there is not enough research funding to satisfy all who want it. Debate takes place over the desirability of concentrating it or distributing it widely. The current trend towards concentration will inevitably weaken the research base in a number of institutions, with consequent effects on the teaching–research link in those institutions, unless funding formulae are amended to support scholarship across the sector.

Do positive links between teaching and research necessarily exist?

The notion that teaching and research within a university are complementary may stem from Humboldt's claim, made in 1809, that 'the teacher does not exist for the sake of the student; both teacher and student have their justification in the common pursuit of knowledge and hence there is a unity of research and teaching' (Humboldt 1970). The assumption that teaching and research are indivisible has persisted, although the existence of this claimed link – which many academics take as axiomatic – is less easily proven in terms of observable outcomes.

In a meta-analysis of 58 studies of the links between teaching and research, Hattie and Marsh (1996) found that the teaching–research relationship can take a number of forms. Analysis showed that some studies found a positive link between teaching and research, sometimes thought to be through common underlying qualities and processes. Others, however, suggest a negative correlation between quality of teaching and learning, perhaps due to the time required for each activity, or because teaching and research require different skills or are rewarded in different ways. Further, some research finds no relationship. In the light of this, the necessary conclusion was that, in the research carried out in this area to date, no strong relationship between quality of teaching and research has been demonstrated and that 'the common belief that research and teaching are inextricably entwined is an enduring myth. At best, research and teaching are very loosely coupled' (Hattie and Marsh 1996).

Despite the lack of hard evidence, there is a strong view within the higher education sector that research–teaching links are beneficial to students, and that this is something to which institutions should aspire (Hughes and Tight 1995). In the UK, the Quality Assurance Agency for Higher Education (QAA) reviews of teaching quality have praised departments for what is often termed 'research-led' teaching. For example:

> The research activities of the staff, who are authoritative in their subject areas, contributed to the development of the curriculum, the excellence of the project and the teaching.
>
> (QAA 1999a)

and in another case:

> The curricula in all programmes . . . are rigorous, challenging to students and informed by staff research and scholarship.
>
> (QAA 1999b)

However, although these statements imply that direct and positive links between teaching and research can be made, the meaning of research-led teaching has seldom been seriously discussed and there has been limited analysis of how it may in fact be beneficial to students.

One problem with the term 'research-led teaching' is that it carries with it particular connotations which are not necessarily helpful. It implies that the focus of concern should be on the content of courses presented to students, and that this should contain up-to-the-minute research outcomes, in some cases relating to the research work being carried out by the academic staff themselves. However, there are many modules where this type of content simply is not appropriate as a main focus. In the early stages of undergraduate degree programmes, it is often necessary for students to develop a broad understanding of key concepts in the discipline. This does, of course involve learning about research outcomes, but they might be decades or centuries old. Particularly in the sciences, but also in other disciplines, it is difficult for students to progress to learning about current research until they have a sound grasp of these core concepts.

In addition, this terminology focuses on the input of staff rather than the needs of students and what they might gain from participating in these courses. This does not fit well with a contemporary broader concern for learners' skills in addition to the learning of propositional knowledge.

It should be noted in passing that the term 'research-led teaching' is also used to refer to teachers adopting a rigorous approach to evaluating and developing their own practice. This is a major and interesting area that is dealt with by Mary Taylor Huber in Chapter 5, but it is not our focus here.

What are the links between teaching and research?

A much wider view of the potential for links between teaching and research would be beneficial, including not only the ways in which links may exist, but also of practical ways in which they can be monitored and improved, to help academic staff review and develop their practice.

Teaching and research activity may be linked through the activities which underpin both, described either as scholarship (Elton 1992) or learning (Brew and Boud 1995). These areas of commonality, which are required of academic staff in both teaching and research, are also those required of a student who wishes to undertake a course of study successfully. This sense that all members of a university – staff and students alike – are engaged in a common enterprise of scholarship and learning is one which can usefully inform our way of thinking about how teaching and research interact.

However, as well as at this general level, more specific or practical links also exist. Neumann's (1992) study of the linkages between teaching and research identifies three main ways in which the two come into contact: the tangible nexus (the transmission of advanced knowledge and the most recent facts); the intangible nexus (the development in students of a critical approach and attitude towards knowledge, and the provision of a stimulating and rejuvenating milieu for academics) and the global nexus (the interaction at a departmental level, with research forming the framework for teaching). Neumann's categories, at least at a basic level, provide a useful way of starting to consider the links between research and learning in our own institutions. However, some of the categories seem problematic. The intangible nexus, for example, appears to include two very different forms of linkage, whilst the global nexus seems somewhat loose and would benefit from further elucidation. This model needs development if it is to provide a useful tool for educational development.

Neumann claims that the nature of the nexus varies according to, for example, the academic level of the students, the nature of the discipline and the type of course concerned. Certainly the importance of disciplinary differences in shaping the nature of teaching–research links requires careful consideration when seeking to develop a model. Differences in the nature of research and how it takes place across disciplines may influence the tightness of the link between research and teaching. In science, for example, the link between the two may not be close at the start of undergraduate programmes, but in the later stages of the degree a greater inter-relationship may develop. In humanities, however, research may feed into teaching from the start but links may not develop as far (Jensen 1988). Moses (1990) reaches a similar conclusion – that fruitful relationships between research and teaching in the sciences exist only at graduate level, whereas in humanities there is a strong relationship between research and undergraduate teaching.

When trying to develop a model for understanding and enhancing links between teaching and research, it is therefore necessary to cater for the differences which exist between disciplines, whilst focusing upon common themes such as scholarship and learning. A model which is too prescriptive or rigid might prove unsatisfactory for all, whilst one which is too vague may be equally ineffective as a tool for supporting educational development.

A framework for developing a research-based curriculum

The links which have been described above provide insight from a theoretical perspective into research–teaching links, but are not immediately useful as tools for supporting staff in developing their practice. They do, however, provide a basis for the development of practical ways of working. At the University of Warwick, interviews were conducted with 20 staff from across the range of disciplines – in humanities, social sciences and sciences – with the aim of developing a useful framework. Members of staff were asked to describe key characteristics of research in their discipline, the nature of degree courses offered by their department, and to indicate how they felt research impacted upon teaching and learning in their department. Four main types of link were described – outcomes, process, tools and context (see Figure 11.1) – which tie in closely both with the notions of scholarship, and the types of teaching–research nexus described above. Drawn together, these four elements provide an overall framework for considering research-based learning, derived from the experience of academic staff. Each of the four elements is described below.

Outcomes, including research outcomes in the curriculum

In many cases, it is possible for recent outcomes of research – developed either within the institution or elsewhere – to be included in the material being taught in modules. Particularly in the later years of undergraduate courses and at master's level, modules may be designed specifically around the areas of research expertise of members of staff. Students often find this highly stimulating and appreciate being taught by researchers who are at the cutting edge in their field, as the enthusiasm which these members of staff have for their subject and their depth of knowledge

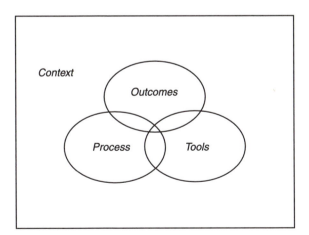

Figure 11.1   Elements of the research-based learning experience

are often conveyed to the students. However, in some cases it is not appropriate for this to take place. The research work may be at too high a level to be accessible to students, or it may not be central to the main focus of the degree programme which students are following. Staff may not be research-active in that, or any, field. In these cases, it may be possible for relevant examples and case studies from research to be brought in to illustrate points being made in modules, thus providing students with an insight into relationships between the course material and current developments in the field.

Process: using research-process-based methods of teaching and learning

Here, students learn by exploring issues, by setting their own questions and finding ways to solve problems and evaluate outcomes in the same way as a researcher tackles a piece of work. This helps students to realize that both at university and in future employment they need to be able to identify where their knowledge needs to be enhanced and to find ways of achieving this. It also helps them to understand that knowledge is constantly developing and there are ultimately very few clear-cut 'right' answers in any subject. This type of research-based learning is commonly done through individual or group project work, and provides a way in which students can become more actively involved in the learning process, leading to enhanced quality of learning. Often, students are set tasks within which they can choose their own topics to pursue, or are asked to respond to case studies describing real-life situations or research issues. Linking research and teaching through process does not require a research-intensive environment: all teaching staff in all institutions can engage in it.

Tools: learning to use the tools of research

In many courses, students are expected to undertake independent research work, which may involve, for example, pinpointing useful journal articles in preparation for essay composition, or for larger pieces of work such as projects or dissertations. In order to be able to undertake research independently, it is important that students develop the skills appropriate for their discipline, which are often also valuable in a range of other contexts. Such skills may include, for example, bibliographic searching, methods of data collection, statistical analysis and use of specialized equipment. Specific training in research methods is often built into degree programmes both at undergraduate and postgraduate levels, and combines general skills with those which are tailored to the particular needs of the discipline concerned.

Context: developing an inclusive research context and culture

This is a less tangible aspect of linking teaching and research, where students and staff are involved in working together in a research environment. This may be achieved by creating opportunities for students to come into contact with the research being undertaken by staff, and for them to feel part of a knowledge-creating community. This can help to break down any perceived division between staff and students and create a greater feeling of all members of the university being part of the common enterprises of scholarship and extending the boundaries of knowledge. In the United States, it is increasingly commonplace for undergraduates to be given the opportunity of participating in a 'live' faculty-led project, at institutions such as Princeton, Stanford, University of California at Berkeley and the University of Delaware. The Reinvention Center at Stony Brook provides a focus for such work (http://www.sunysb.edu/Reinventioncenter/index.html).

Using the framework in curriculum review

As different types of research-based learning lend themselves more easily to different courses, it would not be expected that all four would necessarily be found in every module. However, the four areas described above may offer a vocabulary and framework for reflecting upon how research and teaching are linked across a degree programme as a whole, and finding appropriate ways of enhancing the links. A number of probe questions can initiate this process, by helping staff to clarify what their current position is in relation to linking teaching and research, and to consider possible ways forward:

- Are research and teaching really interlinked in the department, or are they largely independent of each other?
- Are courses designed with an explicit intention to integrate research-based learning? How?
- Are all four types of research-based learning (Figure 11.1) incorporated into degree programmes? Is there scope for development in some areas?
- How, and to what extent, do students come into contact with any research taking place in the department?
- How do students learn research methods and develop research techniques?
- What opportunities are there for students to do their own research projects and self-directed work?
- Does research-based learning take place throughout all years of undergraduate degree programmes? If not, could this be further developed?

In many cases, development consists of making existing practice explicit, as there are often strong links between teaching and research which lie hidden. However, review may identify gaps where few links are apparent. If research–teaching links do not exist, and a member of staff or a department has taken a conscious decision that they need not, this may be entirely appropriate. However, if research–teaching links are claimed but the framework and questions above reveal none, this is a problem which should be addressed.

How do students benefit from a research-based approach to learning?

Although there may be political advantages in ensuring that teaching and research are linked, the pedagogical benefit is of primary importance, that is, that it will enhance students' learning and their experience of higher education. Research into factors affecting the quality of student learning suggests three key aspects.

First, it seems that students' motivation may be enhanced by exposure to advanced and developing subject matter within their degree programmes. Students have been found to enjoy courses in which their lecturer is perceived to be at the forefront of knowledge in their discipline and where relevant examples from their research are used in their teaching (Neumann 1994; Jenkins *et al.* 1998). Since students' levels of motivation and their perception of a learning task, including its interest and relevance, are key factors influencing learning processes (Entwhistle 1981), exposing students to newly developed knowledge and to researchers at the cutting edge of their field can therefore have a positive impact.

Second, effective approaches to learning can be promoted through research-based teaching and learning methods. 'Deep' approaches to learning are characterized by students showing the desire to understand and seek meaning, relating ideas to previous knowledge and experience, looking for patterns and underlying principles, checking evidence and relating it to conclusions, and critically examining logic (Entwistle 1997). Brew and Boud (1995) claim that research, as an activity, demands a deep approach to learning, as it requires the construction of meaning and making sense of phenomena. In addition, Entwistle *et al.* (1992) comment that deep approaches are promoted by encouraging students to develop personal understanding of topics and actively to engage with tasks through problem-solving. These are characteristics which may be included in a research-based approach to curriculum design where students are encouraged to learn through activities which require them to follow the processes of research.

Finally, through adopting research-based methods, particularly those which involve the processes and tools of research, it is also possible to build in the development of transferable skills, such as working collaboratively, oral and written presentation, critical analysis, use of information technology and many other skills, whilst also developing subject-specific knowledge.

Connecting research and teaching at institutional level

In any university there will be a multiplicity of connections between these two key activities, but there may be relatively few formal connections. As we have suggested earlier, whilst there is a strong belief that one informs the other, it has seldom been an act of policy to facilitate those connections. In fact the main level of linkage is at the level of the individual academic who must necessarily find a way of performing the two roles and who may find ways of linking them productively. That task will be eased, and maximum benefit obtained, if institutions and departments act to create the conditions that will encourage links to be made. Hattie (2000) offers a checklist of performance indicators that may be useful in estimating the degree of research and teaching interdependence. Woodhouse (1998) examines ways in which the research–teaching nexus can be audited.

As a starting point for this discussion, it is important to be clear about the nature of the link. This is not easy because, as we have suggested, research and teaching may look rather different from one discipline to another and so, therefore, may the link. So a fairly open model is needed that includes a number of different forms of link and permits the range of practice to be captured. We believe that the model outlined here performs this function. It is also necessary to know what is actually happening in the institution. At one level this may often be no more than putting a name to long-standing practice, but it is likely also to identify significant gaps.

However, in listing cutting-edge research made available to students, problem-based learning projects, the availability of research tools and so on the focus is on 'inputs', on what is done. What outcome measures are there? In other words, if it is believed that research-based learning makes a difference, what sort of difference is it, where would it be seen, and how would it be recognized? This points to a wider problem for higher education. Many institutions are not particularly expert in evaluating the effects of their own practice, in part because it is difficult to do, but also because there is little tradition of evaluating the learning gains that result from particular approaches to teaching, and the skills required to do it may not be widespread in the institution. So one of the tasks for a university is to make sure it is capable, at all appropriate levels, of knowing what happens when teaching practices change (and, indeed, when they stay the same). If it cannot do this then it innovates blindly, moving on to the next fad without finding out the outcome of an innovation. This is not to argue for a monolithic approach to planning and evaluation. James (1997) offers a helpful view of the limitations of extensive pre-planning and the importance of 'trial and error' in development. It is, however, an argument for a culture in which staff are encouraged and equipped continually to question and develop their practice.

For understandable practical reasons, research and teaching are commonly dealt with separately in a university, often assigned to a different pro-vice-chancellor or other senior figure. There will generally be a separate senior committee for each. The funding streams that support them will be separate. It is therefore no one's particular responsibility, at policy level, to deal with research and teaching links. When discussion does occur, it would almost certainly be led from the teaching side. It would be most unusual for a research committee to concern itself with its impact upon teaching, other than to seek to ensure that staff were released from teaching at appropriate times so that they could concentrate on research. A practical step, therefore, would be to ensure that there was overlapping membership of these two committees, with at least one of the members keeping a watching brief on research and teaching connections, and the topic a standing item to be revisited at least annually.

Effective linkages require the active engagement of academic staff. At an institutional level, this can be encouraged through review and appraisal discussions where, once again, in addition to prompts to discuss teaching and research, there could be encouragement to discuss linkages. Promotion procedures offer a stronger point of influence. Many universities have reviewed their promotion criteria in recent years to give greater weight to teaching, but it is not so common for promotion criteria to refer specifically to productive linkages between research and teaching. Such references, supported with advice and guidance on how this might be achieved, are hardly likely to be ignored, especially if that criterion is given sufficient weight in the promotion process. Teaching excellence awards, now relatively commonplace in universities, offer a similar opportunity to reward those who make links between research and teaching.

From the previous discussion on learning processes, it is clear that some forms of curriculum are more likely than others to encourage links with research. It is possible to add to course approval and review processes some questions on linkages – how, when and where they occur, and how they are evaluated. This is mechanistic and likely to lead to token compliance. It can be supported with staff development aimed at broadening the range of teaching approaches which staff feel prepared to use, and exploring their purposes. Course approval panels may also find such discussion useful.

Some forms of curriculum are not necessarily easy to put into place at individual level, since they have organizational and resourcing implications. For example, if inquiry-based learning is to be encouraged, it has to be supported with appropriate learning resources and tools, available to students when and where needed. Where such learning has an interdisciplinary aspect, there are even more significant issues in exploring ways in which students may work across departmental boundaries and have access to an appropriately broad range of staff expertise and resources.

It is less easy to find ways at an institutional level of encouraging research decisions to include teaching concerns. Where there is an internal 'pump-priming' research fund, it is certainly possible to require a 'pedagogic linkage' statement and to weight funding where there is a clear benefit to teaching and learning. Once again compliance threatens, and such an approach requires staff development support if the majority of responses are not to be entirely about the transmission of new knowledge or else complaints, particularly from science departments, that their research is so far removed from the undergraduate curriculum that links cannot be made.

Postdoctoral contract researchers are necessarily heavily engaged in research activity and involved in a research culture. They are also increasingly required to undertake a significant amount of teaching. They offer a major opportunity for making teaching and research links, since there will be a great deal that they can bring to their teaching. Doctoral students, in particular, are likely to be able to relate to undergraduates' difficulties in learning. However, these categories of staff (and doctoral students are staff in so far as they are teaching) are often on the periphery of institutions' and departments' concerns, are not well prepared, in the main, for teaching, and are often subject to significant pressures to give minimal time to teaching. Again, staff development can assist.

At departmental level, there is clearly a tension between curriculum coverage and giving staff the opportunity to teach aspects of their research specialism. However, it may be appropriate to encourage staff to offer their specialism where possible. There are potential problems, of course, in that staff may in a sense be too knowledgeable and find difficulty in gearing down. As already noted, such linkages are generally held to be easier in humanities and social sciences than in sciences.

Departments are generally good at including research students in their research culture. It may be useful to review whether some of the experiences that research students have should be available to undergraduates. These would include the opportunity to engage in 'real' research projects in a junior capacity, participation in research seminars and early training in and access to powerful research tools.

Conclusions

Teaching and research will benefit one another in many ways if institutions, departments and individuals take care to make and reinforce the links. If this is done, students may learn more effectively, and staff may find that some of the damaging tensions between the two activities may be lessened, and that their roles become more satisfying. At the same time, institutions will be safeguarding their reputations as providers of a higher education, and protecting themselves in the educational marketplace, by ensuring that they are offering research-based curricula.

Key learning points

Senior staff

- Review research and teaching committee remits to ensure they adequately support linkages.
- Ensure that promotion and internal funding mechanisms encourage good practice.
- Be prepared to review organization of learning resources to support inquiry-based learning.

Heads of department

- Review current practice.
- Consider how well staff specialisms are being exploited for teaching.
- Make effective use of contract researchers and doctoral students, giving them support to make links.

Professional staff developers

- Explore and define the link between research and teaching, identifying and sharing best practice.
- Develop their own capacity for evaluation of educational innovation and that of the university as a whole.

12

Embedding e-learning practices

Martin Oliver and Jacqueline A. Dempster

Introduction

Recent years have seen a marked increase in the use of information and communi-cations technology (ICT) in Higher Education (HE), both for distance and on-campus education (McConnell 1999). This is a situation that poses challenges as well as opportunities in all areas of learning and teaching. This chapter focuses on the role of staff development in supporting academics' engagement with this process. The wider social agendas influencing this will be outlined, and institutions' readiness to provide support will be considered before looking at different models for staff development. The chapter will conclude by considering the implications for staff developers attempting to embed e-learning practices.

E-learning and the higher education 'market'

The widespread changes affecting HE internationally are nothing new (Taylor 1999), but their intensity and pace have increased, altering the relationship between universities and society in significant ways (Barnett 1994). Many changes reflect the emergence of a market ideology in HE (Holley and Oliver 2000), which is often used as a rationale for adopting e-learning (e.g. Daniel 1996; National Committee of Inquiry into Higher Education (NCIHE) 1997). It is argued that market forces make it vital for institutions to harness technological opportunities to fulfil their strategic mission and provide economic advantage, and that pressures to use ICT to teach more economically underpin 'the rhetorics found within such government-initiated reports as Dearing ([NCIHE] 1997) in the UK and West (1998) in Aus-tralia' (Fox and Herrmann 2000: 73). Fox and Herrmann point out the staff devel-opment implications:

> teachers are . . . reluctant to take up the challenges to use the new online media. Some have deep-rooted concerns about changes in work practices, and others see the huge gap between the rhetoric surrounding technology and the realities of educational settings, while others boldly embrace new media with seemingly little critical pedagogical concern.

This market rhetoric poses problems for staff developers as well as academics: the drive for efficiency introduces the risk of an institution becoming economically led rather than pedagogically led (Bhanot and Fallows 2002). This places staff developers in the difficult position of trying to ensure that e-learning practices are driven by educational rather than technical, economic or administrative considerations.

As a result of these pressures, the last decade has witnessed several major funding programmes and national services aimed at developing and supporting the use of technology in teaching and learning. Many have had embedding as an explicit aim. In the UK, for example, the first two phases of the Teaching and Learning Technology Programme were criticized for developing but not embedding software (Coopers and Lybrand *et al.* 1996), leading to a change of emphasis from creation to implementation in its third phase. Similar priorities appear internationally, for example in the Committee for University Teaching and Staff Development (CUTSD) projects in Australia (Phillips 2001).

What does it mean to 'embed e-learning'?

These pressures have made embedding e-learning a political imperative across the sector. However, the meaning of 'embedding' is ambiguous. It can usefully be contrasted with 'innovation', which involves a shift away from traditional practices, even when this is modest and local (Hannan and Silver 2000); by contrast, embedding involves these once novel practices becoming commonplace. However, this definition remains contested; academics themselves may mean a variety of things by 'embedding' (Harvey and Oliver 2001), including:

- using technology as a mediating artefact (Kuutti 1997) that permits particular educational practices;
- ensuring that ICT is required to achieve a particular learning outcome, rather than being optional;
- using ICT as part of an institutional strategy, rather than simply because it is fashionable;
- widespread use of commonly available technologies, rather than individual 'champions' breaking new ground in isolation;
- use of a particular technology becoming 'expected and natural', rather than worthy of comment.

What is particularly interesting is the variation in focus – from micro-level embedding within specific interactions to the naturalization of technology throughout the institutional culture. However, these definitions share one common feature: they emphasize the difference between embedding (focusing on use) and simply disseminating practice. Changing practice is not simply a matter of information flow, in which staff, once appraised of the latest development, will automatically embrace it – instead, these practices must be adapted, translated and integrated into new disciplinary, pedagogical and institutional contexts through the innovation and creativity of academics (Beetham 2002). In developing their own practice, staff cannot simply reproduce the 'champion' or 'innovative' approaches of others. Whilst representations of practice are useful in raising awareness and providing examples, staff must construct an entirely new set of practical understandings relevant to their own contexts (Beetham 2001).

It is equally hard to define 'e-learning', although current usage implies interaction with resources or communication with fellow learners mediated by electronic technologies (Mason 2002). Analysis of issues and attitudes, stakeholders and strategies reveals a variety of beliefs about what e-learning involves and how it might influence HE (Dempster 2002). As will be argued, however, this ambiguity may be better than creating a precise definition that serves to differentiate e-learning from 'normal' practice.

Institutional structures for supporting e-learning

HE institutions have taken many different approaches to embedding e-learning into academic practice. Some have opted for the large-scale introduction of networked learning, particularly driven by the selection of specific commercial packages (for example, virtual learning environments such as WebCT, Blackboard, Fretwell-Downing's 'le' or Lotus Notes). Others have taken a learning and teaching initiative as a focus. Some have continued to rely on a small number of champion innovators to inspire and drive uptake, whilst others have developed initiatives originally instigated as part of national projects. Others have put sophisticated strategies in place, supported by new development units that work with academics in a client–supplier relationship. There appears no ready model – no single, clearly successful, path – that ensures that e-learning will be embedded. The *operational context* is thus crucial to the choice of tactics that are likely to lead to success.

Early national developments and institutional initiatives have approached technology in teaching and learning with the notion that it is somehow special and different. The consequence has been to concentrate on developing e-learning practices in isolation from other academic development. Such differentiation may be the greatest strategic error of many e-learning development units, and could account for the low level of embedding of ICT in many institutions. All practices involve technology of some kind; the significant difference is simply how familiar we are with their operation (Kuutti 1997), not whether they are electronic. Thus e-learning should not be judged differently because it is 'electronic'; its development must be, first and foremost, educationally valid. It must also therefore be evaluated by academics to ascertain whether resources have been well utilized whilst maintaining or enhancing educational quality. Technical development should thus emphasize the links between pedagogy and technology. The same institutional mechanisms and incentives that reward teaching can also reward e-learning development; special schemes may be divisive, differentiating ICT-based developments from 'normal' practices.

However, the dependence of e-learning developments on ICT infrastructure and technical expertise cannot be underestimated. Fortunately, technologies that were once innovative (e.g. publishing, discussion and assessment tools, videostreaming and videoconferencing facilities) are becoming commonplace enough to allow mainstream support services to be offered. However, progress is often held back not by infrastructure constraints but by issues like motivation, resources and skills (Dempster 2002). These issues are being tackled within staff development units and educational development centres, where the use of the web to support programmes and activities is growing. On-line information and resources are now common-place, including electronic versions of paper-based publications, new web-based journals, guidance materials, resources and links to useful websites. Increasingly, providers of staff development are making more use of the web to offer course support facilities for internal academic programmes, such as course resources, reading lists and discussion boards (Pearson 2002). These have the potential to offer valuable models of good practice in the use of technology to support student activities by giving lecturers a taste of e-learning from the students' perspective (Bennett *et al.* 1999).

Even when both technology and pedagogy are well supported, there may be structural problems that inhibit engagement with e-learning. The division between the two can appear arbitrary and confusing, leading to problems for academics and services alike. An analytical framework (Wills and Alexander 2000) for intro-ducing technology into teaching and learning highlights five factors that must be closely integrated if the introduction of technology is to be successful: strategy; structure; management processes; roles and skills; and the nature of technology itself. Such integration may require changes in operational behaviour: organization and management may need to be restructured or at least work across traditional boundaries, 'so that planning can cut across normal barriers to collaboration in an institution' (Ehrmann 2000). The use of such 'round-table' methodologies is gain-ing popularity as a strategy for developing and evaluating e-learning, explicitly valuing collaboration and negotiation of responsibilities through wider consult-ation with representatives of academic, support and administrative staff together with students. Within institutions where this has worked, strong alliances have emerged between these groups of staff with the shared goal of enhancing stu-dents' learning experience. Such groupings can influence policy to ensure that responses to external requirements, such as widening participation and employ-ability skills, take account of the entire institutional community. These groups can also become a powerful mechanism for organizational learning which, it is argued, may be the key to institutional growth in the current market climate (Sallis and Jones 2002).

Yet institutions often do not review their practices to ensure that such integration takes place. As a result, staff developers may find themselves attempting to balance pedagogic, economic, technical and administrative concerns within structures that do not bind these concerns together. In such a situation, staff developers may need to influence strategy and policy to achieve their ends (cf. Gosling and D'Andrea 2002) by working through committees to establish rewards and incentives such as promotion, recognition of teaching excellence and accreditation for desired forms of practice.

A common alternative to a holistic, institution-wide approach is to create a unit of individuals with complementary expertise who are given the task of promoting, developing and supporting e-learning and managing the process of change. Creation of such a group may indeed contribute to the integration of differing interests noted above; it is certainly an institutional statement of commitment, raising the visibility of e-learning, although without genuine institutional support the unit may find itself given responsibility without resources or authority. Typically, such units arise from technical departments or the library, and may be established in place of or alongside existing staff and educational development groups. Such fractures in support provision are often counter-productive, although they may be politically or technically expedient, because they appear to suggest that e-learning is somehow different from other learning. This may result in technology-driven rather than pedagogically led approaches.

Engaging staff with e-learning

Promoting e-learning can be straightforward if staff developers 'go with the grain' of their own institution, working with specific educational processes or technologies that lecturers are known to be interested in (Dempster and Blackmore 2002). However, *embedding* e-learning practices is not so simple. Whilst appropriate ICT infrastructure and tools are essential (Dempster 2003), the process of engaging staff to make educationally sound changes to their teaching practice requires a sophisticated understanding of curriculum development and change processes. For technology is not neutral in its pedagogic effects. It can enhance and sustain dominant practices such as lecturing, or it can transform and disrupt them (Garrison and Andersen, 2000).

In most institutions, academics' appreciation of the relationship between these processes and e-learning varies considerably, and a one-size-fits-all strategy to encourage embedding is unlikely to succeed. Instead, provision must meet support needs from across a broad spectrum, recognizing subject-specific needs and providing opportunities for staff to be more analytical about their teaching aims (Blackmore *et al.* 2002) so they can make use of technologies where they are most likely to provide benefit. However, provision alone cannot solve the problem. For lecturers to be innovative, they need time for pedagogic analysis, development and exploration – and, as identified in the Dearing report (NCIHE 1997), very little academic time is spent explicitly on such professional development activities.

Because development work can be perceived as complex and unattractive, many initiatives are initially undertaken as exploratory, pilot work. This enables them to be temporarily uncoupled from security and reliability factors, issues that concern central technical support departments when rolling out software and services. For example, in developing a simple web tool with which to try out research-based teaching and learning approaches that lecturers felt were intrinsically interesting, the Technology-Enhanced Learning in Research-Led Institutions project successfully supported lecturers in integrating on-line publishing and discussion in students' learning assignments (Blackmore *et al.* 2001). Had these lecturers been faced with a complex package, particularly one whose support was the responsibility of multiple groups (staff development, technical support, etc.), greater incentives and support would have been required.

Models for developing e-learning practice

Given the variety of institutional structures and the complexities of engaging staff, it is unsurprising that numerous approaches have been implemented to developing e-learning practice. Each reflects particular assumptions, and is designed to meet specific academic needs. In order to make sense of these different models, examples that typify each have been selected; these are presented here in decreasing order of formality.

Formally accredited courses

A drive for professionalism (see NCIHE 1997) has led many institutions to develop accredited teaching development programmes. In the UK, these are increasingly designed as routes to national membership of the Institute for Learning and Teaching in Higher Education. However, few cater fully for developing competence and understanding in the application of ICT to teaching, learning and assessment processes.

The Effective Frameworks for Embedding C&IT with Targeted Support (EFFECTS) project was a UK-based initiative funded under the third Teaching and Learning Technology Programme. Its aim was to embed the use of ICT through programmes of professional development for academic and related staff (Beetham and Bailey 2002) designed to enable staff to engage with ICT in a scholarly, critical manner (Harvey and Oliver 2001). Although each course was designed to address local issues and constraints, an agreed framework of learning outcomes, shared experiences and dialogue between project partners led to courses converging on a common format: a mix of formal training (organized around either locally demanded topics or the learning outcomes) and a reflective account of the process of embedding, which formed the first part of a portfolio of evidence (Smith and Oliver 2000). Thus the programmes promoted a process of curriculum development through action research (Beetham and Bailey 2002).

The project's premise was that accreditation might provide an incentive for academics to commit time to adopting e-learning practices, but this was not true for academics with PhDs. Some did want formal recognition for their effort. Others wanted different things from the course, such as training or access to expert support from the tutors (Smith and Oliver 2000). Participants were particularly concerned to gain career enhancement – a strategic issue that could only be addressed at an institutional level, rather than within the project (Beetham and Bailey 2002). The complex organizational changes that arose from the development of these programmes are also interesting. Technical support and staff development services that had previously remained distant collaborated for the first time on problems that course participants encountered; individuals became perceived as teaching experts within their own departments, or joined institutional teaching-related committees; and numerous local developments took place as 'coursework'. Equally, however, problems arose. The need for different institutional groups to work together led to political tensions about who 'owned' particular areas of concern; individuals' developments pushed the boundaries of established technical systems, causing problems and frustration for all involved; and some course tutors found themselves increasingly in demand from students whose successful working relationship with them had turned into a form of dependency (Harvey and Oliver 2001). Clearly, whilst broadly successful, any attempt to expand such an approach would need to consider the strategic implications for institutional support structures.

Institutional workshops

Many institutions have instigated an informal series of workshops linking pedagogical and technical issues as the focus for staff development. For example, programmes at Southampton and Warwick in the UK have proved an effective way both to motivate and support lecturers and to develop specific ICT and pedagogic competences (Lewis 2001; Warren 2002). Staff develop by engaging in action learning projects, but also through peer learning by discussing and sharing their concerns, needs and approaches as a group. These informal programmes have several advantages:

- They are 'light touch' in terms of time commitments for academics and staff developers, compared with accredited programmes.
- The programme staff provide the necessary technical tools and training at the point of need (sometimes even where centrally supported tools are lacking).
- They can be used to pilot e-learning tools with a diverse or specialized group of course developers/tutors. These can then act as evaluators to inform university decision-making about eventual uptake.
- They develop a set of resources that can be redeployed or adapted for use outside the programme.
- The programme participants' projects form a valuable set of contextually relevant case studies that can provide effective exemplars for future runs of the programme and to engage other staff.

The model is particularly useful when dealing with new and popular approaches. Workshops of this kind can explore and support a number of negotiated pedagogical aims, representing different teaching and learning contexts and a range of discipline areas, through a common technological approach.

Staff secondments and learning technologists

An increasingly common form of educational development involves seconding staff from an institution to work on projects agreed with (and often funded through) central units (Barlow 1995; Elton 1995). Partly, this is because 'the most acceptable form of staff development and the one that probably has had most success is that in which staff developers and academic teachers collaborate with the aim of improving the student learning experience' (Elton 1995: 183). This collaboration is crucial in transforming what might otherwise be a materials development activity into an educational process for those involved. This approach recognizes that 'embedding' practice is a transformative process rather than simply being a matter of adopting technology, developing materials or imparting skills and knowledge. Where this is successful, the academics involved may find that their perception of teaching and learning more generally is changed. Thus whilst embedding e-learning in this way does add to academics' repertoire of skills, it also results in a change in their perception of their role.

Such an approach is central to the work undertaken by learning technologists (Oliver 2002). These individuals' job titles and status differ from institution to institution; however, what they have in common is that their practice:

- centres on collaborative curriculum development, usually initiated by an academic and focused on a particular piece of technology;
- is situated, drawing on the idea of communities of practice, and thus requiring the learning technologist to learn as well as teach during collaboration; and
- involves responsibility without authority, so that they rely on goodwill, expertise and rhetoric to create opportunities for development (both practical and educational) and influence policy.

Their interactions with academics follow a common 'curriculum'. Typically, this starts with the academic's enquiry about the use of a particular type of technology – something that learning technologists see as being relatively unimportant. The first phase of education takes place whilst negotiating the project. During this time, the main burden of learning falls on the learning technologist, who must come to understand the departmental context in which the project is to be implemented. However, this dialogue may also highlight to the academic that taken-for-granted practices and values may be culturally determined rather than general truths.

The next phase of collaboration works along the lines of 'proof of principle' – establishing how a certain approach or tool works in this particular context. During this phase, problems of implementation will be discussed, with the learning technologist learning about this specific context (and thus building up their case lore, and with it their own expertise) whilst teaching through dialogue and the use of cases (often anecdotal) that illustrate principles or problems.

These discussions may, in some cases, lead the academic to question further their assumptions or the problems that arose during the project. This then moves the dialogue into the third phase of the curriculum, wherein general issues (such as theories or counter-examples, rather than additional supporting cases) from educational research are introduced.

Not all collaborations are successful educationally. In part, success is determined by the way in which the learning technologist is viewed. If they cannot establish their credentials with the academics, then it is unlikely that fruitful dialogue will follow, since the collaborator will see them as a service provider rather than an expert.

Informal learning at work

The above sections have all described intentional staff development activities. It is, however, important to recognize that learning is part of our everyday action, an individual process of meaning-making; it is not something that we switch on and off (Billett 1999). Staff are thus constantly learning, constantly being developed, simply through the practices they engage in; this takes place irrespective of whether they are being formally instructed or supported. Any goal-directed activity will reinforce or refine what individuals already know, or lead to new knowledge if the activity is novel (Billett 2002). Thus the very act of introducing new technologies leads to learning, since 'new forms of work practice emerge as workplaces are transformed by changes in technology, global competition and employment practices' (2002: 83). Indeed, such acquisition of practice underpins the development of the kind of intuitive knowledge that marks individuals out as experts (McMahon 2000).

However, this process is not uniformly a good thing. Staff do not just acquire new practices; they also take part in a 'hidden curriculum' that delineates what is considered acceptable, what constitute suitable divisions of labour, and so on. This can perpetuate historical inequalities of power, prejudices, inappropriate short-cuts and misinterpretations just as easily as it can pass on intuitive knowledge (Billett, 1999). There are several ways in which these tendencies can be counteracted. The first is to provide staff with an opportunity to acquire and apply ideas that will help them to conceptualize and analyse their experiences and thus become critical of their own practice (Griffiths and Guile 1999). Alternatively, a more experienced 'other' (typically a colleague, but possibly a mentor such as a staff developer) within the workplace may use instructional interventions (creating situations for learning, then using diagrams, analogies or dialogues) in order to effect a similar process (Billett 1999).

Moreover, the extent to which individuals choose to participate in such educational opportunities varies. This is influenced by each person's history, the perceived benefits, status, links to specific interest groups (Billett 2002) and the perceived credibility of the 'other' who provides the educational opportunity (Billett 1999). Of particular importance is that even where organization-wide opportunities are provided, individuals may not feel able to engage with them – they may feel excluded by virtue of historical inequalities or culturally acquired beliefs about what is appropriate for them to do.

Informal learning thus has considerable power to support embedding, being ongoing, ubiquitous and taking place without the need for additional resources. However, without careful intervention, it can perpetuate injustices and inappropriate activities as easily as fostering desirable values and practices.

Conclusions

Throughout this chapter, a consistent message emerges: to embed e-learning practices effectively, strategic change is required. Practices change constantly, but without 'joined-up' technical and pedagogic support, alongside an appropriate reward scheme, this change will be undirected or even misdirected. Institutional learning and teaching strategies have fostered alliances between academic departments and the centre, but again, these will not succeed in isolation. All too often, staff development remains politically weak (often positioned purely as a service) whilst a complex web of interests makes e-learning high-profile by separating it from other activities, thus making responsibility for its policies and support problematic.

With distinct groups supporting aspects of e-learning practice, considerable confusion can result. This may be compounded by a cultural divide between mainstream staff development and e-learning groups emerging from libraries, ICT services or administrative departments. The former typically assist through consultancy-based exploration and evaluation, acting as 'the conscience of learning and teaching', whilst the latter tend towards a service-focused, client-based approach in order to enable institutional functions (cf. Boud 1995). Both have strengths which, if offered jointly, may provide an institution with a powerful capacity to innovate and to trial, evaluate and embed those approaches that fulfil its strategic mission.

However the structure is arranged, further variation arises from the way in which individuals feel able to engage with support for e-learning. Although the four models outlined above differ in terms of formal structure and intervention, successful staff development in all these forms shares a number of common features. Most obvious is the issue of context, whether disciplinary or institutional (Becher 1989). This shapes individuals' motivations (affecting their willingness to engage) and also influences the acceptability of any of the above models. Also clear is that teaching basic technology skills (how to use something), particularly in isolation, is insufficient. The introduction of technology changes roles and practices (Beetham and Bailey 2002), and unless development work takes these deep-rooted shifts into account it will inevitably lead to conflicts and inconsistencies within the activity being undertaken (Kuutti 1997). Thus any strategy for staff development in e-learning must differentiate between training and development and should aim to build links between training, educational research and practice (Griffiths and Guile 1999).

Provision is only part of the story, however: staff developers must also take into account the complex web of self-interest that surrounds participation. In choosing to support particular activities, they must be aware of the inequalities of the workplace (Billett 2002) and the tendency of individuals to pursue ends that will enhance their career prospects over those that do not (Smith and Oliver 2000; Beetham and Bailey 2002). This latter point highlights why work in this area must be strategic. To succeed, it may prove necessary to include recognition for innovative or excellent teaching practice, or promotional routes for staff who complete particular programmes, as a way of demonstrating the value that the institution places on embedding e-learning practices. However, whilst strategies might provide adequate groundwork for motivating academics, these cannot be relied upon to solve the problem. To do justice to the diversity of individuals' situations, staff developers must also take account of these influences at a tactical level, as part of their day-to-day interactions with staff.

The problems do not end there. Whilst this attention to detail might suffice to embed e-learning within individuals' practices, changing the culture of departments or institutions remains an altogether different proposition. Staff developers run the risk that, through their success, they may simply create new communities of practice organized around particular technologies or e-learning initiatives rather than embedding these new practices into established (typically disciplinary) communities. Hints of this can be seen in the sense of dislocation and dependency reported by some staff who took part in EFFECTS (Harvey and Oliver 2001) and are echoed in concerns about staff who have participated in secondment work (Oliver 2002) or national projects (Dempster and Blackmore 2002). Staff developers must therefore find ways of managing the tension between developing individuals and divorcing them from their colleagues' shared practices.

Key learning points

Senior staff

- Embedding e-learning is a complex process that requires, but goes beyond, provision of technical infrastructure and technical skills training.
- Separating support structures and incentives for e-learning from those for other teaching developments can be divisive and confusing.
- E-learning is often linked to efficiency, in spite of mixed evidence about its ability to save money; this emphasis can lead to economically led rather than pedagogically led developments.

Heads of department

- Learning about e-learning involves a dialogue with other departments and support structures, both to share experiences and to ask for support.
- Trying out pilot developments in safe, simple areas of teaching is a good way to start engaging with e-learning, but issues of staff time and central support will need to be dealt with eventually if these initiatives are to be embedded.
- Singling out an individual as 'the e-learning specialist' may be divisive and counter-productive, as it will make e-learning seem different rather than encouraging everyone to view it as part of their own practice.

Professional staff developers

- There are many possible ways to support e-learning; different combinations will be needed at different times, depending on the institutional context.
- Staff are learning all the time, whether or not they take part in formal courses – however, informal learning can perpetuate bad practice as easily as it can develop what is believed to be good.
- To be effective, initiatives must be aligned with strategic encouragement so that staff are motivated to engage – and achieving this may require staff developers' concerns to be heard at a senior level.

13

Career development for research staff

Marie Garnett and Ruth Goodall

Introduction

For most UK universities the virtually universal use of fixed-term contracts (FTCs) for the employment of researchers is not a strategic choice.[1] It is a consequence of recent circumstances, which have shaped the behaviour of individuals and institutions. These circumstances include a focus on short-term planning, the project basis of public funding for research, an overemphasis on research outputs and a period of financial constraint. It is interesting, however, that, despite similar short-termism and financial constraints in the private sector, employers there have not developed the same attachment to the use of FTCs. In fact, as Bryson (1998: 11) argues in his submission to the Independent Review Committee, only a fifth of companies use FTCs, and even then for no more than 5 per cent of their workforce. Indeed, Keep and Sisson (1992) cite the failure to tackle the issues surrounding FTC researchers as prime evidence of the lack of strategic focus in UK HE human resource management in UK higher education, given the centrality of research to universities.

The impact of FTCs on staff may be compounded in individualistic cultures, especially the pre-1992 universities, where there is a reluctance to take managerial responsibility and where there is often diffuse but powerful resistance to what is seen as intrusive management. Bryson (1999) has argued that this inertia to change may be partly because researchers on FTCs, with their lower ranking in the institution, serve the self-interest of 'traditional' academics by contributing to their professional status and career advancement.

This chapter will briefly outline the recent history of increased attention to the development and career management of FTC researchers in the UK, starting with the 1996 Concordat and finishing with the Joint Negotiating Committee for Higher Education Staff (JNCHES) guidelines of June 2002. First, the chapter discusses and illustrates how to address the staff development issues that arise when large numbers of researchers are employed on FTCs. Second, it explores the issues that might arise if large numbers of FTC researchers are employed on indefinite contracts, including the possibility of greater strategic focus on the needs of research staff. A notable feature of this area is that staff development is often cast within a wider context of human resource management and research supervisor/principal investigator responsibility for 'career development' beyond the current contract and employer.

It is worth noting that a discussion of *strategic* approaches to staff development has been problematic in the case of FTC researchers. In practice the role of staff development, especially in relation to FTC researchers, is more often reactive and is about ameliorating the effects on individuals of the lack of coherent planning. However, the authors believe that staff developers (be they senior managers, heads of department or staff development professionals) have an important role to play in *influencing* and *shaping* cultural change for the improved management and career development of research staff and that new opportunities are arising for this. We focus exclusively on research staff, recognizing that there has been a growth in FTC staff generally, and limit discussion to the UK.

Development of the fixed-term contract researchers' agenda

Stimulated by a government White Paper on research strategy in science and engineering, recognition of the need for significant improvement in the employment conditions of FTC researchers was signalled in 1996 by the signing of the so-called 'Concordat' (Committee of Vice-Chancellors and Principals *et al.* 1996). This was a highly significant and unique event, as all six major research councils, the three main bodies representing institutional chief executives and the Royal Society and British Academy signed it. The Concordat focused on enhancing career management and development within higher education institutions and was enforced primarily through agreed changes to research grant conditions (requiring applicants for grants to demonstrate compliance). The Concordat has since been reviewed and updated by the Research Careers Initiative (RCI) Strategy Group.

Since 1996, the government has provided significant funding of initiatives to develop resources for, and best practice in relation to, the better management and career development of FTC researchers. This period has also seen the release of important government and other national recommendations, regulations and guidance which have had the combined effect of both enabling and compelling universities to review the ways in which they manage and develop FTC researchers.

The following paragraphs provide a brief assessment of the key initiatives, recommendations, regulations and guidance that have contributed to the current context for FTC research in universities.

The Scottish Higher Education Funding Council was much quicker than its English counterpart in responding to the challenges laid down by the Concordat and subsequent RCI reports. As early as 1996 significant funding was given to support a number of excellent initiatives to encourage and disseminate good practice in the employment of FTC researchers. The outputs of these early initiatives were disseminated south of the border and provided a basis for later work undertaken in England.

Following the Concordat the RCI group, chaired by Sir Gareth Roberts, issued regular reports targeted at research councils and universities and making concrete recommendations towards more widespread implementation of the Concordat. Graduate schools were established, training courses on research launched and in some cases local departments encouraged to find ways of placing key researchers on longer or permanent contracts (for example, at University of Nottingham). Nonetheless the somewhat downbeat conclusion of the third interim RCI report (RCI Strategy Group 2001) was that although progress had been made it was slower than expected and, slightly more worryingly, improvements had begun to level off.

Although on a superficial level it was easy for universities to convince themselves that they were adequately meeting its terms and to satisfy the requirements of paper-based research grant applications, this trend gave cause for concern. The RCI Group concluded that a cultural change was needed at institutional level, and a project funded by the Higher Education Funding Council for England (HEFCE), Good Management Practice for Contract Research Staff (GMPCRS), was launched in 2000 to produce the framework and tools to underpin this cultural change. Although the framework and tools are inherently useful, the project provided little insight into how to manage the change process needed to implement them (http://www.sheffield.ac.uk/~gmprcs/).

The White Paper on science and innovation (Department of Trade and Industry 2000) stressed that with 30,000–40,000 FTC researchers now employed in UK universities, the high quality of science cannot be sustained without attention to career management issues. The Roberts Review (Roberts 2002) into the supply of scientists and engineers in the UK reaffirmed the belief that cultural change was needed in higher education to ensure that nurturing staff became a priority. The Review made concrete recommendations to revise career structures for FTC researchers in relation to career stability and the wastage of time and resources created by the current system of research funding.

In a sense the recommendations of the Roberts Review have already been superseded by the JNCHES (2002) guidelines. This landmark agreement was forged by the trade unions and the Universities and Colleges Employers' Association, in the light of the fixed-term employment regulations from the European Union. The guidance proposes that new staff, including researchers, be automatically appointed on indefinite contracts. The acceptance of these guidelines is still subject to local negotiations; there is effectively a four-year lead in time (before legal claims can be made by individuals), and a 'get-out' clause whose significance is unknown (see below). FTC researchers could conceivably become a 'thing of the past'. What is more likely, however, is that the balance of employment will shift towards indefinite contracts but that FTC researchers will continue to be employed in smaller numbers.

Irrespective of whether they are employed on fixed-term or indefinite contracts, it will soon become much more difficult for universities to evade the pressure to improve the management and development of their research staff. The Fixed Term Employees Regulations (EU Directive 99/70/EC) will undoubtedly impact on universities' use of successive employment contracts, although the precise nature and extent of the impact will remain uncertain until the caveat to their use 'where there is objective justification' has been tested in the courts. Rumoured changes to the research assessment exercise will propose an increased focus on people management, which will be directly linked to funding. This may come shortly after the planned launch of Concordat Mark II, signatories to which will agree to deliver principled institutional human resource strategies for research. Market forces, too, should not be underestimated. Many universities are eager to secure a competitive edge in the recruitment and retention of high-calibre researchers, by improving the attractiveness of the employment packages that they offer. In short, there are a number of converging pressures, including from initiatives launched within the sector itself, for improved employment packages and expanded career development opportunities for researchers.

Advantages and disadvantages of fixed-term contracts

Universities may be reluctant to forgo the advantages to the institution of the widespread use of FTCs. FTCs enable universities to match the length of contract precisely to the period of funding available, thus eliminating the financial risk for the institution. They also enable universities to 'buy in' research skills as and when required. Researchers are too often complicit in this arrangement as they may view a contract, however short, as more desirable than the disruption caused by uprooting and relocating to take up a new post. This enables universities to appoint known and able individuals to very short contracts (sometimes as short as one week) which offer little career progression and for which they would not be able to attract external candidates.

The use of FTCs also enables universities, traditionally collegial and non-managerial in culture, to side-step uncomfortable management decisions should they so wish. In evidence to the House of Lords Select Committee senior managers from higher education suggested the following reason for the use of FTCs: 'A research worker who goes off the boil or loses enthusiasm or skill can be easily removed without any contractual or redundancy problems' (Bryson 1998: 19).

Although the employment of large numbers of researchers on indefinite contracts will undoubtedly bring its own set of challenges, the authors believe that the disadvantages of using FTCs are substantial enough to merit this fundamental change.

FTCs might offer flexibility to the institution, but an ever changing workforce can threaten an institution's ability to build its capability and manage its knowledge base. This is especially true for fixed-term research contracts where the new knowledge developed by researchers can be lost to the institution at the end of a contract unless proper strategies for knowledge management are in place.

Although difficult to measure, the amount of time lost to an FTC by staff seeking their next contract, or through lack of motivation arising from their transitory relationship with the institution or the assignment, must be significant. When the time lost to a single contract is multiplied by the number of FTCs operated by an institution it becomes difficult to justify the inefficiency of this type of employment contract. Between September 2000 and August 2001, the University of Warwick made 288 new appointments to FTCs, 34 per cent of all the new appointments made in that period. One hundred and twenty-one of the new FTC appointments were on contracts of 12 months or less, and all except three were to contracts of three years or less in length. Given an estimated average cost of recruitment of approximately £5000 per post, including advertising, application processing, selection, interviewing and payment towards relocation costs, the University of Warwick alone has invested £605,000 in recruiting staff that will have left its employment within the year.

Another disadvantage of FTCs, alluded to by Bryson (1998: 12), is their impact on quality. As he points out, the lack of continuity engendered by the use of FTCs makes it difficult to monitor quality and the task of assuring quality often falls as an additional burden on permanently employed members of staff.

The preceding paragraphs have focused on the advantages and disadvantages for institutions arising from the use of FTCs. The disadvantages for the individual employee are no less persuasive in the argument against widespread use of FTCs.

In a recent survey (Anderson 2000) at the University of East Anglia (UEA) researchers were asked about their feelings towards being employed on FTCs. The 176 survey responses highlighted concerns about job insecurity, lack of identifiable career structure and perceived lack of commitment from the institution, which they said resulted in low motivation towards their work. These concerns are not trivial. Individuals on FTCs often find it difficult to gain access to financial services, including mortgages and other loans. The continued need to relocate in order to find work can have detrimental effects on families and relationships. As already mentioned, this might lead to the individual's continually accepting very short-term contracts and forfeiting scarce opportunities for career progression in order to avoid having to relocate. The lack of institutional commitment to the individual's long-term development can also have detrimental effects on the individual's ability to extend their expertise.

Issues for institutions employing fixed-term contract researchers

This section outlines the results of a study of FTC researchers' and their supervisors' perceptions of the career development-related issues that arise for FTCs (Dumelow *et al.* 2000). The study was carried out at the universities of Warwick, Birmingham, Aston and Coventry between September 1999 and June 2000. Forty-two FTC researchers and 21 supervisors from the four universities were interviewed. A further 95 supervisors were surveyed via questionnaire. The project findings identified six key issues affecting researchers' career development.

Developing general research-related skills

Although researchers acknowledged that they were developing specialized research skills and knowledge from working on their project, some actually felt less employable at the end of their contracts than they did at the beginning.

They said that they had had limited opportunities to develop general research skills useful for career advancement and that they had had little time to keep up to date with new developments in their field. One researcher commented:

> There isn't the opportunity to use new technologies or explore new technologies that are coming up, which if I was in the commercial world, I would be expected to use. So there is a slight worry that when the contract is finished . . . I suddenly find myself with skills that were not up-to-date.
>
> (Dumelow *et al.* 2000: 9)

Discussing and gaining acknowledgement of career goals and direction

The majority of researchers participating in the study were on contracts of three years or less. One of their key needs was to be given the opportunity to discuss their careers with someone, either a careers advisor or their supervisor, and to have their career needs acknowledged. Having their career needs acknowledged meant sitting down with the supervisor, identifying how their development needs might be met within the contract and planning how other needs might be met by course attendance or other staff development opportunities.

Managing the fixed-term contract researchers' experience

Interviewees felt that the process of being a FTC researcher should be better managed, with proper induction into the department, the setting out of clear expectations and an agreed strategy for dealing with the end of the contract. They also felt that universities should provide them with more support to help them remain in university employment, if that was appropriate.

Communication of relevant information

FTC researchers felt that many university policies had been written with permanently contracted staff in mind and that often much of the information provided was inappropriate to the short-term nature of their employment. The sort of information that they felt that they were lacking included that on entitlement to appraisals, policies on staff development, other resources and support available within the institution:

One thing which is clearly lacking that I've found with this contract is the lack of appraisal. I know I haven't been here that long, but you should get an appraisal at least once a year shouldn't you? Whether I have and I should have asked for it, I don't know. But my rights haven't been made clear on that. I think I was actually talking to someone in Personnel and they said you could have had an appraisal if you wanted it. Well, surely I shouldn't have to ask for it?

(Dumelow *et al.* 2000: 15)

Ensuring that what universities promise is being done

Essentially, FTC researchers were frustrated by their perception that the universities were not checking that policies in place for researchers were actually being implemented. The following comment sums up the consensus view:

I think there isn't a strong enough explanation as to what staff members' responsibilities are, what [supervisors'] responsibilities are and what the mechanism is if that process fails. There's provisions made but they're not active provisions. They don't make things happen. It's like the university's written a lot of words which they can show to somebody and say look we're doing well with these provisions but it never happens because no-one ever bothers checking.

(Dumelow *et al.* 2000: 17)

Support networks

Being an FTC researcher was perceived to be an isolating experience and many felt that opportunities to liaise with other researchers in the same discipline or other disciplines would be immensely helpful. Additionally, some researchers felt isolated from their departments and unsure of where to turn for support and guidance.

Although supervisors felt a responsibility to help researchers to network with other researchers working in their discipline, they felt unable to help promote more general networking.

Addressing the issues of employing researchers on fixed-term contracts

The issues raised in the preceding case study provide a useful starting point for consideration of how the institution, through its senior managers, heads of department and staff developers, can improve the management and career development of researchers employed on FTCs, at least in the eyes of FTC researchers and their supervisors.

Developing general research-related skills

The Warwick-led research found that supervisors were willing to help researchers to develop general and specialized research skills. However, this begs the question of which skills should be developed and how.

As a starting point, the institution, its FTC researchers and their supervisors should agree on the general and research skills that researchers can expect to develop during their employment. Through extensive consultation with researchers and research supervisors, the Research Career Builder (HEFCE Good Management Practice Project) has identified a number of useful skills.

Provision should then be made for the supervisor and researcher to plan jointly which skills should be developed and how. Institutions may find that skills development through courses has limited impact unless training is supported by opportunities to use and develop the skills 'on the job'. This indicates an important role for staff development professionals in helping supervisors to identify opportunities for researchers to develop a broader range of skills than hitherto, within the research context.

Discussing and gaining acknowledgement of career goals and direction

The supervisor questionnaire survey and interviews demonstrated that supervisors were willing to take on more responsibility for talking to researchers about their career goals and direction. This is welcomed, given the large numbers of FTC researchers and the limited brief of many careers offices, which typically do not offer one-to-one guidance for members of staff.

However, any increase in this aspect of the supervisor's role needs to be clarified by the institution and fully supported. Training and development is needed to ensure that supervisors can confidently fulfil their responsibilities whilst recognising the limits of their role. The institution also needs to ensure that detailed information is available to supervisors about the myriad of other resources available to support the career development of FTC researchers.

Heads of department can play a valuable role in initiating and promoting staff development events to meet both individual and departmental needs. For example, at both UEA and Warwick, several departments have requested a seminar for supervisors focusing on the personal and career development issues for FTC researchers.

Managing the fixed-term contract researchers' experience

Supervisors acknowledged that they should be responsible for providing the link between researchers and the department. This role involves ensuring that the researcher is properly integrated into the work of the department, facilitating the flow of information between the department and the researcher and implementing national and university policies relating to the employment of the researcher. Although not mentioned by the supervisors themselves, few of them have ever received formal support for their management role. This may be because many universities, certainly the pre-1992 ones, have traditionally prized academic capability over management skill. Support for the development of supervisors' general management skills is important, but this needs to be championed by senior managers, reinforced by heads of department and recognized by institutional mechanisms for reward and recognition.

Communication of relevant information

The responsibility clearly lies with the institution to ensure that its policies are equally inclusive and that they are communicated effectively to relevant members of staff. As we discovered at UEA, FTC researchers can be difficult to communicate with. Some may be disadvantaged by too great a reliance on electronic communication. However, the alternative, to use quickly out-of-date mailing lists, is also less than satisfactory.

In order to ensure that institutional policies are inclusive, senior managers need accurate information about the nature of the total research workforce. Without data it is easy to act on the basis of inaccurate assumptions and to generate strategies which are inappropriate or incomplete. Particular care needs to be given to ensure that institutional policies and procedures do not disadvantage or discriminate against researchers on FTCs by unconsciously taking as the norm full-time staff on indefinite contracts. Areas for attention might include: induction, appraisal, recruitment, selection and promotions criteria, and access to staff and careers development guidance.

Staff developers also need to evaluate their own provision to ensure that it is easily accessible to FTC researchers. Length and timing of events can be critical. At UEA most events are offered as short lunchtime sessions which researchers feel they can legitimately attend because it is in their own time.

Ensuring that what universities promise is being done

In some senses this is the most important, and the most difficult issue for institutions to address. The successful implementation of policy depends to a large degree on the head of department. In the case of researchers, heads of department need to ensure that supervisors are given the resources and the relevant support (training and development, etc.) to enable them to implement institutional policy. In their turn, senior managers need to monitor and develop practice at departmental level in order to improve the chances of matching policy to practice.

The only reliable method of ascertaining that policies are being implemented is to ask the researchers directly about their experiences. Current national piloting of the Contract Research Online Survey tool, which will enable institutions quickly and easily to survey staff, will soon make this possible.

Support networks

Both UEA and the University of Warwick have developed successful networks for FTC researchers. The success of the networks has been largely due to the ability of senior management to recognize, from an early stage, their potential to motivate and mobilize the FTC researcher population. The creation of a genuine partnership between the network members who set the agenda and the staff development functions at both institutions, which provide funding and active support, has also proved immensely useful.

Addressing the issues of employing researchers on indefinite contracts

Discussion in this section is necessarily indicative as the only institution, to date, with the experience of transferring *all* its researchers to indefinite contracts is Robert Gordon University (in 2002), a small university with relatively small numbers of research staff. However, the experience of some universities engaged in a much smaller-scale transfer of a percentage of their researchers to indefinite contracts (on the basis that overall institutional research income is likely to remain stable over much longer periods than traditional research contracts currently offer) enables us to anticipate some of the issues that institutions must address.

Institutions already engaged in limited moves to transfer a number of their existing FTC research staff to indefinite contracts have faced problems in identifying which staff should be transferred. Should the university identify the research skills that are generalizable across the broadest range of research and then offer indefinite contracts to researchers with those skills, or should it offer indefinite contracts to those researchers with the specialist skills that it would find most difficult to replace?

In some senses the JNCHES recommendations provide some clarity by looking at the converse and stating very clearly the limited circumstances under which new researchers should be offered an FTC. However, the recommendations will be difficult to implement without changes in some of the prevailing characteristics of institutional career structures, culture and research funding mechanisms.

Human resource planning

Centralized mechanisms will need to be put in place at the institutional, faculty and departmental level to facilitate the transfer of research staff between projects. This will mean an increased emphasis on record keeping to enable the individual's research skills and experience to be matched quickly and accurately to new research assignments. This process of centralization and 'bureaucratization' may well be controversial itself in decentralized systems and be opposed by research grant holders for the reasons alluded to by Bryson.

Second, this process may be much easier in the arts and social sciences where it is acknowledged that research skills are much more generalizable. It may prove much more difficult to redeploy researchers in some areas of the sciences. This may give rise to industrial relations issues if the unions will not accept this as justification for more science researchers to be employed on FTCs. In that case institutions may need to take legal advice to enable them to make the redundancy process more manageable, or they may need to persuade (and prove to) science research supervisors that they do not always require a highly trained specialist in a given subject to successfully undertake the research. None of these scenarios suggests that a transition of this type will be easy to achieve in the sciences.

Appropriately resourced staff development professionals will also need to work closely with research supervisors to provide prompt and appropriate training and support for researchers as they take up a new role. It will become ever more necessary for research supervisors to be active in identifying training needs and guiding the research project through its early stages.

Career structures

The widespread use of FTCs has traditionally meant that researchers progress much more slowly up the pay scales than their academic colleagues. Indefinitely employed researchers should, however, have access to progression and promotion opportunities that equal those of their academic colleagues. This may cause some tensions for the institution as academics see, with envy, that their colleagues are receiving equal pay for the luxury of being able to work full-time on their research.

Research funding issues

Research supervisors are under pressure from their funders to produce high-quality research to short deadlines, often with little time given to training and development. If research staff are being redeployed from one research contract to another a substantially larger investment in their training and development will be required, including by supervisors. This will inevitably require extra time and research funders should reasonably be expected to share the burden of cost that this will place on institutions. The likelihood of opposition from supervisors to the changes required will increase without such provision.

Joining the community of practice?

Previous chapters have drawn attention to the importance of social learning within communities of practice (see Chapter 10). FTC researchers' membership of such communities has always been problematic, and indeed will continue to be so. The prospect of a core of permanent or semi-permanent research staff should enable integration into such local cultures to occur, provide a louder voice for their concerns in departments and generally permit enhanced staff development opportunities. There is also the possibility of researchers beginning to create their own 'community of practice' within institutions.

Conclusion

The employment of researchers on FTCs is widespread in UK higher education. Although there are some obvious advantages to universities in employing FTC researchers, the authors are convinced that the costs to the individual, and consequently the impact on their contribution to the institution, outweigh the benefits. Converging national initiatives, including the JNCHES (2002) guidelines may move UK higher education away from the widespread use of FTCs and present an opportunity to put the development of all researchers on to a new basis. However, many of the issues are likely to be enduring whether researchers are employed on a fixed-term or an indefinite basis, and institutions need to pay proper attention to their management and career development.

Note

1   The authors have chosen to refer to 'fixed-term contract' (FTC) researchers throughout this chapter in keeping with the desire of policy leaders to move away from the more derogatory term 'contract research staff' which, nonetheless, is still commonly used and appears in many UK government publications.

Key learning points

Senior staff

- Recognize and champion the importance of good management practice in relation to research staff and offer incentives for staff, especially principal investigators, to become good managers.
- Monitor institutional policy and develop strategies for dealing with tensions that changes in policy might create.
- Ensure that institutional policies and procedures are relevant and communicated effectively at all levels. The prospect of a new core of semi-permanent research staff enables a new strategic approach to development.

Heads of department

- Recognize and value management skill and ensure supervisors acquire the skills they need.
- Initiate and promote relevant staff development activity. Ensure that researchers are included in the community, and invited to meetings, awaydays and so on, so that they can participate fully.
- Provide the resources and support necessary for principal investigators and research staff themselves to implement institutional policy.

Professional staff developers

- Help staff to think more creatively about what staff development is. Support the integration of researchers into local departmental communities.
- Review staff development provision in relation to training for research, including research council requirements, and equality of opportunity.
- Act promptly to provide useful and appropriate training opportunities at institutional level. This will require co-ordination and partnerships with graduate schools and departments. Support researchers in developing their own networks and communities.

Part IV

Case studies

In this part of the book we present a number of substantial institutionally focused case studies, each of which meets a number of criteria. First, it deals with a substantive development likely to be of interest in its own right. Second, it illustrates or exemplifies a key issue or theme from the book, without repeating previous chapters. Third, each chapter is drawn from a different context in order to interest a range of readers.

Chapter 14 focuses on the departmental level in a post-1992 English institution, De Montfort University, Leicester. The creation of research capacity in a UK system that awards funding through a periodic assessment of research has been a major issue. In common with other former polytechnics, the University was not funded to undertake research before 1992. The late Ian Beardwell gives a highly readable, experiential account of the development of a local research culture. His analysis indicates the importance of locating strategies within the emerging opportunities provided by disciplinary and institutional contexts and the progressive building of an inclusive culture, in stages, over time. It concludes with a reflective section making explicit the role of informal staff development and indicating potential alternatives and additions to his approach. The case study exemplifies the social learning/community-of-practice paradigm, discussed in Chapters 1 and 10 and elsewhere, in which learning is embedded in practice.

Chapter 15 focuses on the interests of all staff in a pre-1992 research-intensive Scottish university. It concerns an initiative undertaken at institutional level but largely outside traditional staff development structures, focused particularly on staff not normally active participants in staff development. It is an explicit attempt, therefore, to address, with an institution's own staff, some of the concerns about the 'learning divide' and social exclusion that underlie public discussion of lifelong learning, the articulation of targets for widening participation and so on featured in Chapter 3. The study underlines the importance of broadening definitions of staff development, drawing attention to its increasing dispersal within higher education institutions, also discussed in Chapter 1. The authors carefully chart the programme's outcomes in which 'soft, long-term' intangible gains in morale and motivation (see also Chapter 10) emerge as critical. This is an inclusive vision and a chapter that ideally should be read by all managers who persist in the view that the only legitimate and organizationally useful staff development for support staff is narrowly focused, job-specific training.

The final chapter returns to the quality agenda, which is often a major reason for the growing size and role of staff development (Chapter 1). It focuses on the alignment of development processes with institutional mission, based on an explicit student learning perspective, at the University of Sydney, Australia. The case illustrates how institutional quality assurance processes may be taken beyond mere regulation to produce participative learning and desirable educational out-comes. The chapter's focus on quality, institutional alignment and organization learning returns the book to key issues for strategic staff development raised in Chapter 1.

14

Creating a local research culture

Ian Beardwell

Introduction

The focus of this chapter is on the generation and maintenance of a research culture that can provide a major contribution to the academic process in its own right, while acting as an integral part of the wider work of departments and faculties. In large part it has been the product of many questions from colleagues around the theme 'How did you do it for your department?' and my attempts to think through some of the processes and respond to those questions with an assessment that might help them frame their own plans. It is thus a personal account in the style set by other heads of department (Slowey 1995) in an area of limited literature. It concludes with a reflective section on some potential alternatives and additions to the informal staff development approaches and mechanisms that I adopted.

Contextual and institutional factors

In order to examine this issue in some depth it is necessary to identify some assumptions and organizational contexts at the outset. The experience outlined in this chapter is based on a decade of development within one particular department which is a core part of a business school. The Department of Human Resource Management was formally created on 1 April 1989. Its immediate composition was that of a small core of personnel and training specialists who had mainly taught at the postgraduate and post-experience level, one individual who had taught psychology to undergraduates and the author – at that point the newly appointed head who had arrived from setting up a similar department at Kingston Business School in 1985. The department had grown, in 2001, to 23 staff in total with 5 chairs, 3 senior research fellows, and research staff attached to externally funded research projects. It is important to appreciate that it was not set up as a research-based unit with dedicated funding and staffing; rather, it has had to grow within a large, busy and diverse provider of a range of undergraduate, professional and postgraduate programmes. In this mix it has had to make its contribution to generalist as well as specialist courses and, in common with other academic groups, it has had to address the regulatory requirements of internal and external teaching quality audit and the growing significance of the research assessment exercise (RAE).[1] In addition, it has had to satisfy the external accreditation process of a professional body – in this case the Chartered Institute of Personnel and Development.

Taking account of the culture: the research antecedents of human resource management

The antecedents of human resource management (HRM) lie in a multidisciplinary past. Prior to the 1980s the HRM domain had been composed of a variety of subdisciplinary groupings – each with its own research traditions. Perhaps the longest-established branch of UK analysis was that centred around trade union studies and the role of collective bargaining. In the 1950s both labour law and labour economics began to develop their respective analyses of the employment relationship, with industrial sociology assuming some prominence by the late 1960s and early 1970s. Alongside this growth in the academically oriented research antecedents of the subject, there was an equally strong tradition of applied work in personnel management and organizational psychology. Finally, from the late 1970s onwards, a focus on labour process analysis began to emerge which looked to explain and examine the employment relationship from a critical and analytical account of managerial processes in the management of labour.

In the 1980s a particular approach to presenting and analysing this area of academic enquiry emerged within a number of major American business schools, notably Harvard. This new approach sought to break with past research traditions and to replace them with an integrated approach to 'managing human resources'. This was focused around the relationship between the strategic intent of the organization, the manner in which human resources could contribute to that intent, and the extent to which – together with business strategy – they could help deliver better performance for the organization. This HRM approach has been at the heart of the intellectual debate surrounding the subject since its emergence over the past fifteen years.

This brief, and necessarily selective, outline of the contributory research traditions in the area indicates two issues: first, that these approaches were firmly rooted in social science traditions (whether or not they were analytical or prescriptive); and second, that there were a number of key centres which became dominant in research, analysis and dissemination within the UK. Developing a research culture, therefore, has had to take into account the disciplinary backgrounds that staff brought to the creation of the department, and the influence of the predominant research centres in the setting of UK research agendas within the subject. An overriding consideration was the desire (and the necessity!) to avoid jurisdictional disputes, factions and groups that can distort the work of a department. To a large degree, the institutional context has played an important part in shaping those agendas.

The institutional context: De Montfort and the department

Teaching and research in the traditional disciplines pre-dating HRM were heavily concentrated in a small number of significant specialized departments within the pre-1992 university sector. Indeed, the two major departments at the London School of Economics and Warwick provided the majority of academically trained specialists by means of their master's and doctoral programmes. In the main, the post-1992 or former polytechnic sector was largely geared towards teaching on professional programmes for personnel and training specialists on general management qualifications (for example, the Diploma in Management Studies), and on some undergraduate programmes (notably the BA in Business Studies). By and large there was no tradition of research within the polytechnics, although they were great consumers of research output for their teaching programmes. The creation of a specialized department at Kingston Business School in 1985 was the first occasion on which such a recognized grouping had emerged within that sector. The Department of Human Resource Management at what was to become De Montfort in Leicester was only the second.

A significant factor in creating the new department was the identification of HRM as a key component in a new business school structure with the explicit goal of building a research capability in the subject. The idea of growing a department with complementary teaching and research objectives was unique in that part of the higher education sector at that time. A much more common model was that of a small (often individualized) research output running alongside a large volume of teaching, with any spare staff capacity often being directed to 'consultancy' – more often than not a training activity delivered off-site. Thus there were high volumes of activity, but little systematically planned research. It was this set of institutional issues which the author, as the newly appointed head of department, addressed to create a very different kind of environment.

Setting it up: Initial steps in building a department

There are clearly benefits in starting with a relatively clean sheet of paper. It was not quite like that, of course. There were five current members of staff who had been brought together into the new structure, only one of whom had an active research record. As the new head, I was an unknown quantity to them. The staffing plan for the new department envisaged a full complement of 16 lecturing staff, a reader and the head as a professor. Thus there was a large recruitment 'gap' to fill. It was this gap which provided the opportunity to introduce a new ethic into the institutional context. Indeed, in the first year or so there was much questioning of the new focus on research from those who saw their role as primarily teaching and applied training. Managing those expectations alongside the new emphasis on research from the newly arriving appointees was to be a major task, involving 'awaydays', interactive discussion and other informal SD.

If the clean sheet was not entirely to hand, then at least there was considerable scope and discretion in recruiting and selecting staff with research capability. From the outset, job advertisements noted that applicants were invited to specify their research interests at the time of applying. Equally important was the requirement that every short-listed applicant should be prepared to present their work to the department on the morning of the interview. In today's climate it is difficult to remember just how unusual that requirement was. Many appointments were still made with just a brief meeting between applicants and potential colleagues over lunch prior to the interviews. Quite often, and particularly where interviews took place in vacations, this interaction might not have occurred at all.

The principal aim of the recruitment programme was to build up a team of staff which could cover the formal teaching requirements and start to build a research capacity, with individual attributes which would make the department distinctive. Thus it was important to ensure that some new appointees had strong professional skills which would ensure continuation of the greatly valued (and market-sensitive) Centre of Excellence status awarded by the Chartered Institute of Personnel and Development, while others displayed interests in small business and HRM, the labour market, international HRM and so forth. Although none of these specialist interests was strong enough in its own right to warrant recognition comparable to established centres, they were a way of putting the department on the map amongst the various peer groups. The first main recruitment phase occurred across the two-year period 1990–1992. During that time some eight staff joined the department, taking it up to 14 in total. This significantly increased both its size and its mix: the new appointments reflected the priorities which have been identified above, with two staff having a strong professional background, four having a wide variety of experience, and two being very young 'new blood' postgraduates on whom we took a chance.

By 1993, some four years after its formation, the department had reached its expected size and had some useful strength. But it is probably true to say that it was still a group of individuals in terms of research capacity. It would take another five years before further additions and natural development within the existing staff would really see the research culture established.

Establishing credibility: The middle period of development

In 1993, with the main structure of the department nearly complete, a meeting amongst the staff led to a very important decision. Towards the conclusion of a day-long review of our own work, the idea began to emerge of a book which would serve both the needs of the academic discipline and our own desire to establish our name and our credentials. This was at a critical point in the debate over the emergence of the term 'HRM' to describe and encompass the work covered by the department. At the time there was no systematic textbook to cover how the subject, and its contributory elements, were emerging from that debate. Although there were a number of very highly regarded texts available, most of these addressed the component elements of HRM. A text which sought to review the developments in the subject, while providing students with good research-based material that covered key aspects, was badly needed by many colleagues in the subject at many other centres. The outcome was the decision to write a major textbook, drawing on the contributions from the department and with the author and a senior colleague as the joint editors.

Textbooks are a risky venture, especially viewed from today's perspective. The RAE in the UK does not generally regard them as contributions to knowledge, and publishers are now anxious to guarantee success for their own titles because the price of bringing an unsuccessful book to market is that much higher. However, nearly a decade ago, the discipline was looking for such a book and publishers were anxious to produce one. In those circumstances the department found itself with a firm proposal that readily established itself in the market and which, today, is the biggest selling HRM text in the UK and a substantial seller overseas.

It is important to appreciate that there were substantial benefits to be gained from pursuing such a venture. Setting aside the general publicity and positioning in the market which accrued to the department, there were major issues of research and SD which arose from the book. The first, and in many ways the most immediate, was that a text with a dozen authors who were all immediate colleagues gave a sense of community to a group who were growing both in size and impact; many different talents were on display in the first edition of 1994, which mirrored the department. Connected with this was the 'safe haven' the book provided for those who had not written extensively before. For the great majority of the book's authors, this was a new venture. For those who had not written for a professional audience before, it was the route to developing writing skills and cutting their teeth within the obligations of a publishing deadline. For those who had written before, it was a test of bringing their expertise to bear in a way that would benefit the less experienced through informal coaching and mentoring. The manuscript was delivered on time one year after the book was commissioned – no mean feat!

It is no exaggeration to say that the publication of the book gave a huge boost to the department. It encouraged some to register for PhDs; it encouraged others to develop their own writing further and it gave rise to further collaborative work between colleagues which would otherwise have taken longer to develop. This is not to say that one book, published in this way, is the key to creating a research culture. But it was an important element in putting together an environment in which systematic writing was seen as the usual thing to do. And it helped to consolidate that effort at the right time.

A further boost was received from the result of the 1992 RAE. Although it had come a little early in the life of the department, there was still enough work produced for eight colleagues to be entered – approximately half the department. A 2 rating allowed the university to identify the department as worth investing in, and it was able to appoint a senior research fellow and two research students in the autumn of 1993. This added to research capacity to an extent that could not be achieved by simply helping existing colleagues with their own work, and lifted the volume and quality of output of research.

Further growth took place when in 1995 the university made further substantial investments in HRM research on the strength of the 1992 RAE outcome. It awarded a further chair to the department and two additional research student-ships, and a major researcher in organizational behaviour was appointed in the autumn of 1995. The addition of a well-known 'name' gave colleagues a huge boost and added nationally and internationally recognized research expertise. For individual members of staff it meant that research agendas could be explored and research expertise tapped into, which helped many projects and writing plans. The discussion and analysis of research activities became a common topic amongst colleagues.

The consolidation period enabled the department to bridge the gap between intent and outcome successfully. Without it, and without the investment that went into it, including informal SD, it is very unlikely that the step-change in research activity that occurred across that period would have been achievable. The outcome for the department was that it went into the 1996 RAE in a strong position.

Integrating research culture: Locating research at the heart of things

The period since 1997 has seen a considerable shift towards a structured and integrated research culture. As a result of the 1996 RAE (in which a 3b rating was obtained) the university again invested in the department. In 1998 it was awarded a further chair and in 1999 it gained two further chairs and two more senior research fellowships. Each of the chairs was again a significant arrival, and the pattern of professorial appointment meant that, since 1995, the four chairs had all come from schools which were rated 4 or 5 in RAEs (5* being the top rating). The effect was that research played an increasingly central role in the expectations, atmosphere and culture of the department. One observable outcome was that one of the departmental research groups obtained a £140,000 award from the Economic and Social Research Council in collaboration with researchers in Spain and Germany and further funds were awarded by the Anglo-German Foundation to carry out the German section of the work.

As a consequence, preparations for the 2001 RAE were different from both the two preceding rounds. This time the department made some painful but pretty sophisticated judgements on whether the overall quality of each individual's output would, in fact, fully meet the panel's criteria. This meant some difficult choices, and some colleagues were not entered as a result. In 1996 that would have been even more painful and in 1992 it would have had a catastrophic effect on the growing culture within the department. In large measure this has demonstrated the extent to which we have changed as a group, and a complete understanding and acceptance that as our level of performance has improved so has the overall 'batting average' elsewhere. The department received a 3a rating.[2]

From the perspective of a decade of development there is a story to tell. It is that it is still possible, despite all the constraints and financial restrictions currently bedevilling British higher education, to build a research culture which is embedded and which has the capacity to look to the next stage of development. There are very important matters that still need to be addressed, and it is to these that the next section is devoted.

Assessing the move to a research culture: Winners, losers and those who get lost along the way

One important consideration in all this is the extent to which those who have had the 'lived experience' of this shift in culture do actually feel that they have had a chance to take part personally and to enhance their own research capability. This is probably where many attempts fail – particularly in the post-1992 sector in the UK. However, my own department does not strictly categorize 'researchers and others'. All incoming staff, whatever their status, carry out teaching and supervisions and contribute to the life of the department. This may mean that a senior colleague will convene a meeting and prepare and circulate a note of that meeting, just as readily as they will supervise a student project or have a research meeting with their own team. Equally, almost all the lecturing staff are engaged in active research; those who are not have explicitly decided not to, and that is recognized and understood. It is in managing this set of expectations, including thorough SD, that a great deal of the difficulty, and the success, of developing a culture resides.

Perhaps the greatest mistake that has occurred in the UK is to believe that research culture can be 'grafted on' in some way. This has almost always led to tensions and resentments. When staff are recruited whose sole obligation is to research, there are understandable criticisms from staff whose teaching and administration are burdensome – while the researchers may feel resentful that their efforts are not appreciated by their colleagues. At its most extreme a 'two-cultures' environment may grow, in which one culture does not recognize and address the interests and concerns of the other. The key thing to establish in these circumstances is that the culture of the department as a whole is one in which *all* these activities are seen to have a place; if the baseline culture of the department is not aligned to accommodate that spread of activity, then no amount of subsequent adjustments can replace it. To this extent, the creation of the department at De Montfort always had the research expectation built in – even before it was at a measurable level of activity.

The recruitment strategy is also vital. Many of the staff at De Montfort have not had the 'classic' track record of postgraduate work followed by a research post and then a lectureship. The staff mix has meant that the idea of a 'hybrid' route to an academic role, one in which a variety of prior experience has been accrued, has actually enriched the research culture. For many staff the development of a research role is an experience which has expanded their personal skills and horizons. The department does not necessarily look for a narrow focus in making appointments but would want to be assured that the overall 'fit' of the person to the department was right. The process of the departmental assessment of candidates for a half-day prior to interviews is a critical part of the process – even if that assessment is not binding on the appointment panel, as a result some candidates for chairs have not been selected.

This emphasis on the philosophy of the department is carried over into SD funding and promotions. Focusing SD funds has been an important part of developing the research strategy, so that every major conference at which a paper is to be given has always been supported. Nevertheless, there are plenty of occasions when a non-research-based activity needs support and it is as important to that individual as conference support is to another. This approach also colours our assessment as to whether or not someone is 'research-active'. We have not drawn formal distinctions within the department, but see this categorization as an artefact for the RAE. Where individuals have not been entered for RAE 2001 they are still eligible for SD and travel funds and can apply for small grants when available. Within the department currently there are three individuals who are wholly committed to teaching and administration. This has been discussed and agreed with them, and their contribution to the work of the department is encompassed within the overall philosophy. All other staff receive quite substantial relief for research activity where it has been identified and agreed; this is not simply contingent on RAE entry, but on whether within the department it is recognized that they are playing a research role.

Promotion and accelerated increments are dealt with on university criteria, but the decisions are arrived at by each faculty. Again, it would be unusual for such a promotion or advancement to be solely on the one criterion of research, except where, after careful career construction, an individual was applying for either a readership or a chair. In those circumstances the normal criteria of external refereeing and advisers would come into play – as at any other university. Thus, for general promotion, research would be seen as a key attribute alongside others.

Reflections

In the forgoing account I have stressed the need for consistent effort over time to create a balanced departmental culture in which research is seen as one integral component and not simply 'grafted on'. Staff development, conceived as largely informal discussion at routine and special meetings, informal support by established researchers of other colleagues and so on, was important to achieving support for and commitment to the new philosophy and the development of appropriate skills. It was and is integrated into the life of the department – 'part of the furniture', if you like, in line with the broader discussion of informal learning in Chapter 10. Table 14.1 sets out explicitly these forms of SD and some additional ideas about SD.

Clearly I enjoyed some advantages in context, notably in creating a new department with a largely clean sheet and arguably in personal skill sets (a background in

Table 14.1 Staff development for research

Staff development measures	Purpose	Possible alternatives and additions	Comments
Self-organized 'awaydays' and discussion in routine meetings	Developing, agreeing and reviewing the philosophy. Gaining staff commitment and 'ownership'.	'Awaydays' planned with external SD unit or consultant and facilitated by them.	Some institutional SD units provide this service or can find outside consultant support. Keep space for discussion in routine meetings.
Textbook project	Building the team and focusing effort on a clear product.	Writing groups (Murray 2001) to get inexperienced staff writing; short course training (e.g. on applying for research monies; dealing with journals); seminars with successful external 'new' researchers. Formal mentoring arrangements and joint writing projects.	There are a range of alternative ways of enhancing colleagues' confidence and skills available. Most need to be in-house but utilize any external provision in the institution or discipline, including 'small grant' funding. Requires funding or generating some resource. Monitor impact of support activities on the active researchers.
Remission from teaching; resourcing of conference participation	Provides time for research and writing; and opportunities for dissemination and networking.	Study leave and sabbatical arrangements.	Need to agree formula/ procedures and priorities. This support should not be at the expense of other activities/colleagues
Recruitment and selection policy and process	Getting the right people for the department – overall 'fit'; involving colleagues in applying the philosophy in practice.	Processes are now fairly common in UK.	Important for ensuring good decisions that maintain support of colleagues for philosophy. Also department's own HRM processes need to be congruent with its philosophy.
New head of department with appropriate leadership and management background	To effect development and change.	Collective leadership by senior team; leadership and management development for existing heads (see Chapter 9); greater external support (see above).	It is for others to judge the merits of my approach, however, I do believe leadership and management is important locally.

HRM). Attempting to change an established departmental culture and group of staff will be a longer, harder job, especially for heads for whom managing and promoting informal SD does not come naturally. The textbook project will not be available to many current departments. Fortunately, there are some supportive resources within the external environment, at least within the UK. I believe an environmental scan of the 'outer context' of the development of the discipline, other departments in the discipline, priorities of potential funders of research and the opportunities that provides is essential. Second, the scan needs to address the 'inner context' of institutional strategy, and the opportunities for investment of funds and availability of other support and resources (for example, from a SD unit). 'Going it alone' is not an easy or prudent course in most instances.

Conclusions

From all that has gone before, the conclusions follow quite naturally. It is possible to build a research culture that is supportive of individuals and supported by them, as well as integrated into the general life of the institution. It need not be either onerous or oppressive. It is vital to clarify what the overall philosophy of the department is or could be and to develop a 'culture' around that philosophy. Key components of that, in my experience, are appointing individuals with skills and aptitudes that permit at least some of that philosophy to be realized, and creating an atmosphere in which individual members of staff know that it is their own colleagues who are setting the pace and the context. In this, SD, broadly conceived, is critically important.

The rest is down to support from the institution, luck and a realization that it takes about ten years for all these factors to work together and produce results. If you happen to be in the fortunate position of managing that process and seeing it come to fruition, then you will have experienced one of the most satisfying jobs in higher education!

Key learning points

Senior staff

- Institutional context is critical. Those institutions with research aspirations must provide realistic levels of resourcing, and reward success with investment in new posts. Funds for selective poaching can be helpful provided it is part of an integrated strategy and not 'bolting on' experienced researchers.
- Ensure a supportive service environment, including management training for heads of department and staff development with an organizational focus for departments without sufficient internal resources.
- Remember that it takes time.

Heads of department

- Undertake an environmental scan and position your efforts carefully within the 'outer' and 'internal' contexts. Develop plans which align with institutional mission and resources.
- Seek to integrate research within overall departmental culture and avoid the development of two separate cultures through reliance on quick-fix importation of experienced researchers. Stay focused on priorities, and remember it takes time to effect cultural change.
- Ensure staff input, support and ownership of this philosophy through discussion, 'awaydays' and other informal staff development. Utilize formal and informal staff development to develop skills and aptitudes of existing staff (including yourself) and recruit new staff that 'fit' the emergent culture.

Professional staff developers

- Develop capacity to design and facilitate awaydays and similar internal consultancy processes and/or contacts with external consultants able to provide such services in a higher education context.
- Provide leadership and management development for heads of department (and research group leaders) that includes specific material on developing research capacity and culture.
- Provide 'light touch' guidance, drawing upon examples from academic units, and support for internal key processes such as mentoring and study leave.

Notes

1 The Research Assessment Exercise in the UK is carried out by funding bodies every 4–5 years. Departments are ranked by panels of peers on a scale of 1, 2, 3, 3a, 3b, 4, 5 and 5*. This ranking, along with a volume multiplier based on the proportion of staff submitted, determines the level of public funding allocated over the next 4–5 year period for research. As there is no equivalent exercise for teaching and learning which is formula-driven, the effect has been to ensure all institutions and departments in the UK must aspire to RAE success and funding. In this respect the UK differs from most other higher education systems, notably the system in USA.
2 When this chapter was written, it was unclear whether departments with a 3a rating would receive any funding. Subsequently it became clear that they would not. At the time of going to press the RAE was under review, partly as a result of this funding out-turn in which some improving departments received less or no funding (editors).

15

'The best hundred pounds': Learning Works in the University of Glasgow

Graeme Davies and Kathy Maclachlan

Headline results of the 1999 NIACE [National Institute of Adult and Continuing Education] adult learning survey show that the learning society is still a distant dream. . . . Social class and the length of initial education continue to show a powerful effect on adults' participation, and . . . the more you get, the more you want, for 76 per cent of current learners say they are likely to take up learning, but 87 per cent of people who have done no learning since they left school are unlikely to do so in the future.

(Tuckett and Sargant 1999: 5)

The learning divide not only continues but is growing, as the learning rich become richer and the learning poor become poorer in most parts of the UK.

In stark contrast, as the world of work is rapidly changing, and as the demands on employees are concomitantly shifting, continuing learning has never been so important both to the organization and the staff that it employs. For in addition to the job-specific skills that are an essential part of their work function, employees of today and tomorrow are increasingly required to possess an array of 'key' or 'soft' skills such as confidence, communication, teamworking, flexibility and creativity that will, it is believed, enable them to adapt and grow in these changed and changing work environments.

For those involved in staff development in universities, these two learning vignettes, viewed together, pose a very real problem, particularly in relation to the training and development needs of lower-skilled members of staff where a disproportionate number of disaffected learners are located. They also raise the question of the role of the universities in encouraging the broad spread of lifelong learning, as discussed by Parker in Chapter 3.

This chapter will examine the structure and impact of an initiative founded in the University of Glasgow in 1997 that aims not only to help reverse the trends evident in the adult learning survey, but also to contribute to the creation of a culture of lifelong learning amongst all members of staff, particularly, but not exclusively, those who would not normally engage in a structured learning activity.

The initiative, Learning Works, is an employee development scheme (EDS) through which certain categories of staff are entitled to an annual learning allowance of £100 to spend on the learning of their choice as long as that learning is *not* job-specific, that is, concerned with a skill that is required for their particular post. Glasgow was the first university in Scotland, and only the third in the UK, to implement such a scheme, and in so doing it drew from innovative staff development practice that had been steadily growing in the corporate sector for almost a decade beforehand.

Employee development schemes

The history of EDSs in the UK dates back to 1989, when they were imported from the United States by the Ford Motor Company. Born of collective bargaining agreements in the mid-1980s, Ford's Employee Development and Assistance Programme (EDAP) reflected a recognition on the part of both management and unions that 'future competitiveness (and hence jobs) depended upon the skills and abilities of employees' (Department for Education and Employment (DfEE) 1995: 1) and that these skills and abilities extended beyond the parameters of the functional and the job-specific. Ford understood that what was required were 'broad transferable skills and conceptual and cognitive abilities which develop through the process of learning itself' (Beattie 1997: 13), and so introduced a programme that was specifically geared towards encouraging the habit of learning amongst its staff. Through EDAP, each employee is entitled to an allowance of up to £200 per year for any structured learning activity that is concerned with personal rather than professional development. Since Ford's lead in 1987, the UK has witnessed a remarkable spread of EDSs. A recent UK research survey (Parsons *et al.* 1998) estimated that around 2275 firms were involved in EDSs, and this figure does not include those operating in Scotland.

Although one of the most interesting aspects of these initiatives is the huge diversity of scheme design and structure as each has evolved uniquely in response to local needs and local contexts, their essence can be summarized as follows:

- They provide a broad learning menu of personal development opportunities that are not directly job-related.
- They are entirely voluntary.
- They are employee-led and often jointly negotiated between management, workforce and unions.
- They provide 'customized doorstep learning provision' programmed around work patterns and imaginatively delivered to cater for the needs of new learners.
- They provide access to guidance and advice about learning.
- They are wholly or partially financed by the employers.
- Most presume the bulk of the learning will take place in the employee's own time (DfEE 1995; Payne 1996; Lee 1999; Maclachlan 1999).

If almost 3000 organizations, from all sectors in Britain, are funding EDSs, what spurs them to do so, particularly in an economic climate where the emphasis is upon the lean and the cost-effective? Why do they, for example, pay for a cleaner to learn to swim when equipment needs replacing or buildings need refurbishing? The simple answer is that participating organizations recognize that their greatest asset is their people. They see their employees as an investment rather than a cost, and they know that competitive advantage depends as much upon investment in people as it does upon infrastructure and information technology.

Less simplistically, research into EDSs over the past seven years has identified a range of particular benefits that are distinct from but complementary to those accrued through vocational and skills training. The difference between the two, according to Payne (1996: 230) is that 'where job-specific training has a present perspective, employee development schemes have a future perspective'. The most obvious of the benefits is the number of employees that they encourage to return to learning, in particular the numbers in low-skilled or unskilled occupations, the learning poor from the survey who are traditionally the least likely to engage in continuing education or training. Beattie's (1997: 34) evaluation at Ford found that 'since EDAP was introduced, participation among manual workers is more than twice the national average . . . and . . . more than half are taking part in formal learning for the first time since leaving school'.

Because (a) they are geared towards the interests of the adult rather than the short-term needs of the organization, (b) their systems build supported, easy steps into learning for the tentative returner, and (c) they remove some of the most commonly cited barriers to learning, they are particularly successful in reaching those whom adult education and training does not. And if, as the literature suggests, the ability to learn is a fundamental prerequisite for the effective employee, they may well therefore be one of the most sound long-term investments an organization can make.

The corporate sector is not renowned for its grand gestures of employee altruism. Companies must know with a fair degree of confidence that there will be a positive return on their investments, so over the last decade, a number of comparative and single-scheme studies (Metcalfe 1992; Beattie 1997; Parsons *et al.* 1998; Lee 1999) have sought to evaluate EDSs and identify the observable benefits that they bring to the organization. They have classified these into ones that pertain to the individual employee, and ones that relate to the organization as a whole. One noticeable feature of these studies is their remarkably positive conclusions, and, with the exception of those dealing exclusively with small businesses which have very distinct cultures and needs, they all observe clear identifiable outcomes from this type of investment in learning. For individual members of staff, the benefits are recorded as

- enhanced confidence and self-esteem;
- increased job satisfaction;
- an increased sense of belonging at work;
- increased motivation;
- the generation of an excitement about learning;
- a willingness to continue learning;
- greater responsiveness to work-related training.

Parsons *et al.* (1998: 49) observed that 'the most common benefit cited by employees was greater confidence in their ability to learn which crossed age, gender and occupation but which was greatest for those with no qualifications'.

In relation to the organization, the benefits are commonly clustered into

- quantitative, directly measurable features;
- indirectly attributable benefits;
- behavioural benefits.

The first and second of these categories include indices such as numbers of new and repeat learners, qualifications achieved, progression in learning, reduced absenteeism and staff turnover, and increased productivity. With the exception of the Ford EDAP scheme (Beattie 1997), hard evidence of these indices was scarce in the early days of EDSs in Britain, because companies did not record it. However, more recent studies (Parsons *et al.* 1998; Lee 1999) have begun to provide quantitative data evidencing these benefits in other organizations throughout the UK. Whilst not denying the importance of these factors, it is in many ways the third cluster that signifies the real difference that EDSs can make, because it relates to how employees respond to their job, to their colleagues and to the organization as a whole. This third cluster includes

- improved teamworking;
- increased motivation;
- a greater involvement in change;
- a sense of being recognized and valued at work;
- a greater confidence in work-related learning;
- a broadening of skills;
- greater internal dialogue and communication.

These are, in summary, almost the totality of those key or core skills that policy directives cite as necessary for organizations and nations to survive and to thrive in the knowledge-based global economy.

However, the move to introduce EDSs as an integral part of staff development policies in higher education is not wholly driven by examples of practice in the corporate world. It also comes from directives and recommendations within the higher education sector itself. The Dearing Report (National Committee of Inquiry into Higher Education 1997) challenged higher education institutions to consider the Investors in People award, in which the training and development needs of *all* staff are addressed. Bett (1999: 90) confirmed the 'need, across the sector and in most institutions, for greater investment of time and resources in the training and development of **all** groups of staff' and the Higher Education Training Organisation (THETO 1999: 21) recommended that:

> In order to allow traditionally more disadvantaged staff to participate in the new learning and skills agenda, higher education institutions should consider the introduction of 'work-based' employee development schemes, with the aim of extending life-long learning opportunities to **all** staff within the higher education sector. (Emphasis added)

Given these sectoral leads, if universities, whose very business is the promotion of learning, cannot support this same learning amongst all their staff, what message do they send to other organizations whose values and objectives are not so educationally rooted?

This section has sketched both the background and recorded benefits of EDS, and has shown how they can complement the training elements of a balanced staff development strategy in higher education institutions. One purpose of this book, however, is to consider how examples of practice in universities are managed and operated within these strategies, so it is to the details of Glasgow's EDS, Learning Works, that the discussion now turns.

Learning Works in the University of Glasgow

Why Glasgow?

The University of Glasgow recognized that it was fitting for a learning institution to include all its staff in its community of learners. It also wished to signal a public commitment to its employees and send a clear message about the extent to which it values them as individuals, and about the value and potential of lifelong learning in enhancing their lives, particularly those who have not previously benefited from such opportunities. Ultimately, however, it saw the scheme as a win–win initiative, where the individual would gain an increased sense of confidence in their abilities, greater motivation to learn new things and a stronger sense of belonging in the workplace. Departments would gain as a result of these changes in individuals, and the University would gain more committed motivated members of staff as well as an enhanced image as a caring organization.

Structure and management

In designing the particular nature of the scheme, its Management Group made a principled decision to limit it in the first instance to the manual, ancillary, clerical and secretarial staff – those on the lowest pay scales who have traditionally had least access to and success in learning. Technical staff were subsequently included in the second year (1998–9), and the number of eligible staff now stands at over 2900.

Any member of staff in these categories can claim a learning allowance of up to £100 per year which may be spent on the learning activity or activities that they choose. The only stipulations are: that it is a structured learning activity; that it takes place in their own time; and that it is not job-specific, because that would impinge on the activities of the Staff Development Services. Learning choices are kept as broad as possible to encourage maximum participation. An extensive programme of short courses on campus is offered, designed specifically for the scheme, but if staff prefer, they may access any courses run through the Department of Adult and Continuing Education's Open Programme, in local colleges, universities or community centres, or indeed one-to-one tuition in leisure or sports activities. Every effort has been made to keep the systems as simple as possible whilst at the same time recognizing the need to be accountable to the University's quality auditing procedures. Essentially, once staff receive their brochure they can register for their allowance, and if they have decided upon their choice of activity they are sent a learning voucher which they take to the course or to the relevant institution. If they have not made the decision, their allowance is secured for them until the end of the year and at any time they may contact the Learning Works team to receive their voucher.

Day-to-day management and administration are undertaken by a small team that also includes the part-time services of a guidance officer and a researcher, but they would have minimum authority or impact without the support and guidance of a university-wide Management Group. This group has nurtured Learning Works from very tentative beginnings and has brought to it a mix of expertise, experience and skills from across the institution, but particularly from its former Personnel and Staff Development Services. Other representatives are from all the campus trade unions, and from departments, such as the Computing Service or the Sport and Recreation Service, that provide courses for the brochure. The group is chaired by the vice-principal responsible for staffing matters. Without this Management Group – or, more accurately, without its specific vertical and horizontal representation – the scheme could not have achieved the results it has since its inception. The unions offer their unique knowledge of staff and give it credibility amongst their members. The different departments contribute their subject expertise and their facilities. The Staff Development Service likewise assists with the programme, but what it and the vice-principal uniquely contribute is a strategic synergy that has established Learning Works solidly within Glasgow's staff development strategy, and has enabled its two functions of personal and professional development to complement rather than to compete with each other.

Having the vice-principal as chair of the Management Group has been another critical factor for Learning Works, not only because of his staffing remit but also because of his position in the senior management team where strategic visions and financial decisions affecting the entire institution are made. The combination of these efforts at both strategic and operational levels has undoubtedly played a key part in the successful integration of Learning Works within Glasgow, but they too were dependent upon another level of support that could only come from the top, that is, from the principal of the university. All the research previously cited points to the critical role of a 'champion' from a very senior level within an organization, whose lead and support at an institutional level make a difference at all stages of a scheme's development.

Before considering other factors that have contributed to the success of Learning Works, it is perhaps timely to indicate what some of its outcomes have been in relation to both individual staff and to the organization as a whole.

Outcomes

Evaluating the impact of EDSs requires a multidimensional approach which reflects the range of indices discussed above. Learning Works tracks both quantitative and qualitative outcomes through its registration database, its end-of-course evaluation forms, staff surveys and focus groups, and through surveys with managers across the university.

Quantitative data accumulated from the beginning of the scheme show a steady rise in registration rate from 43 per cent in its first year, to 56 per cent of all eligible staff in 1999–2000 (1675 registrations). Although it must be recognized that these figures represent registration and not uptake, they do signal an intention to learn. As such they can be compared with the NIACE survey referred to above which recorded an 'intention to take up learning' rate of 38 per cent throughout the UK, and only 33 per cent in Scotland. Learning Works is therefore generating an interest in learning that is two-thirds higher than the Scottish norm. In addition, it is attracting a higher percentage of social groups C2/D/E (skilled manual/semi-skilled, unskilled) workers than the national average, for only 31 per cent of the NIACE survey indicated an intention to learn, whereas the registration rate for the manual and ancillary staff, which is the nearest approximation that can be made, was 40 per cent.

In common with all EDSs, there is a discrepancy between the registration rate and actual participation in a learning activity. Learning Works' participation figures in 1999–2000 were 1066, which represented 36 per cent of all eligible staff and an encouraging 23 per cent from the manual and ancillary groups. A comparison between these figures and the NIACE survey produces further evidence of the successes of Learning Works: the current learning rate for adults in Scotland is 18 per cent, while for Learning Works it is 36 per cent; the rate for men throughout the UK is 24 per cent (Learning Works 30 per cent); and for women throughout the UK 21 per cent (Learning Works 38 per cent).

In relation to the learning experience, the dedicated Learning Works courses are very popular, particularly with women and those staff with lowest levels of educational attainment. Data from 384 end-of-course evaluation forms showed that 25 per cent of those completing the forms had school education only, and 79 per cent of them took the Learning Works courses. Similarly, 47 per cent had post-school but not higher education experience, and 82 per cent of them also opted for these courses. This would appear to confirm an emergent trend of the courses providing a safe, non-threatening step into learning for adults who have been least successful at the initial schooling stages.

Qualitative data from these evaluation forms indicate very positive responses to the learning, for half had encouraged others to undertake a learning activity as a result of their experience in the scheme. As well as encouraging others, the nature of this experience appears to be stimulating a desire to continue learning, for 77 per cent of the learners have previously taken courses through Learning Works, and 21 per cent were specifically influenced to learn more by their experience in the previous year.

Other trends which are beginning to emerge are concerned with issues of motivation and gain in relation to the learning, for 'being keen to do more learning' emerged as the second most popular outcome from participants' experience. As staff utilize the opportunities offered through Learning Works to broaden their interests, they appear to become 'hooked' on learning in the process. Furthermore, though specific job-related gains were low down on the list of outcomes, as would be expected given the non-vocational nature of the scheme, the gains reported by the learners were ones that relate directly to those key or soft skills that are increasingly required in the workplace: 'a keenness to continue learning' (18 per cent); 'a greater sense of self confidence' (18 per cent); and 'a recognition of my ability to achieve what I set out to achieve' (15 per cent). So, whilst the participating members of staff are enjoying the opportunity to develop new interests in their personal lives, they are also acquiring the learning, confidence and communication skills that are equally important in their working environments. Proof that these skills are already manifesting themselves at work can be found in a Learning Works survey of management staff (Maclachlan 1999) which reported 34 per cent of the 50 managers interviewed as having observed evidence of positive change amongst staff after less than two years of the schemes' operation. For example:

> They're already more confident in speaking to me and dealing with queries from the floor.
>
> (Library)

> They're working better together and communicating better as a team.
>
> (Catering)

Anecdotal evidence from other unpublished research also shows members of the manual and ancillary staff feeling more positive about themselves and about the university as an employer:

> It makes you feel more part of something.

> I found myself speaking to this huge audience and I'd never have done that before the course.

> It shows they recognise that we may not have the qualifications, but we've got brains too.

> a kind of personal touch – the company's interested in you.
>
> (Maclachlan 2001)

Whilst it would be unwise to attribute too much to the data at this stage in the life of Learning Works, the cumulative and consistent feedback does suggest that the soft, longer-term outcomes noted in national evaluation studies are beginning to emerge amongst participating staff in the University of Glasgow. Furthermore, it demonstrates that universities can successfully address issues of social inclusion and accessibility in learning that Parker highlights in Chapter 3, for their staff as well as for their student body.

Employee development schemes in other universities

Evidence of similar initiatives in European universities has not been identified, perhaps because of the different nature of the universities, and/or the different labour relations in the countries. However, Snell (2001) has mapped the range of EDSs currently operating in higher education institutions within the UK. What she found was 'a number of ambiguities [and] a great deal of confusion within the sector about what was actually being discussed' (Snell 2001: i). Her survey shows that only 3.5 per cent of the higher education sector operates full EDSs, though a further 2 per cent 'indicated some level of formal support for learning and educational development'. The five full schemes are located in the universities of Glasgow, Leeds, Oxford Brookes, Derby and Warwick, and though all contain key elements of the classic definition as outlined above, each has developed its own variant of the model. The University of Leeds, for example, has incorporated the trade union UNISON's Return to Learn programme in its scheme. Derby concentrates on those who have been away from learning for two or more years. Oxford Brookes (the first in the UK) targets workers earning less than £14,000 and links with other work-based learning and essential skills initiatives, whereas Warwick confines its learning opportunities to those provided by its internal departments or its Open Programme.

One of Snell's conclusions that is of particular relevance to the theme of this book is that

> The breadth, take-up and financial investment in the schemes appears to bear little relationship to the size or type of institution, but owes significantly more to the vision of senior management and the ethos of the institution with regard to learning and development.
>
> (Snell 2001: 14)

Senior management hold the master key that can open a wide range of personal development opportunities for staff, but Snell's survey and the experience of the Glasgow Learning Works team point to a range of additional factors that are equally critical to the implementation of a successful EDS within a university environment. At a strategic level these include:

- a strong committed 'champion' at senior management level;
- dedicated central funding that is independent of departmental or faculty budgets;
- the active involvement of the senior manager with a responsibility for staff development;
- broad representation on the scheme's management group which must include staff development personnel;
- an integration into the university's staff development strategy, which can only be achieved through the previous two factors;
- high-profile publicity and feedback so that heads of faculties and departments

are kept informed of the aims and outcomes, and may therefore be more proactive in their support for the scheme.

At an operational level they are:

- an adequate lead-in time that allows for broad consultation relating to the nature of the scheme and the learning interests of the employees;
- the appointment of dedicated staff to run the scheme, including a guidance element, which Learning Works has found to be of increasing importance;
- close liaison between these staff and other staff development personnel;
- user-friendly systems that will not deter the tentative learner;
- a broad range of learning choices that include short taster courses at times and locations that are most convenient to potential learners;
- good, clear, ongoing publicity that is taken to employees at their various workplaces;
- worksite co-ordinators who perform an advocacy, support and communication function for less confident members of staff;
- and finally, a sense of enthusiasm and of excitement – a sense that learning can be fun as well as useful, and that it need not replicate the experiences that many unfortunately endured during their initial schooling.

Conclusion

The senior management team in the University of Glasgow and the four other universities in the UK have demonstrated through their employee development schemes a commitment to the vision of an inclusive community of learners in their institutions. It is a vision and a reality that is replicable in other institutions, albeit at a cost, but when the institutional budgets are being formulated, we at Glasgow would suggest that the question to be asked is not 'what is the cost of investing this amount in staff?', but rather 'what is the cost of *not* investing it?' For, to conclude with words of one of Glasgow's janitors:

> People like myself couldn't afford these things. I couldn't have done it on my own you know. That hundred pound's the best thing that ever happened as far as I'm concerned.

Key learning points

Senior staff

- EDS need a strong committed 'champion' at <u>senior management</u> level together with dedicated central funding that is independent of departmental or faculty budgets.
- EDS need high profile publicity and feedback so that heads of departments are

kept informed and are therefore able to be more proactive in their support for the scheme.

- EDS require the appointment of dedicated staff including a guidance element, to run the scheme, with close liaison between these staff and other staff development personnel.

Heads of department

The learning points for Heads of Departments concern their potential role in actively promoting learning amongst their staff.

- Successful employee development schemes require that as managers, they provide a strong and continuing encouragement to both prospective and existing participants.
- Reviewing and discussing the achievements of their staff and assisting them with their plans for futher participation in the scheme are critical tasks.
- At an organizational level they are uniquely positioned to assist in the identification of worksite co-ordinators who can perform an advocacy, support and communication function amongst work colleagues.

Professional staff developers

For staff development specialists, the learning relates to operational and institutional issues.

- At an operational level they would need to maintain a close, ongoing liaison with the staff who run the scheme.
- At an institutional level they should recognize the potential impact of achievement in *any* learning process on the potential to participate in work-related development.
- At an institutional level, they should work towards the incorporation of the EDS into the University's overall staff development strategy.

16

Using a student-focused learning perspective to align academic development with institutional quality assurance

Michael Prosser and Simon Barrie

Introduction

Much has been written about quality assurance processes in teaching and learning in recent years (Harvey and Knight 1996; Woodhouse 1999). While there has been a great deal of debate as to the definition of quality and the evidence upon which to base decisions about the quality of higher education, there has been little written about the concept of learning which underpins quality processes. Nor has there been any consideration of how the variety of quality processes and indicators are aligned within themselves and how they are aligned with institutional policies and processes for academic development in teaching and learning. In this chapter we will suggest that such alignment is the key to effective quality improvement in higher education. In order to achieve such alignment, a clear theoretical underpinning of the policies and processes is required – it is this theoretical underpinning which can provide the coherence within and between policies and processes across an institution. In this chapter we outline the theoretical perspective from which we, and our university, have been working in developing its quality improvement policies and processes – the so-called student learning perspective (Prosser and Trigwell 1999; Ramsden 2003). We will then outline some of the institutional quality assurance processes that are being implemented consistent with this theoretical perspective, and describe some of the academic development activities designed to support these processes and further improve quality.

Theoretical underpinning of policies and processes: student learning perspective

Research on student learning has shown that students adopt qualitatively different approaches to their studies, depending upon their prior experiences of studying and the particular context in which they find themselves. These different approaches lead to qualitatively different learning outcomes. Surface approaches, in which students focus on reproducing the content and processes they are studying, seem to be associated with experiences of high workload and of assessment demands being able to be met by reproductive learning. Deep approaches, on the other hand, seem to be associated with student experiences that the teaching is good, that the goals are clear, and that there is some freedom of choice in how and what they learn. Deep approaches to study are in turn associated with an understanding of the subject matter which can broadly be described as relational, while in surface approaches the understanding can be described as multistructural (Biggs 1999). That is, students can understand the outcomes of the course and what the course was about in terms of a coherent or of an unrelated set of ideas and procedures. Student approaches to study are not stable aspects of cognitive structure, but are conceived of as relations between the student and the context; see Ramsden (2003) for a recent discussion of this. The way institutions structure the teaching and learning contexts of students has an important impact on what and how students learn.

A model describing the results of much of this recent research on student learning is shown in Figure 16.1. It shows that students' experiences of teaching and learning contexts are a function of both their prior experiences of teaching and learning and of the present context. It is in relation to these experiences that they approach their studies. In order to improve their learning outcomes, we need to be concerned about both the context and their experiences of that context. Institutional policies and practices of student evaluation of teaching would be expected to have substantial effects on the way staff approach their teaching and structure the teaching and learning context. If the focus of evaluation is on

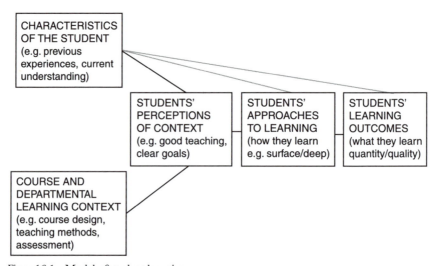

Figure 16.1   Model of student learning

presentation and not on student learning, then staff will structure the context of their teaching around presentation issues.

More recently, the focus of some of this research has changed to how teachers conceive of and approach their teaching, and how such conceptions and approaches affect student learning. Broadly speaking, it seems that university teachers conceive of teaching on the one hand as transmitting information to students, with a focus on what the teacher does, and on the other as helping students develop an understanding, with the focus being on what the students do as a result of the teaching. There is substantial and growing evidence that these conceptions and approaches to teaching are associated with students' approaches to learning in a way that would be expected. That is, subjects in which teaching is seen as being about transmission of information are more likely to have students adopting surface approaches to learning, while subjects that see teaching as being about changing students' understanding are more likely to have students adopting a deep approach. Again, there is evidence that institutional policies and practices of student evaluation of teaching would have a substantial effect on staff conceptions and approaches to teaching (Ramsden 1998).

What are the implications of such a view of student learning and teaching for institutional policy-makers? If institutions wish to encourage students to focus on understanding and not reproduction, then they need to establish their policies and practices with an explicit view of student learning in mind.

This chapter addresses some of these issues in relationship to current research on student learning and describes and critically discusses how one university is attempting to institutionalize these ideas into its practices. But before describing these practices, some comments on the current Australian context for higher education are warranted.

National context

The Australian university system, like many others in the Western world, is experiencing a dramatic increase in external quality review processes and an unprecedented focus on 'bottom-line' accountability for expenditure (Woodhouse 1999; Karmel 2000). The factors driving such changes are many and varied, but those mentioned frequently include the massification of higher education and the explicit linking of government's education and employment agendas (Harvey and Knight 1996). University education is seen more in terms of its role as a key to socio-economic growth than as contributing the outcomes of inquiry to the intellectual and ethical growth of society as in Newman's ideal. There is a growing perception by government of universities as production houses, turning out employable graduates for consumption by an economic rationalist society (Coady 2000).

In a time of shrinking public funding (Karmel 2000), government quality assurance agendas are being brought to bear on the unfamiliar target of university teaching. Such quality assurance agendas are based primarily on an economic-rationalist interpretation of quality and seek to assure that such teaching represents value for money.

While claims of quality teaching, on the part of universities and the people who work in them, are not new, the introduction of processes to explicitly measure and demonstrate teaching quality are. In the past, teaching was to a large extent a private activity that took place behind the closed doors of the classroom. It was a transaction between teacher and student that was not open to public scrutiny or critique and was not subject to 'corporate management'.

Changing roles of academic development units

Given this changing context, how are academic development units reacting? In Australia, at least, there is a shift away from the more traditional staff development focus on individual members of staff to a more strategic focus on the institution's strategic plans and objectives. Rather than a focus on helping individuals become better teachers, the focus of many units' activities is on working with academic and other staff to help achieve the institution's mission. Often this means working more on an outcomes basis (for example, improving the first-year experience of students, improving the institution's retention rates, enhancing the institution's quality assurance processes and monitoring their outcomes). As well, some units are taking a more student-focused perspective, consistent with the model of student learning referred to previously. The point here is that any institutional process of academic development has, either implicitly or explicitly, underlying models, values and theories of student learning built in. Often the different processes and outcomes are not well aligned – partly because the underlying theory is not well explicated. Given the generally good acceptance of John Biggs's concept of constructive alignment for student learning, it would be expected that issues of alignment of institutional academic development processes and outcomes would be a key focus for academic development units.

This is certainly the case at the University of Sydney, where an explicit student-focused perspective based upon the student learning theory referred to previously has been explicitly adopted by the institution, and the academic development activities of the institution's academic development unit have been aligned with this perspective. In the following sections some aspects of this alignment will be described and analysed

Institutional context

The University of Sydney is a large, research-intensive, multidisciplinary university. It has a student enrolment of about 40,000, with about 28,000 enrolled in bachelor's degree programmes and about 10,000 in graduate and postgraduate programmes. It has a total of about 5000 staff, with about 2500 academic staff. It is the oldest university in Australia.

Sydney appointed its inaugural pro-vice-chancellor (teaching and learning) in 1999. This appointment signalled its desire to lift its performance in the key area of teaching and learning. The pro-vice-chancellor, in co-operation with the chair of the Academic Board, has instituted a number of institutional-level initiatives. These include:

- a performance-based funding model for teaching and learning (about $A3.2 million, or about 3.5 per cent of the allocation for undergraduate teaching – this will increase to about $A7 million in 2005);
- faculty teaching and learning plans;
- a teaching improvement fund to support key aspects of the faculty's teaching and learning plans (about $A1.3 million);
- a scholarship of teaching index used to identify and reward scholarly activities in teaching and learning in higher education (about $A600,000);
- and, more recently, Academic Board reviews of faculties' teaching and learning.

These changes have not been, and are not being, introduced without substantial dissatisfaction, discussion and debate. The strongest initial reaction was to the performance-based funding model. The model was initially proposed by the pro-vice-chancellor. The Institute for Teaching and Learning (ITL) established a faculty-based working group to support the consultations and discussions about the model. In the process, a number of changes were made to the model – mainly focused on accounting for field-of-study variations in the indicators. Two years later, there is general acceptance of the model, if not enthusiastic support. In order to qualify for funding from the model, the teaching improvement fund and the scholarship of teaching index, each faculty has to produce a faculty teaching and learning plan, approved by the Academic Board. Once the plan is approved, faculties can then apply for a teaching improvement fund grant to support various aspects of their teaching and learning plan. The plan itself needs to be based upon evidence of performance, including the teaching performance indicators. These strategic links are meant to tie the various initiatives together, so that they all act in consort.

All of this, in many ways, constitutes Sydney's response to the emerging quality debate in higher education. It has adopted a perspective that its quality assurance processes need to be academic-led, evidence-based and scholarly in nature, consistent with the its vision of itself as a research-intensive university.

In the next section we will briefly describe how the ITL, Sydney's academic development unit, has responded to these quality issues, given such an institutional context, and the changing role of academic development units as described previously.

Academic development processes

In line with the arguments made earlier, the ITL has substantially changed its mission and strategic plan to better align its activities with the changing focus of the university. In the following sections we will focus on one aspect of the ITL's response, student evaluation of teaching, and illustrate how this response embodies the use of common theoretical underpinning to provide coherence to the ITL'S academic development work. The key principles upon which this work is based include:

- that the activities of the ITL are strategically aligned with the university's teaching and learning strategic initiatives;
- that the activities are research-led and scholarly in nature;
- that the focus is not so much on academic staff development as on project-based initiatives aimed at enhancing student learning experiences and outcomes.

In ensuring that its work is informed by these three principles, the ITL has drawn upon the student learning research discussed earlier in this chapter. This does not mean that any particular model or theory of learning is used to the exclusion of all others. Rather the student-focused approach which we have described provides an overarching framework within which other theories and models of learning and teaching can be drawn upon. Indeed, the explicit use of this student-focused theoretical perspective has promoted much valuable debate and discussion amongst both the staff of the unit and our academic colleagues teaching in the faculties. Such debate is a valuable aspect of any research-led and scholarly academic development process.

Such an approach to academic development means that the academic staff of the ITL need to be research active – supervising postgraduate research students, applying for research grants, and publishing the results of their work regularly in refereed journals. It also means that we maintain active contact with other academic staff in the institution and engage them as collaborators in the strategically aligned projects.

Student evaluation of teaching

As noted previously, Sydney's quality assurance and quality improvement policies are informed by a view of student learning which is student-focused. In such a view of learning the students' experiences of learning are central to determining the quality of the outcomes of learning and as such the student experience sits at the heart of the university's quality assurance strategies. The challenge for the ITL was to develop processes to gather information on students' learning experiences which would be helpful in the context of these quality assurance policies while ensuring that such data would also be helpful for the university community in seeking to improve these experiences.

Over the past three years the ITL has devoted considerable resources to the development of a student evaluation-of-teaching system which is theoretically aligned with such a view of learning (Barrie 2001). The system is aligned with institutional policies in terms of the theoretical perspective on learning embodied in the items used in the survey tools. The system is multilayered, incorporating feedback for individual teachers, unit-of-study evaluation, student course experience, and graduate course experience (see http://www.itl.usyd.edu.au/teval). The data gathered at the four different levels of the institution are aligned and theoretically related to data gathered at other levels, as all surveys are based on a student-focused view of learning. For the three higher levels there is also a correspondence between the psychometric structure of the actual surveys. In this way, data gathered at the level of feedback for individual teachers and quality improvement data on individual units of study (subjects) are aligned with university quality assurance data gathered on students' experiences of their overall course and with national data on graduates' overall university experience. We will now briefly consider the alignment between three of these levels.

The Australian government's emerging national higher education quality assurance strategy incorporates data from a survey of graduates on their experiences of university. This information is gathered using the Course Experience Questionnaire (CEQ) and has been conducted nationally in Australia for many years. There is a considerable body of published research on both the theoretical basis for the survey and the psychometric validity of the CEQ (Ramsden 1991). The CEQ is based on the same student-focused view of learning which underpins Sydney's quality assurance policies and was used as the basis for the development of its internal survey of current students, the Student Course Experience Questionnaire (SCEQ). The SCEQ factor scale data contribute to the bulk of the performance indicator information used in Sydney's internal quality assurance strategies. As a result of the close alignment between the SCEQ and the CEQ, these internal performance indicator data are directly comparable with the national data set for benchmarking purposes. The SCEQ gathers data on students' experiences of their overall degree courses, yet clearly these courses comprise diverse combinations of subjects (or units of study, as they are called in our university). There is a need for departments to be able to see how students' learning experiences in different units of study might contribute to the overall learning experience of the degree. This information is gathered by another level of the ITL system, the Unit of Study Evaluation (USE) system. At this level there is a need for richer and more explanatory data on students' learning experiences to inform curriculum and teaching development, yet such data must still relate to the quantitative data gathered for quality assurance purposes. In designing the USE survey the underlying theoretical perspective on learning in the SCEQ and CEQ is mirrored in the survey items. The items also correspond to the aspects of the learning experience tapped in the SCEQ and CEQ factor scale scores that are used in calculating the performance indicators for allocating the teaching performance fund. This system encourages academics to focus teaching improvement and curriculum development efforts on relevant aspects of the student learning experience. Because of the alignment between the different levels of the system the outcomes of curriculum developments in the different units that comprise a course, as measured by improvements in the student learning experience on the USE survey, should be echoed in changes to the student learning experience as measured by the factor scale scores on the SCEQ.

As an example of the articulation between these three levels of survey, consider the following items from the CEQ, SCEQ and USE respectively, which relate to the Clear Goals and Standards Scale of the national CEQ survey. Practices characteristic of this scale involve the establishing of clear aims and objectives for a course and clear expectations of the standard of work expected from students.

CEQ (survey of graduates' experiences of their whole university degree):

- I usually had a clear idea of where I was going and what was expected of me in this course.
- It was always easy to know the standard of work expected.
- The staff made it clear right from the start what they expected from students.
- It has often been hard to discover what was expected of me in this course.

SCEQ (survey of current students' experiences of their degree course):

- I have usually had a clear idea of where I am going and what is expected of me in this course.
- It is always easy to know the standard of work expected.
- The staff made it clear right from the start what they expected from students.
- It has often been hard to discover what is expected of me in this course.

USE (survey of current students' experiences of a particular subject):

- The learning outcomes and expected standards of this unit of study were clear to me.
- Please explain the reasons for your rating.

In supporting academic development within the university, the teaching evaluation system also provides a mechanism which facilitates alignment of the ITL's academic development work with institutional strategies and priorities. Moreover, it provides a sound theoretical and research basis for scholarly work by members of the academic community in the area of teaching and learning. To facilitate such academic development work the ITL has established a number of working groups with representation from each faculty of the university. Through these groups the ITL works collaboratively with faculties to identify and progress strategic projects aimed at improving the student learning experience. This process involves the support of the members of the faculty in understanding and interpreting the data on the student learning experience gathered by such surveys and then supporting academic development activities to target particular aspects of the student learning experience. This work is research-led and based on current student-focused learning theories as well as being strategically aligned with institutional priorities through its basis in Sydney's quality assurance processes and policies. We believe this alignment allows the academic development work of the ITL to be more effective at an institutional level and contributes to the ITL demonstrating the quality of its work with the university community.

Like most such units, the academic development work of the ITL covers many areas, for example the first-year Experience, learning technologies, graduate attributes, as well as teaching formal courses in the discipline of higher education. The teaching evaluation system provides a common student-focused perspective as a basis for many of the academic development initiatives undertaken by the ILTHE. The explicit recognition of a student-focused view of teaching that informs these diverse activities provides a congruence and synergy between the different activities, which contributes to the effective team approach of the unit in supporting a range of projects.

We will now briefly consider some particular examples of this alignment and congruence between institutional quality assurance and the academic development work of the ITL.

Academic staff development

The first example is in the redesign of the ITL's three-day programme on teaching and learning and the graduate certificate in higher education. The three-day programme is compulsory for all new members of the academic staff and is a constituent part of the graduate certificate. The student-focused perspective underlying the design of the student evaluation system also underlies the design of the three-day programme and the graduate certificate. The three-day programme begins by asking the participants to reflect on how their students approach their studies and how they would like them to approach their studies, and to complete John Biggs's Study Process Questionnaire (Biggs 1987), the scales of which represent surface and deep approaches to study. Invariably, they would prefer students to adopt deeper and less surface approaches. They then discuss in groups why students may adopt one approach or the other. The results of the research literature are then summarized in terms of the relationships between students' experiences of their learning environment (as indicated by CEQ indicators) and approaches to study (Study Process Questionnaire indicators). The university's CEQ and SCEQ results are then examined. This half-day provides the context for examining, in the remaining two-and-a-half days, the importance of aims and objectives, active teaching and learning methods, assessment focusing on understanding and not reproduction, and the importance of students developing an understanding of the standards applied in assessment. In the process we examine various aspects of the university's student-focused policies on teaching and learning.

The graduate certificate has two key aspects. The first is to engage participants in an examination of their teaching and learning practices from the student learning perspective referred to above. The second is to engage them in the scholarship of teaching focusing on some aspects of their teaching. Here we will refer to the first aspect only. The first task is for participants to interview three students about how they approach their studies and why (Gibbs 1992). This exercise strongly reinforces the within-individual variation in approaches to study and how that variation relates to variations in experiences of the teaching and learning context. For example, the participants invariably find that virtually all students adopt surface approaches when preparing for examinations – no matter how they approach other aspects of their studies. They then examine the aims and objectives, teaching and learning methods and assessment methods of one of the units of study they are teaching during that semester, from a student-focused learning perspective.

The next example focuses on our use of working groups to support our academic development work.

First Year Experience Working Group

The First Year Experience Working Group was established substantially to address issues emerging from the analyses of the student evaluations relating to first-year students. The SCEQ results suggested that much first-year teaching was more teacher-focused than student-focused. The students had little understanding of the overall goals and standards to be achieved in their programmes. Many saw the assessment processes focusing on reproduction rather than understanding. Key performance indicators suggested some of the retention rates for some of the first-year programmes needed to be improved. As a result, the ITL established a working group with representatives from each of the faculties to support the development and implementation of first-year experience plans at the faculty level. One of us had had experience of such a working group in another institution, and it was judged that this would be an appropriately strategic way of addressing the issues referred to above (Pitkethly and Prosser 2001). Since the establishment of the Working Group, most of the faculties have developed first-year experience plans outlining the ways in which they orientate their students to their programmes of study, and how they will support them throughout their first year of study. The plans have been designed to address issues emerging from the ongoing student evaluation of their first-year programmes. The university is supporting many of these plans via strategic funding initiatives through the office of the pro-vice-chancellor (teaching and learning).

The ITL has established a number of other working groups to work with the faculties to address other strategic issues such as the university's graduate attributes policy, the university's policies on research-led teaching and the scholarship of teaching and online learning strategies. In all of these initiatives we have aligned the activities with the emerging university policies on teaching and learning, and, in particular, student-focused approaches to teaching and learning.

Discussion and conclusion

The University of Sydney has developed a quality assurance system, including processes and performance indicators, that is explicitly based on a student-focused theoretical model of teaching and learning. This is unusual in Australian universities. As the academic development unit of the university, the Institute for Teaching and Learning supports this quality assurance system and the university community in further improving the quality of teaching and learning. To do this the ITL has developed teaching evaluation systems and academic development initiatives which are also in alignment with the theoretical perspective of the university's quality assurance systems. This has several benefits, both for the institution and for the ITL.

The shared theoretical perspective underpinning academic development initiatives undertaken with individuals, course teams and faculties, means that the work of the ITL is aligned and congruent with institutional policies. Therefore ITL activities are more likely to be effective and efficient because they complement one another and they are supported by institutional initiatives, priorities and rewards. For example, issues raised with new staff in the context of the three-day induction programme may find synergies with the theoretical basis for faculty-wide initiatives to improve the first-year experience. The common underlying perspective means that staff can easily relate their own learning about student learning to such initiatives, and such initiatives are transparently related to university priorities.

The common theoretical stance allows the work of the ITL to be 'relational'. That is, it is more holistic and the separate elements are integrated in a whole, rather than being 'multistructural', or comprising discrete elements. Because of its central role, both in the university quality assurance processes and as a driver for curriculum development and teaching improvement, the ITL's teaching evaluation system is explicitly student-focused. Moreover, the different components of the system which are designed to provide feedback to different levels of the university community, are interrelated in terms of the shared perspective underpinning the various surveys. We have found that the explicit student focused perspective embodied in the teaching evaluation system provides a powerful mechanism for supporting the use of a shared perspective in academic development initiatives, both by the ITL and by colleagues working independently in the faculties.

In a climate of shrinking university resources, academic development units are often vulnerable to challenges as to their worth and efficacy, as evidenced by the closure in recent years of many such units in Australian universities. In much the same way that universities are being asked to demonstrate their effectiveness and relevance through quality assurance, academic development units must also be accountable for their activities. We have found that the use of a theoretical perspective to align our collaborative academic development work with individuals and faculties and with the institutional quality assurance processes has contributed to the improved perception by our academic colleagues of the relevance of such development work. It also provides a strategic basis for our prioritization of such work as well as ready access to a considerable body of research upon which to base such work.

Such a clear alignment with a single theoretical perspective might be seen by some to be unnecessarily restrictive. We have not found this to be the case. The student-focused perspective discussed in this paper is one that can accommodate a variety of models of learning – constructivism, collaborative learning, situated cognition, and models of learning communities. As such it is a broad perspective rather than a narrow theoretical base, and we have found it a helpful model in which to ground our work.

Key learning points

Senior staff

- Formulate teaching and learning policies with an explicit theoretical and conceptual perspective on what constitutes quality teaching and learning.

- Ensure that the senior academic manager responsible for developing and implementing institutional policies in teaching and learning has a scholarly understanding of key issues in teaching and learning.

Heads of department

- Recognise the value of, and engage with, the institution's teaching and learning policies and the systems and strategies designed to support the policies.
- Encourage the collaboration between academic staff and the university's academic development unit in the implementation of the institutional policies.
- Facilitate the engagement by departmental staff in the scholarship of teaching and learning.

Professional staff developers

- Reconceptualize the role of the unit as being an academic development unit working with the institution, its faculties and departments, in developing and implementing the institution's teaching and learning policies rather than being a staff development unit.
- Ensure that academic development policies and practices are informed by research and aligned with the institution's policies on teaching and learning.
- Work collegially with the academic departments/faculties and senior academic management to develop academic quality assurance and development systems aligned with the institution's teaching and learning policies.

References

Adams, J.C. (1997) *Championing 'Investors in People' in Higher Education*. Briefing Paper 46. Sheffield: HESDA.

Altbach, G. (1995) Problems and possibilities: the US academic profession, *Studies in Higher Education*, 20(1): 3–19.

Altbach, G. and Finkelstein, M. (1997) *The Academic Profession: The Professoriate in Crisis*. New York: Garland.

American Association of University Professors (1994) The work of faculty: expectations, priorities, and rewards, *Academe* (Jan./Feb.).

Anderson, G.L. and Herr, K. (1999) The New Paradigm Wars: Is there room for rigorous practitioner knowledge in schools and universities?, *Educational Researcher*, 28(5): 12–21, 40.

Anderson, J. (2000) Survey of CRS perceptions of career development at UEA and the Norwich Research Park. ResNet Report, Centre for Staff and Educational Development, University of East Anglia, Norwich.

Andresen, L. (1996) The work of academic development – occupational identity, standards of practice and the virtues of association, *International Journal for Academic Development*, 1(1): 38–49.

Arora, V.K. and Faraone, L. (2001) 21st century engineer-entrepreneur, in *Proceedings of the 2001 American Society for Engineering Education Annual Conference*. ASEE Annual Conference, Albuquerque, New Mexico, June 23–27, 2001.

Askling, B. and Stensaker, B. (2001) Quality as institutional development: A leadership issue? Paper presented at European Association for Institutional Research Conference, Porto, 9–12 September.

Aspin, D. and Chapman, J. (2000) Lifelong learning: concepts and conceptions, *International Journal of Lifelong Education*, 19(1): 2–19.

Balderson, S. (1997) *Investing in People: An Individual Perspective on a Collective Commitment and Achievement*. Briefing Paper 51. Sheffield: HESDA.

Baldwin, R. and Blackburn, R. (1981) The academic career as a developmental process, *Journal of Higher Education*, 52(6): 48–64.

Baldwin, T. and Ford, J. (1998) Transfer of training. A review and directions for future research, *Personnel Psychology*, 41(2): 63–105.

BankBoston Economics Department (1997). *MIT: The Impact of Innovation*. Available at www.mit.edu/newsoffice/founders (accessed 9 November 2002).

Bargh, C., Bocock, J., Scott, P. and Smith, D. (2000) *University Leadership: The Role of the Chief Executive*. Buckingham: SRHE/Open University Press.

Barlow, J. (1995) Releasing staff on projects, in A. Brew (ed.) *Directions in Staff Development*. Buckingham: SRHE/Open University Press.

Barnett, R. (1994) *The Limits of Competence*. Buckingham: SRHE/Open University Press.

Barnett, R. (1997) *Higher Education: A Critical Business*. Buckingham: SRHE/Open University Press.

Barrie, S. (2001) Reflections on student evaluation of teaching: Alignment and congruence in a changing context, in E. Santhanam (ed.) *Student Feedback on Teaching: Reflections and Projections. Proceedings of Australian Teaching Evaluation Forum*. Perth: University of Western Australia.

Bass, R. (1999) The Scholarship of Teaching: What's the Problem? *Inventio: Creative Thinking about Learning and Teaching* 1(1). http://www.doit.gmu.edu/Archives/feb98/randybass.htm (accessed 26 November 2002).

Baume, C. and Baume, D. (1996) A national scheme to develop and accredit university teachers, *International Journal of Academic Development* 1, (2) 51–8.

Baume, C., Martin, P. and Yorke, M. (eds) (2002) *Managing Educational Development Projects*. London: Kogan Page.

Beattie, A. (1997) *Working People and Lifelong Learning*. Leicester: NIACE.

Becher, T. (1989) *Academic Tribes and Territories: Intellectual Inquiry and the Cultures of Disciplines*. Buckingham: SRHE/Open University Press.

Becher, T. (1999) *Professional Practices: Commitment and Capability in a Changing Environment*. New Brunswick, NJ: Transaction Publishers.

Becher, T. and Trowler, P.R. (2001) *Academic Tribes and Territories*, 2nd edn. Buckingham: SRHE/Open University Press.

Beckhard, R. (1989) A model for the executive management of transformational change, in J.W. Pfeiffer (ed.) *The 1989 Annual: Developing Human Resources*. San Diego: University Associates Inc.

Bednarzik, R.W. (2000) The role of entrepreneurship in U.S. and European job growth, *Monthly Labor Review*, July, 3–13.

Beer, M., Spector, B., Lawrence, P.R., Quinn Mills, D. and Walton R.E. (eds) (1984) *Managing Human Assets*. New York: Free Press.

Beer, M., Spector, B., Lawrence, P.R., Quinn Mills, D. and Walton, R.E. (eds) (1985) *Human Resource Management: A General Manager's Perspective*. New York: Free Press.

Beetham, H. (2001) How do representations of our practice enable change to happen?, *Educational Developments*, 2(4): 19–22.

Beetham, H. (2002) Developing learning technology networks through shared representations of practice, in C. Rust (ed.) *Proceedings of the 9th International Improving Student Learning Symposium*. Oxford: Oxford Centre for Staff and Learning Development.

Beetham, H. and Bailey, P. (2002) Professional development for organizational change, in R. Macdonald and J. Wisdom (eds) *Academic and Educational Development: Research, Evaluation and Changing Practice in Higher Education*. London: Kogan Page.

Belanger, P. (1998) Learning society in the making, *Education for the 21st Century: Issues and Prospects*. Paris: UNESCO.

Bennett, S., Priest, A. and Macpherson, C. (1999) Learning about online learning: an approach to staff development for university teachers, *Australian Journal of Educational Technology*, 15(3): 207–21.

Benson, S. (2001) Defining the scholarship of teaching and learning in microbiology. Focus on microbiology education, *American Society for Microbiology Newsletter*, 7(3): 1–6.

Bergquist, W.H. (1992) *The Four Cultures of the Academy*. San Francisco: Jossey-Bass.

Bernstein, D. (1999) Project Report. Oral Presentation at the Carnegie Academy for the Scholarship of Teaching and Learning. Menlo Park, CA. June, 1999.

Bernstein, D.J. (2000) Bernstein Project Summary. *Peer Review of Teaching.* http://www.unl.edu/peerrev/bernstein/

Bett, M. (1999) *Independent Report into Pay and Conditions for Staff in Higher Education.* London: The Stationery Office.

Bhanot, R. and Fallows, S. (2002) ICT: a threat to the traditional university?, in S. Fallows and R. Bhanot (eds) *Educational Development through Information and Communications Technology.* London: Kogan Page.

Bhidé, A.V. (2000) *The Origin and Evolution of New Businesses.* New York: Oxford University Press.

Biggs, J.B. (1987) *The Study Process Questionnaire (SPQ) Users' Manual.* Hawthorne, Vic.: Australian Council for Educational Research.

Biggs, J. (1999) *Teaching for Quality Learning in Higher Education.* Buckingham: SRHE/Open University Press.

Bilimoria, D. and Fukami, F. (2002) The scholarship of teaching and learning in the management sciences: disciplinary style and content, in M.T. Huber and S.P. Morreale (eds) *Disciplinary Styles in the Scholarship of Teaching and Learning: Exploring Common Ground.* Washington, DC: American Association for Higher Education and Carnegie Foundation for the Advancement of Teaching.

Billett, S. (1999) Guided learning at work, in D. Boud and J. Garrick (eds) *Understanding Learning at Work.* London: Routledge.

Billett, S. (2002) Workplaces, communities and pedagogy: an activity theory view, in M. Lea and K. Nicoll (eds) *Distributed Learning: Social and Cultural Approaches to Practice.* London: RoutledgeFalmer.

Binney, G. (1992) *Making Quality Work: Lessons from Europe's Leading Companies.* London: The Economist Intelligence Unit with Ashridge Management Guides.

Blackmore, P. (1999) A categorisation of approaches to occupational analysis, *Journal of Vocational Education and Training,* 5(1): 61–76.

Blackmore, P. (2000) Some problems in the analysis of academic expertise, *Journal of Teacher Development,* 4(1): 45–63.

Blackmore, P. (2001) Accredited provision in research-intensive institutions. Unpublished paper, Standing Conference on Academic Practice, Warwick.

Blackmore, P., Gibbs, G. and Shrives, L. (1999) *Supporting Staff Development within Departments.* Oxford: Oxford Centre for Staff Development.

Blackmore, P., Roach, M. and Dempster, J.A. (2002) The use of ICT in education for research and development, in S. Fallows and R. Bhanot, R. (eds) *Educational Development through Information and Communications Technology.* London: Kogan Page.

Blackwell, R., Channel, J. and Williams, J. (2001) Teaching circles: a way forward for part-time teachers in higher education?, *International Journal for Academic Development,* 6(1): 40–53.

Blackwell, R. and McLean, M. (1996a) Peer observation of teaching and staff development, *Higher Education Quarterly,* 50(2): 156–71.

Blackwell, R. and McLean, M. (1996b) Mentoring new university teachers, *International Journal for Academic Development,* 1(1): 80–5.

Blackwell, R., and Preece, D. (2001) Changing higher education, *International Journal of Management Education,* 1(3): 4–14.

Blampied, N.M. (2001) University teacher accreditation in New Zealand and the Association of University Staff: a policy of watchful waiting, in D. Woodhouse (ed.) *The Profession of Tertiary Teaching: Contemporary International Debate on Accreditation.* AAU Series on Quality No. 7. Wellington: Academic Audit Unit.

Blyton, P. and Turnbull, P. (ed.) (1992) *Reassessing Human Resource Management.* London: Sage.

Booth, C. (1998) Final report of the Planning Group for Accreditation and Teaching in Higher Education, May 1998. Bristol: HEFCE.

Boud, D. (1995) Meeting the challenges, in A. Brew (ed.) *Directions in Staff Development.* Buckingham: SRHE/Open University Press.

Boud, D. (1999) Situating academic development in professional work: using peer learning, *Internal Journal for Academic Development,* 4(1): 3–10.

Boud, D. and McDonald, R. (1981) *Educational Development through Consultancy.* Guildford: SRHE.

Box, M. and Thackwray, R. (eds) (2002) *Effective Investors in People Assessment of Higher Education Institutions.* Sheffield: HESDA.

Boyer, E. (1990) *Scholarship Reconsidered: Priorities of the Professoriate.* Princeton, NJ: Carnegie Foundation for the Advancement of Teaching. Princeton University Press.

Boyer Commission on Educating Undergraduates in the Research University (1998) *Reinventing Undergraduate Education: A Blueprint for America's Research Universities.* Stony Brook, NY: State University of New York at Stony Book for the Carnegie Foundation for the Advancement of Teaching.

Boyer Commission (2001) Reinventing Undergraduate Education: Three Years After the Boyer Report. New York: Stony Brook University.

Brew, A. (ed.) (1995) *Directions in Staff Development.* Buckingham: SRHE/Open University Press.

Brew, A. and Boud, D. (1995) Teaching and research – establishing the vital link with learning, *Higher Education,* 29: 261–73.

Brewster, C. (1993) The integration of human resource management and corporate strategy: evidence from 14 countries. Paper presented at British Academy of Management, Milton Keynes, 20–22 September.

Brewster, C. and Hegewisch, A. (1994) *Policy and Practice in European Human Resource Management.* London: Routledge.

Brown, R. (2002) *What Should be the Role of Research in Higher Education?* Series on Learning, Teaching and Higher Education, 1, Working Paper No. 12. Southampton: Southampton Institute Academic Development Service.

Bryson, C. (1996) *The use of Fixed-Term Contracts in Higher Education – not such a flexible solution for all parties?* 14th Annual International Labour Process Conference, Aston University, 27–29 March.

Bryson, C. (1998) *Evidence to the Independent Review Committee: The Use of Short Term and Temporary Employment in UK Universities.* Nottingham: Nottingham Trent University.

Bryson, C. (1999) Contract research: the failure to address the real issues, *Higher Education Review,* 32(2): 29–50.

Buchanan, D. and Badham, R. (1999) *Power Politics and Organisational Change: Winning the Turf Game.* London: Sage.

Burgoyne, J. (1992) Creating a learning organisation, *RSA Journal,* 140, April: 321–36.

Calder, L., Cutler III, W.W. and Mills Kelly, T. (2002) History lessons: historians and the scholarship of teaching and learning, in M.T. Huber and S.P. Morreale (eds) *Disciplinary Styles in the Scholarship of Teaching and Learning: Exploring Common Ground.* Washington, DC: American Association for Higher Education and Carnegie Foundation for the Advancement of Teaching.

Cambridge, B.L. (2001) Fostering the scholarship of teaching and learning: communities of practice, in D. Lieberman and C. Wehlburg (eds) *To Improve the Academy,* Vol. 19. Bolton, MA: Anker.

Cambridge, B.L. (2002) Linking change initiatives: the Carnegie Academy for the Scholarship of Teaching and Learning in the company of other national projects, in D. Lieberman and C. Wehlburg (eds) *To Improve the Academy,* Vol. 20. Bolton, MA: Anker.

Candy, P. (1996) Promoting lifelong learning: academic developers and the university as a learning organization, *International Journal for Academic Development*, 1(1): 7–19.

Cervero, R.M. (2001) Continuing professional education in transition, *International Journal of Lifelong Education*, 20(1–2): 16–29.

Charney, A. and Libecap, G.D. (2000) *The Impact of Entrepreneurship Education: An Evaluation of the Berger Entrepreneurship Program at the University of Arizona, 1985–1999.* Tucson, AZ: Karl Eller Center, University of Arizona.

Chaston, I. (1994) Are British universities in a position to consider implementing total quality management?, *Higher Education Quarterly*, 48(2): 118–34.

Clark, P. (2000) The ILTHE: the Challenge and the Opportunity. Open Lecture, Open University, 22 February.

Clarke, B. (1983) *Higher Education Systems: Academic Organisation in Cross-national Perspectives.* Berkeley: University of California Press.

Coady T. (2000) Universities and the ideals of inquiry, in T. Coady (ed.) *Why Universities Matter.* Sydney: Allen & Unwin.

Coaldrake, P. and Stedman, L. (1998) *On the Brink: Australian Universities Confronting Their Future.* St Lucia: University of Queensland Press.

Collett, P. and Davidson, M. (1997) Renegotiation autonomy and accountability: the professional growth of developers in a South African institution, *International Journal for Academic Development*, 2(2): 28–34.

Commission of the European Communities (1994) *Competitiveness, Employment, Growth.* Luxembourg: Office for Official Publications.

Commission of the European Communities (1995) *Teaching and Learning: Towards the Learning Society.* Luxembourg: Office for Official Publications.

Committee of Vice-Chancellors and Principals *et al.* (1996) A concordat to provide a framework for the career management of contract research staff. Available from Universities UK.

Coopers & Lybrand, Institute of Education and Tavistock Institute (1996) *Evaluation of the Teaching and Learning Technology Programme.* Report M21/96. Bristol: Higher Education Funding Council for England. http://www.hefce.ac.uk/pubs/hefce/1996/m21_96.htm (accessed 9 November 2002).

Cranton, P. (1998) Effectiveness and ethics: three perspectives, *International Journal for Academic Development*, 3(2): 107–8.

Critten, P. (1993) *Investing in People: Towards Corporate Capability.* Oxford: Butterworth Heinemann.

D'Andrea, V. (2001) *Peer Review of Teaching in the USA.* York: LTSN Generic Centre. http://www.ltsn.ac.uk/genericcentre/ (accessed 9 November 2002).

D'Andrea, V. and Gosling, D. (2001) Joining the dots: reconceptualising educational development. *Active Learning*, 2(1): 64–80.

Daft, R.L. (1997) *Management.* Fort Worth, TX, 5th edition. Chicago: Dryden Press, 2000.

Dale, M. (2000) *Towards the End of Teaching? Innovative Methods in Teaching Adults Today.* Gothenburg: Nordic Folk Academy.

Daniel, J. (1993) The challenge of mass higher education, *Studies in Higher Education*, 18(2): 197–203.

Daniel, J. (1996) *Mega-universities and Knowledge Media: Technology Strategies for Higher Education.* London: Kogan Page.

Daniel, M.J. (2001) Institutional self evaluation: The development and use of internal audit teams, in M. Box and R. Thackwray (eds) HESDA 2001 *Investors in People in Higher Education* (2nd edn). Sheffield: HESDA.

Davies, J.L. (1996) *Higher Education Management Training and Development. Quality Indicators*. New Papers on Higher Education No. 18. Paris: UNESCO.

De Corte, E. (2000) Marrying theory building and the improvement of school practice, *Learning and Instruction*, 10: 249–66.

DeBats, D. and Ward, A. (1998) Degrees of difference: reshaping the university in Australia and the United States. Sydney: Australian Centre for American Studies.

Deem, R. and Johnson, R. (2000) Managerialism and university managers: building new academic communities or dismantling old ones?, in I. McNay (ed.) *Higher Education and its Communities*. Buckingham: SRHE/Open University Press.

Dempster, J.A. (2002a) Are institutions ready for collaborative learning on the web? *Interactions* 6(1). http://www.warwick.ac.uk/ETS/interactions/vol6no1/ed.htm (last accessed 27/8/02).

Dempster, J.A. (2002b) Developing and supporting research-based learning and teaching through technology. Chapter VII, pp. 128–158, in Ghaoui, C. (ed.) *Usability Evaluation of Online Learning Programs*. Hershey Idea Group Publishing, USA.

Dempster, J.A. and Blackmore, P. (2002) Developing research-based learning using ICT in HE curricula: the role of research and evaluation, in R. Macdonald and J. Wisdom (eds) *Academic and Educational Development: Research, Evaluation and Changing Practice in HE*. London: Kogan Page.

Department for Education and Employment (DfEE) (1995) *Employee Development Schemes: Developing a Learning Workforce*. London: DfEE.

Department for Education and Employment (DfEE) (1997) *Higher Education in the Learning Society (the Dearing Report)*. London: The Stationery Office.

Department for Education and Employment (DfEE) (1998) *The Learning Age: A Renaissance for a New Britain*, Cm 3790. London: The Stationery Office.

Department for Education and Skills (2000) *The Excellence Challenge*. Nottingham: DfES.

Department of Employment, Education, Training and Youth Affairs (1998) *Uniserve Australia. Background Report*. Canberra: Department of Employment, Education, Training and Youth Affairs.

Department of Trade and Industry (2000) *Excellence and opportunity – A Science and innovation Policy for the 21st century*, Cm 4814. London: The Stationery Office.

Devanna, M.A., Fombrun, C.J. and Tichy, N.M. (1984) A framework for strategic human resource management, in C.J. Fombrun, N.M. Tichy, and M.A. Devanna (eds) *Strategic Human Resource Management*. New York: Wiley.

Diamond, R.M. and Adam, B. (eds) (1995) *The Disciplines Speak: Rewarding the Scholarly, Professional, and Creative Work of Faculty*. Washington, DC: American Association for Higher Education.

Diamond, R.M. and Adam, B. (eds) (2000) *The Disciplines Speak II: More Statements on Rewarding the Scholarly, Professional, and Creative Work of Faculty*. Washington, DC: American Association for Higher Education.

Donald, J.G. (2002) *Learning to Think: Disciplinary Perspectives*. San Francisco: Jossey-Bass.

Duke, C. (2002) *Managing the Learning University*. Buckingham: SRHE/Open University Press.

Dumelow, C., Garnett, M. and Blackmore, P. (2000) *Career Development Provision for Contract Research Staff: A study of career-related needs, roles, responsibilities and current provision at four universities in the West Midlands Region*. Sheffield: UCoSDA.

Ehrmann, S. (2000) Technology and revolution in education: ending the cycle of failure, *Liberal Education*, Fall, 40–9. http://www.tltgroup.org/resources/V_Cycle_of_Failure.html (last accessed 27/8/02).

Ellington, H., Percival, F. and Race, P. (1993) *Handbook of Educational Technology*. London: Kogan Page.

Elliott, J. (1993) *Reconstructing Teacher Education*. Sussex: Falmer Press.

Elton, L. (1992) Research, teaching and scholarship in an expanding higher education system, *Higher Education Quarterly*, 46(3): 252–68.

Elton, L. (1995) An institutional framework, in A. Brew (ed.) *Directions in Staff Development*. Buckingham: SRHE/Open University Press.

Elton, L. and Partington, P. (1993) *Teaching Standards and Excellence in Higher Education*. Sheffield: CVCP/Universities Staff Development Unit.

Ember, L.R. (2000) Encouraging entrepreneurship. *Chemical and Engineering News*, 8 July.

Entwistle, N.J. (1981) *Styles of Learning and Teaching*. Chichester: Wiley.

Entwistle, N.J. (1997) Contrasting perspectives on learning, in F. Marton, D. Hounsell and N.J. Entwistle (eds) *The Experience of Learning*, 2nd edn. Edinburgh: Scottish Academic Press.

Entwistle, N., Thompson, S. and Tait, H. (1992) *Guidelines for Promoting Effective Learning in Higher Education*, Centre for Research on Learning and Instruction, University of Edinburgh.

Eraut, M. (2000) Non formal learning and tacit knowledge in professional work, *British Journal of Educational Psychology*, 70: 113–36.

Farnham, D. (ed.) (1999) *Managing Academic Staff in Changing University Systems*. Buckingham: SRHE/Open University Press.

Fenn, D. (2000) The profit-minded professor, *INC Magazine*, 16 May.

Finkelstein, M.J., Seal, R.K. and Schuster, J.H. (1998) *The New Academic Generation: A Profession in Transformation*. Baltimore, MD: Johns Hopkins University Press.

Fox, R. and Herrmann, A. (2000) Changing media, changing times: coping with adopting new educational technologies, in T. Evans and D. Nation (eds) *Changing University Teaching: Reflections on Creating Educational Technologies*. London: Kogan Page.

Fraser, K. (2001) Australasian academic developers' conceptions of the profession, *Internal Journal of Academic Development*, 6(1): 54–64.

Freidson, E. (1973) *The Professions and Their Prospects*. London: Sage.

Freidson, E. (1994) *Professionalism Reborn*. Cambridge: Polity Press.

French, W. and Bell, C. (1983) *Organization and Development: Behavorial Science Interventions for Organizational Improvement*. Englewood Cliffs, NJ: Prentice Hall.

Gallison, P. (1997) *Image and Logic: A Material Culture of Microphysics*. Chicago: University of Chicago Press.

Garavan, T.N. (1991) Strategic human resource development, *Journal of European Industrial Training* 15(1): 17–30.

Garavan, T.N., Heraty, N. and Morley, M. (1998) Actors in the HRD process, *International Studies of Management and Organisation*, 28(1): 11–35.

Garrison, R. and Andersen, T. (2000) Transforming and enhancing university teaching: stronger and weaker technological influences, in T. Evans and D. Nation (eds) *Changing University Teaching: Reflections on Creating Educational Technologies*. London: Kogan Page.

Gibbons, M., et al (1994) *The New Production of Knowledge: The Dynamics of Science and Research in Contemporary Societies*. London: Sage.

Gibbs, G. (1992) *Improving the Quality of Student Learning*. Oxford: Technical and Educational Services Limited.

Gibbs, G. (1996a) Preparing university teachers: an international overview of practices and issues. Paper presented at the Conference on Improving University Teaching, Nottingham.

Gibbs, G. (1996b) Supporting educational development within departments, *International Journal for Academic Development*, 1(1): 27–37.

Gibbs, G. (2000) Are the pedagogies of the disciplines really different?, in C. Rust (ed.) *Improving Student Learning through the Disciplines*. Oxford: Oxford Centre for Staff and Learning Development.

Gibbs, G. and Habeshaw, T. (2002) *Recognising and Rewarding Excellent Teaching*. Milton Keynes: TQEF National Co-ordination Team and Centre for Higher Education Practice.

Gibbs, G., Holmes, A. and Segal, R. (2002) *Funding Innovation and Disseminating New Teaching Practices*. Milton Keynes: TQEF National Co-ordination Team and Centre for Higher Education Practice.

Glassick, C.E., Huber, M.T. and Maeroff, G.I. (1997) *Scholarship Assessed: Evaluation of the Professoriate*. San Francisco: Jossey-Bass.

Gmelch, W. and Miskin, V. (1995) *Chairing an Academic Department*. Thousand Oaks, CA: Sage.

Gorard, S., Rees, G., Fevre, R. and Furlong, J. (1998) Learning trajectories: travelling towards a learning society, *International Journal of Lifelong Education*, 17(6): 400–10.

Gordon, G. (1999) *Interim Report of the UCoSDA Management Survey: An Overview of Good Practice*, in UCoSDA Mini-Conference Report.

Gordon, G. (2000) *The Strathclyde Journey to Recognition: Linking Mission and Strategic Objectives to Individual views and Aspirations*. Briefing Paper 80. HESDA.

Gordon, G., Durrani, T. and Sutherland, W. (2001) Developing the leaders for tomorrow: A case study. Paper presented at EAIR Conference, Porto, 10 September.

Gosling, D. (2001) Educational development units in the UK – what are they doing five years on?, *International Journal for Academic Development*, 6(1): 74–90.

Gosling, D. (2002) Models of peer observation of teaching and their implications. Birmingham: Key Note Address, Peer Observation of Teaching in HE conference, LTSN Generic Centre, 29 May 2002.

Gosling, D. and D'Andrea, V. (2002) How educational development/learning and teaching centres help HE institutions manage change, *Educational Developments*, 3(2): 1–3.

Griffiths, T. and Guile, D. (1999) Pedagogy in work-based contexts, in P. Mortimore (ed.) *Understanding Pedagogy and its Impact on Learning*. London: Paul Chapman.

Grossman, P.L., Wilson, S.M. and Shulman, L.S. (1989) Teachers of substance: subject matter knowledge for teaching, in M.C. Reynolds (ed.) *Knowledge Base for the Beginning Teacher*. New York: Pergamon Press.

Guest, D.E. (1987) Human resource management and industrial relations, *Journal of Management Studies*, 24(5): 503–21.

Guest, D.E. (1989) Personnel and HRM: can you tell the difference?, *Personnel Management*, January, 48–51.

Guest, D.E. (1992a) Employee commitment and control, in J.F. Hartley and G.M. Stephenson (ed.) *Employment Relations: The Psychology of Influence and Control at Work*. Oxford: Blackwell.

Guest, D.E. (1992b) Human resource management in the UK, in B. Towers (ed.) *The Handbook of Human Resource Management*. Oxford: Blackwell.

Halsey, A.H. (1992) *Decline of Donnish Dominion*. Oxford: Oxford University Press.

Hannan, A. and Silver, H. (2000) *Innovating in Higher Education: Teaching, Learning and Institutional Cultures*. Buckingham: SRHE/Open University Press.

Harvey, J. and Oliver, M. (2001) EFFECTS external evaluation. Unpublished project report.

Harvey, L. (1994) Continuous quality improvement: a system-wide view of quality in higher education, in P.T. Knight (ed.) *University-Wide Change, Staff and Curriculum Development*. SEDA Paper 83. Birmingham: Staff and Educational Development Association.

Harvey L. and Knight, P. (1996) *Transforming Higher Education*. Buckingham: SRHE/Open University Press.

Hattie, J. (2000) Performance indicators for the interdependence of research and teaching, in S. Paewai and G. Suddaby (eds) *Towards Understanding the Interdependence of Research and Teaching*. Palmerston North, New Zealand: Massey University.

Hattie, J. and Marsh, H.W. (1996) The relationship between research and teaching: a meta-analysis, *Review of Educational Research*, 66(4): 507–42.

Higher Education Funding Council for England, 2001a is *HEFCE* 01/40 Foundation degrees; report on refunded projects, June Bristol: *HEFCE*.

Higher Education Funding Council for England, 2001b is *HEFCE* News; Press release 19 October 2001. Bristol: *HEFCE*.

Henkel, M. (2000) *Academic Identities and Policy Change in Higher Education*. London: Jessica Kingsley.

HESDA (2001) *Investors in People in Higher Education* (Second Edition), Sheffield: HESDA.

HESDA (2002) *Senior Management Development: Eight Case Studies*. Sheffield: HESDA.

Hess, D.J. (1997) *Science Studies: An Advanced Introduction*. New York: New York University Press.

Hicks, O. (1997) Career paths of directors of academic staff development units in Australian universities: the emergence of a species?, *International Journal for Academic Development*, 2(2): 56–63.

Hicks, O. (1998) Challenging assumptions about effectiveness and ethics, *International Journal for Academic Development*, 3(2): 110–13.

Hicks, O. (1999) Integration of central and departmental development – reflections from Australian universities, *International Journal for Academic Development*, 4(1): 43–51.

Higher Education Funding Council for England (1998) *An Evaluation of the Computers in Teaching Initiative and the Teaching and Learning Technology Support Network* (chair Atkins). Report 98/47. Bristol: HEFCE.

Higher Education Funding Council for England (2000) *Rewarding and Developing Staff in Higher Education*. HEFCE Consultation 00/56. Bristol: HEFCE.

Higher Education Funding Council for England (2001a) *Widening Participation*. www.hefce.ac.uk (accessed 18 November 2001).

Higher Education Funding Council for England (2001b) *Widening Participation*. www.hefce.ac.uk (accessed 27 November 2001).

Higher Education Staff Development Agency (2001) *Top Management Programme Prospectus*. Sheffield: HESDA.

Higher Education Staff Development Agency (forthcoming) Senior Managers' Project: Case-Studies of Practice. Sheffield: HESDA.

THETO (1999) *Labour Market Information Project: A Survey of Human Resource Development, Qualifications and Skills within the Higher Education Sector*. Sheffield: THETO.

THETO (2000a) *National Occupational Standards for Higher Education Managers and Administrators*, Sheffield: THETO.

Hodkinson, P. and Isitt, M. (eds) (1995) *The Challenge of Competence*. London: Cassell.

Holley, D. and Oliver, M. (2000) Pedagogy and new power relationships, *International Journal of Management Education*, 1(1): 11–21.

Hounsell, D. (1994) Educational development, in J. Bocock and D. Watson, *Managing the University Curriculum: Making Common Cause*. Buckingham: SRHE/Open University Press.

House, D. and Watson, D. (1995) Managing change, in D. Warner and E. Crosthwaite (eds) *Human Resource Management in Higher and Further Education*, pp. 9–19. Buckingham: SRHE/Open University Press.

Huber, M.T. and Morreale, S.P. (eds) (2002) *Disciplinary Styles in the Scholarship of Teaching and Learning: Exploring Common Ground*. Washington DC: American Association for Higher Education and Carnegie Foundation for the Advancement of Teaching.

Hudson Institute, Inc. (1999) Mechanical engineering in the 21st Century: Trends impacting the profession. Report prepared for the Committee on Issues Identification, Council on Public Affairs, American Society of Mechanical Engineering.

Hughes, C. and Tight, M. (1995) Linking university teaching and research, *Higher Education Review*, 28(1): 51–65.

Hughes, P. (1999) *Appraisal in UK Higher Education*. Bristol: University of Bristol.

Humboldt, W. (1970) On the spirit and the organizational framework of intellectual institutions in Berlin, *Minerva*, 8: 242–67. (Original work published 1809.)

Hutchings, P. (1996) *Making Teaching Community Property. A Menu for Peer Collaboration and Peer Review*. Washington DC: American Association for Higher Education.

Hutchings, P. (ed.) (1998) *The Course Portfolio: How Faculty Can Examine Their Teaching to Advance Practice and Improve Student Learning*. Washington, DC: The American Association for Higher Education.

Hutchings, P. (ed.) (2000) *Opening Lines: Approaches to the Scholarship of Teaching and Learning*. Menlo Park, CA: The Carnegie Foundation for the Advancement of Teaching.

Hutchings, P. (2001) The scholarship of teaching and learning: What it's not; what it is. Handout for CASTL Residency, June.

Hutchings, P. and Shulman, L.S. (1999) The scholarship of teaching: new elaborations, new developments, *Change*, 31(5): 10–15.

Hyland, T. (1996) Professionalism, ethics and work-based learning, *British Journal of Educational Studies*, 44(2): 168–80.

Institute for Learning and Teaching (1999) *ILTHE Consultation: The national framework for higher education teaching*. York: ILTHE.

Jacobs, D. (2000) A chemical mixture of methods, in P. Hutchings (ed.) *Opening Lines: Approaches to the Scholarship of Teaching and Learning*. Menlo Park, CA: Carnegie Foundation for the Advancement of Teaching.

James, R. (1997) An organisational learning perspective on academic development: a strategy for an uncertain future, *International Journal for Academic Development* 2(2): 35–41.

Jenkins, A. (1996) Discipline-based Educational development, *International Journal for Academic Development*, 1(1): 50–62.

Jenkins, A., Blackman, T., Lindsay, R. and Paton Salzberg, R. (1998) Teaching and research: student perspectives and policy implications, *Studies in Higher Education*, 3(2): 127–41.

Jensen, J.J. (1988) Research and teaching in the universities of Denmark: does such an interplay really exist?, *Higher Education*, 17(1): 17–26.

Johnston, I. and Peat, M. (1998) *UniService Science. Final Report to CUTSD 1995–1997*. Department of Employment, Education, Training and Youth Affairs, Australia.

Joint Negotiating Committee for Higher Education Staff (2002) *Fixed-Term and Casual Employment. Guidance for Higher Education Institutions*. London: JNCHES.

Karmel, P. (2000) Funding universities, in T. Coady (ed.) *Why Universities Matter*. Sydney: Allen & Unwin.

Keep, E. and Sisson, K. (1992) Owning the problem: personnel issues in higher education policy making in the 1990s, *Oxford Review of Economic Policy*, 8(2): 67–78.

Keep, E., Storey, J. and Sisson, K. (1996) Managing the employment relationship in higher education: quo vadis?, in C. Cuthbert (ed.) *Working in Higher Education*. Buckingham: SRHE/Open University Press.

Kelly, T. (1992) *A History of Adult Education in Great Britain*. Liverpool: Liverpool University Press.

Kennedy, H. (1997) *Learning Works: Widening Participation in Further Education*. Coventry: Further Education Funding Council.

Kinman, G. (1998) *Pressure Points. A Survey into the Causes and Consequences of Occupational Stress in UK Academic and Related Staff*. London: Association of University Teachers.

Kirsch, G. (1992) Methodological pluralism: epistemological issues, in G. Kirsch and P. Sullivan (ed.) *Methods and Methodology in Composition Research*. Carbondale: Southern Illinois University Press.

Knapper, C. (1998) Is academic development a profession?, *International Journal for Academic Development*, 3(2): 93–6.

Knight, P. (2002a) A systemic approach to professional development: learning as practice, *Teaching and Teacher Education*, 18: 229–41.

Knight, P. (2002b) *Being a Teacher in Higher Education*. Buckingham: SRHE/Open University Press.

Knight, P. and Trowler, P. (1999) It takes a village to raise a child: mentoring and the socialisation of new entrants into the academic professions, *Mentoring and Tutoring*, 7(1): 23–34.

Knight, P. and Trowler, P. (2000) Department-level cultures and the improvement of learning and teaching, *Studies in Higher Education*, 25(1): 69–83.

Knight, P. and Trowler, P.R. (2001) *Departmental Leadership in Higher Education*. Buckingham: SRHE/Open University Press.

Knight, P. and Wilcox, S. (1998) Effectiveness and ethics in educational development: changing context, changing notions, *International Journal for Academic Development*, 3(2): 97–106.

Kogan, M. and Hanney, S. (2000) *Reforming Higher Education*. London: Jessica Kingsley.

Kogan, M., Moses, I. and El-Khawas, E. (1994) *Staffing Higher Education: Meeting New Challenges*. Paris: OECD.

Kotter, J. (1990) *A Force for Change: How Leadership Differs from Management*. New York: Free Press.

Kouwenburg, A. and Thackwray, R. (1999) *Nijmegen University Project Report: UFB*. (VSNU Netherlands).

Kubr, M. (ed.) (1986) *Management Consulting*. A guide to the profession. Second Edition. Geneva: International Labour Organization.

Kuutti, K. (1997) Activity theory as a potential framework for human–computer interaction research, in B. Nardi (ed.) *Context and Consciousness: Activity Theory and Human–Computer Interaction*. Cambridge, MA: MIT Press.

Land, R. (2001) Agency, context and change in academic development, *International Journal for Academic Development*, 6(1): 4–20.

Langley, J. (2000) Working with multiple partners in social work, in T. Bourner, T. Katz and D. Watson (eds) *New Directions in Professional Higher Education*. Buckingham: SRHE/Open University Press.

Lave, J. and Wenger, E. (1991) *Situated Learning: Legitimate Peripheral Participation*. Cambridge: Cambridge University Press.

Laycock, M. (1997) QUILTHE – A whole Institution Approach to Quality Improvement in Learning and Teaching in Higher Education, in S. Armstrong, G. Thompson and S. Brown (eds) *Facing up to Radical Changes in Universities and Colleges*. London: Kogan Page.

Learning and Teaching Support Network (2001) What is the LTSN? www.ltsn.ac.uk/index.asp?id=8 (accessed 26 November 2002).

Learning Works (2001) *Learning Works' Annual Report, 1999/2000*. Glasgow: University of Glasgow.

Lee, C. (1999) *Learning from Employee Development Schemes*. Employment Brief No. 41. Institute for Employment Studies.

Lee, M. (2001) A refusal to define HRD, *Human Resource Development International*, 4(3): 327–42.

Legge, K. (1978) *Power, Innovation and Problem Solving in Personnel Management*. London: McGraw-Hill.

Legge, K. and Exley, M. (1975) Authority, ambiguity and adaptation: the personnel specialist's dilemma, *Industrial Relations Journal*, 6(1).

Lewis, G. (2001) Support for the development of e-learning resources. *Interactions* 5(2). http://www.warwick.ac.uk/ETS/interactions/vol5no2/lewis.htm (last accessed 27 August 2002).

Lewis, K.G. (1996) Faculty development in the United States: a brief history, *International Journal for Academic Development*, 1(2): 26–33.

Lifelong Learning News (2001) Secretary of State sets out a vision, *Lifelong Learning News*, issue 2, Summer.

Luby, A. (1997) *Towards an Accreditation System for Professional Development for Academic Practice in Higher Education, Volume 1: The Project Report*. Sheffield: UCoSDA.

Lumsdaine, E., Lumsdaine, M. and Shelnutt, J.W. (1999) *Creative Problem Solving and Engineering Design*. New York: McGraw-Hill.

Maclachlan, K. (1999) *Learning Works: A View from Within. A Survey of Management Staff at the University of Glasgow*. Glasgow: University of Glasgow.

Maclachlan, K. (2000) Learning Works – Employee Development in the University of Glasgow, in *Work-Based Learning Opportunities (WBL) in Higher Education*. Sheffield: THETO.

Maclachlan, K. (2001) Better than bingo: Tipping the balance towards participation in workplace learning. Unpublished MPhil dissertation, University of Glasgow.

Magin, D.J. (1998) Rewarding good teaching: a matter of demonstrated proficiency or documented achievement?, *International Journal for Academic Development*, 3(2): 124–35.

Malcolm, J. and Zukas, M. (2000) Becoming an educator: communities of practice in higher education, in I. McNay (ed.) *Higher Education and Its Communities*. Buckingham: SRHE/Open University Press.

Marchese, T. (1991) TQM reaches the academy, *Bulletin of the American Association for Higher Education*, 44: 3–14.

Marginson, S. and Considine, M. (2000) *The Enterprise University: Power, Governance and Reinvention in Australia*. Cambridge: Cambridge University Press.

Martin, E. (1999) *Changing Academic Work*. Buckingham: SRHE/Open University Press.

Maslen, G. (2002) Stress hits half down under, *Times Higher Education Supplement*, 26 July: 9.

Mason, R. (2002) E-learning: what have we learnt? in C. Rust (ed.) *Proceedings of the 9th International Improving Student Learning Symposium*. Oxford: Oxford Centre for Staff and Learning Development.

Matheson, C. (1981) *Staff Development Matters*. London: Co-ordinating Committee for the Training of University Teachers.

Mattson, J. and Simon, M. (1996) *The Pioneers of NMR and Magnetic Resonance in Medicine: The Story of MRI*. Bar-Ilan UP in Jericho, Israel and Dean Books, New York.

Mazur, E. (1997) *Peer Instruction*. Upper Saddle River, NJ: Prentice Hall.

McConnell, D. (1999) Guest editorial: networked learning. *Journal of Computer Assisted Learning*, 15(3): 177–8.

McCracken, M. and Wallace, M. (2000) Towards a redefinition of Strategic HRD, *Journal of European Industrial Training* 24(5): 281–90.

McGoldrick, J., Stewart, J. and Watson, S. (2001) Theorising human resource development, *Human Resource Development International*, 4(3): 343–56.

McInnis, C. (1992) Change in the nature of academic work, *Australian Universities' Review*, 35(2): 9–12 FAUSA.

McInnis, C. (1996) Change and diversity in the work patterns of Australian academics, *Higher Education Management*, 8(2): 105–17.

McInnis, C. (1998) Academics and professional administrators in Australian universities: dissolving boundaries and new tensions, *Journal of Higher Education Policy and Management*, 20(2): 161–73.

McInnis, C. (2000a) Changing academic work roles: the everyday realities challenging quality in teaching, *Quality in Higher Education*, 6(2): 143–52.

McInnis, C. (2000b) *The Work Roles of Academics in Australian Universities*. Canberra: Department of Education, Training and Youth Affairs.

McInnis, C. (2000c) Towards new balance or new divides? The changing work roles of academics in Australia, in M. Tight (ed.) *International Perspectives on Higher Education Research*. London: JAI/Elsevier.

McInnis, C. (2001) Promoting academic expertise and authority in an entrepreneurial culture, *Higher Education Management*, 13(2): 45–55.

McMahon, A. (2000) The development of professional intuition, in T. Atkinson and G. Claxton (eds) *The Intuitive Practitioner: On the Value of Not Always Knowing What One Is Doing*. Buckingham: Open University Press.

McNay, I. (1993) The evolving university: four cultural models. Paper presented at EAIR Conference, Turku, Finland, August.

McNay, I. (1995) From the collegial academy to corporate enterprise: the changing cultures of universities, in T. Schuller (ed.) *The Changing University?* Buckingham: SRHE/Open University Press.

Metcalfe, H. (1992) *Releasing Potential. Company Initiatives to Develop People at Work*, Vols 1 & 2. Sheffield: Department of Employment.

Meyerson, D. and Scully, M. (1995) Tempered radicalism and the politics of ambivalence and change, *Organisation Science*, 6(5).

Middlehurst, R. (1991) The changing roles of university managers and leaders: implications for preparation and development. Sheffield: CVCP/USDTU.

Middlehurst, R. (1993) *Leading Academics*. Buckingham: SRHE/Open University Press.

Middlehurst, R. and Barnett, R. (1994) Changing the subject: the organization of knowledge and academic culture, in J. Bocock and D. Watson (eds) *Managing the University Curriculum: Making Common Cause*. Buckingham: SRHE/Open University Press.

Middlehurst, R. and Garrett, R. (2001) Interim Report to HESDA of survey on senior management development in UK Higher Education. HESDA, Sheffield.

Mills, D.Q. and Friesen, B. (1992) The Learning Organisation, *European Management Journal*, 10(2): 146–56 (June).

Mintzberg, H. (1978) Patterns in strategy formation, *Management Science*, 24(9): 934–48.

Morreale, S.P., Applegate, J.L., Wulff, D.H. and Sprague, J. (2002) The scholarship of teaching and learning in communication studies, and communication scholarship in the process of teaching and learning, in M.T. Huber and S.P. Morreale (eds) *Disciplinary Styles in the Scholarship of Teaching and Learning: Exploring Common Ground*. Washington, DC: American Association for Higher Education and Carnegie Foundation for the Advancement of Teaching.

Moses, I. (1987) Educational development units: a cross-cultural perspective, *Higher Education*, 16: 449–79.

Moses, I. (1990) Teaching, research and scholarship in different disciplines, *Higher Education*, 19(3): 351–76.

Moses, I. and Roe, E. (1990) *Heads and Chairs. Managing Academic Departments*. St Lucia: University of Queensland Press.

Murray, R. (2001) Integrating teaching and research through development for students and staff, *Active Learning in Higher Education*, 2(1): 31–45.

National Advisory Group for Continuing Education and Lifelong Learning (1997) *Learning for the Twenty-First Century* (the Fryer Report). London: NAGCELL.

National Committee of Inquiry into Higher Education (1997) *Higher Education in the Learning Society*. (Chair Sir Ron Dearing.) London: HMSO.

Neave, G. and van Vught, F. (ed.) (1991) *Prometheus Bound. The Changing Relationship between Government and Higher Education in Western Europe*. Exeter: BPCC Wheatons.

Neumann, R. (1992) Perceptions of the teaching–research nexus: a framework for analysis, *Higher Education*, 23(2):159–71.

Neumann, R. (1994) The teaching–research nexus: applying a framework to university students' learning experiences, *European Journal of Education*, 29(3): 323–39.

Newman, J.H. (1852) *The Idea of a University*, Notre Dame, Indiana: University of Notre Dame Press.

Nicholls, G. (2001) *Professional Development in Higher Education*. London: Kogan Page.

Nixon, J. (1996) Professional identity and the restructuring of higher education, *Studies in Higher Education*, 21(1): 5–16.

Nixon, J. (2000) A new professionalism for higher education, in G. Nicholls (ed.) *Professional Development in Higher Education*. London: Kogan Page.

Nummedal, S.G., Benson, J.B. and Chew, S.L. (2002) Disciplinary styles in the scholarship of teaching and learning: a view from psychology, in M.T. Huber and S.P. Morreale (eds) *Disciplinary Styles in the Scholarship of Teaching and Learning: Exploring Common Ground*. Washington, DC: American Association for Higher Education and Carnegie Foundation for the Advancement of Teaching.

Oliver, M. (2002) What do learning technologists do?, *Innovations in Education and Teaching International*, 39(4): 1–8.

Organization for Economic Co-operation and Development (1996) *Lifelong Learning for All*. Paris: OECD.

Organization for Economic Co-operation and Development (1998) *Combating Social Exclusion through Adult Learning*. Paris: OECD.

Parker, S. (1998) The wider context of continuing education, in F. Quinn (ed.) *Continuing Professional Development in Nursing*. Cheltenham: Stanley Thornes.

Parsons, D., Cocks, N. and Rowe, V. (1998) *The Role of Employee Development Schemes in Increasing Learning at Work*. Research Report No. 73. London: Department for Education and Employment.

Parsons, T. (1954) The professions and social structure, in T. Parsons (ed.) *Essays in Sociological Theory*, rev. edn. Glencoe, IL: Free Press.

Partington, P. (1994) Human resource management and development in higher education. Paper presented at Quinquennial Conference of the Conference of European Rectors, Budapest. Sheffield: UCoSDA.

Payne, J. (1996) Lifetime learning and job-related training: The twin pillars of employee development, *Adults Learning*, June.

Pearson, A. (2002) Web-based staff development, *Educational Developments*, 3(2): 17. http://www.seda.demon.co.uk/eddevs/vol3/sd.html (accessed 27 August 2002).

Pedler, M., Boydell, T. and Burgoyne, J. (1991) *The Learning Company: A Strategy for Sustainable Development*. Maidenhead: McGraw-Hill.

Pennington, G. (1999) Towards a new professionalism: accrediting higher education teaching, in H. Fry, S. Ketteridge and S. Marshall (eds) *A Handbook for Teaching and Learning in Higher Education*. London: Kogan Page.

Perkin, H. (1989) *The Rise of Professional Society: England since 1880*. London: Routledge.

Pettigrew, A. (1985) *The Awakening Giant: Continuity and Change at ICI*. Oxford: Blackwell.

Pettigrew, A.M. (1992) The character and significance of strategy process research, *Strategic Management Journal*, 13, Special Issue: 5–16.

Phillips, R. (ed.) (2001) Learning-centred Evaluation of Computer-Facilitated Learning Projects in Higher Education. Perth: Murdoch University. http://cleo.murdoch.edu.au/projects/cutsd99/ (last accessed 26 November 2002).

Pickard, J. (1991) What does the 'Investors in People' award really mean?, *Personnel Management Plus*, 2(3): 18–19.

Piper, D.W. (1993) *Quality Management in Universities*. University of Queensland: Australian Government Publishing Service. Canberra: Department of Employment, Education and Training.

Pitkethly, A. and Prosser, M. (2001) The First Year Experience Project: a model for University wide change, *Higher Education Research and Development*, 20: 185–98.

Planet Research (1999) *Satisfaction at Work*. London: Investors in People UK.

Porter, M. (1980) *Competitive Strategy: Techniques for Analysing Industries and Competitors*. New York: Free Press.

Porter, M. (1981) The contributions of industrial organisations to strategic management, *Academy of Management Review*, 6(4): 609–20.

Porter, M. (1985) *Competitive Advantage: Creating and Sustaining Superior Performance*. New York: Free Press.

Prosser, M. and Trigwell, K. (1999) *Understanding Learning and Teaching: The Experience in Higher Education*. Buckingham: SRHE/Open University Press.

Quality Assurance Agency (1999a) Subject Review Report: University of Sussex, Molecular Biosciences. http://www.qaa.ac.uk/revreps/subjrev/All/q68_00.pdf (accessed 14 September 2001).

Quality Assurance Agency (1999b) Subject Review Report: King's College London, Nursing, Midwifery and Gerontology. http://www.qaa.ac.uk/revreps/subjrev/All/q114_99.pdf (accessed 14 September 2001).

Ramsden, B. (2001) *Patterns of higher education institutions in the UK*. London: Universities UK.

Ramsden, P. (1991) A performance indicator of teaching quality in higher education: The Course Experience Questionnaire, *Studies in Higher Education*, 16: 129–50.

Ramsden, P. (1998) *Learning to Lead in Higher Education*. London: RoutledgeFalmer.

Ramsden, P. (2003) *Learning to Teach in Higher Education*, 2nd edn. London: RoutledgeFalmer.

Research Careers Initiative Strategy Group (1998) *RCI Report*. London: Office of Science and Technology and Universities UK.

Research Careers Initiative Strategy Group (2000) *RCI Report*. London: Office of Science and Technology and Universities UK.

Research Careers Initiative Strategy Group (2001) *RCI Third (Interim) Report*. London: Office of Science and Technology and Universities UK.

Roberts, Sir Gareth (2002) *SET for Success: The Supply of People with Science, Technology, Engineering and Mathematics Skills*. London: HM Treasury.

Reynolds, P., Hay, M. and Camp, S.M. (1999) Global Entrepreneurship Monitor. Executive Report. Ewing Marion Kauffman Foundation, Center for Entrepreneurial Leadership.

Rhoades, G. (1997) *Managed Professionals: Restructuring Academic Labor in Unionised Institutions*. Albany: State University of New York Press.

Rix, A., Parkinson, R. and Gaunt, R. (1994) *Investors in People: A Qualitative Study of Employers*. Research Series Report No. 21, January. Moorfoot, Sheffield: Research Strategy Branch, Department of Employment.

Roach, M., Blackmore, P. and Dempster, J. (2001) Supporting high level learning through research-based methods: a framework for course development, *Innovations in Education and Training International*, 38(4): 369–82.

Rose, J. (2001) *The Intellectual Life of the British Working Classes*. New Haven, CT and London: Yale University Press.

Rust, C. (1998) The impact of educational development workshops on teachers' practice, *International Journal for Academic Development*, 3(1): 72–80.

Salaman, G., Cameron, S., Hamblin, H., Iles, P., Mabey, C. and Thompson, K. (eds) (1992) *Human Resource Strategies*. London, Sage, in association with the Open University.

Salem, A. and Michael, R. (2002) Calculus conversations: Making student thinking visible. A Scholarship of Teaching and Learning Project for the Carnegie Foundation for the Advancement of Teaching. http://cte.rockhurst.edu/carnegie_project/index.htm (accessed 26 November 2002).

Sallis, E. and Jones, G. (2002) *Knowledge Management in Education: Enhancing Learning and Education*. London: Kogan Page.

Salvatori, M.R. (2000) Difficulty: the great educational divide, in P. Hutchings (ed.) *Approaches to the Scholarship of Teaching and Learning*. Menlo Park, CA: The Carnegie Foundation for the Advancement of Teaching.

Sargant, N. (2000) *The Learning Divide Revisited*. Leicester: National Institute of Adult Continuing Education.

Sawbridge, M. (1996) *A Politics and Organisational Complexity of Staff Development for Academics: A Discussion Paper*. Sheffield: UCoSDA.

Schon, D. (1983) *The Reflective Practitioner: How Professionals Think in Action*. New York: Basic Books.

Schuetze, H.G. and Slowey, M. (2000) Traditions and new directions in higher education. A comparative perspective on non-traditional students and lifelong learners, in H.G. Schuetze and M. Slowey (eds) *Higher Education and Lifelong Learners. International Perspectives on Change*. London: RoutledgeFalmer.

Schwab, J. (1964) Structure of the disciplines: meanings and significances, in G.W. Ford and L. Pugno (eds) *The Structure of Knowledge and the Curriculum*. Chicago: Rand McNally.

Scott, I. (2001) Imperatives and stumbling blocks in professionalising higher education in a developing country: a view from the South. Paper presented at the Second Annual Conference of the ILTHE, York.

Scott, P. (1995) *The Meanings of Mass Higher Education*. Buckingham: SHRE/Open University Press.

Scott, P. (2000) The death of mass higher education and the birth of lifelong learning, in J. Field and M. Leicester (eds) *Lifelong Learning: Education across the Lifespan*. London: RoutledgeFalmer.

Senge, P.E. (1993) *The Fifth Discipline*. London: Century.

Seymour, E. (2001) Tracking the processes of change in US undergraduate education in science, mathematics, engineering, and technology, *Science Education*, 86: 79–105.

Shulman, L.S. (1987) Knowledge and teaching: foundations of the New Reform, *Harvard Educational Review*, 57(1): 1–22.

Shulman, L.S. (1999) Taking learning seriously, *Change*, July/August: 11–17.

Sisson, K. (ed.) (1989) *Personnel Management in Britain*. Oxford: Basil Blackwell.

Slowey, M. (ed.) (1995) *Implementing Change from within Universities and Colleges*. London: Kogan Page.

Smith, G. (1992) A categorisation of models of staff development in higher education, *British Journal of Educational Technology*, 23: 39–47.

Smith, G. (1902) 'Responsibility for staff development', *Studies In Higher Education*, 17(1), 27–41.

Smith, H. and Oliver, M. (2002) University teachers' attitudes to the impact of innovations in ICT on their practice, in C. Rust (ed.) *Proceedings of the 9th International Improving Student Learning Symposium*. Oxford: Oxford Centre for Staff and Learning Development.

Smith, J. and Oliver, M. (2000) Academic development: a framework for embedding learning technology, *International Journal of Academic Development*, 5(2), 129–37.

Snell, S. (2001) *Employee Development Schemes in Higher Education Institutions*. Sheffield: Higher Education Staff Development Association.

Sporn, B. (1999) *Adaptive University Structures*. London: Jessica Kingsley.

Stace, D.A. and Dunphy, D.C. (1991) Beyond traditional paternalistic and developmental approaches to organizational change and human resource strategies, *International Journal of Human Resource Management*, 2(3): 263–83.

Storey, J. (ed.) (1989) *New Perspectives on Human Resource Management*. London: Routledge.

Storey, J. (1992) *Developments in the Management of Human Resources: An Analytical Review*. Oxford: Blackwell.

Sveiby, K. (1992) The knowledge company: strategy formulation in knowledge-intensive industries, *International Review of Strategic Management*, 3: 37–48.

Swinnerton-Dyer, P. (1991) Policy on higher education and research, the Rede Lecture 1991, *Higher Education Quarterly*, 45(3): 204–18.

Sykes, C.L. (1988) *Profscam: Professors and the Demise of Higher Education*. Washington DC: Regnery Gateway.

Tamkin, P. and Hillage, J. (1999) *Employability and Employers: the Missing Piece of the Jigsaw*. IES Report 361. Brighton: Institute for Employment Studies.

Tann, J. (1995) The learning organization, in D. Warner and E. Crosthwaite (eds) *Human Resource Management in Higher and Further Education*, pp. 44–55. Buckingham: SRHE/Open University Press.

Taylor, P. (1999) *Making Sense of Academic Life*. Buckingham: SRHE/Open University Press.

Taylor, P. and Thackwray, R. (2001a) *Investors in People Explained*, 4th edn. London: Kogan Page.

Taylor, P. and Thackwray, R. (2001b) *Investors in People Maintained*, 2nd edn. London: Kogan Page.

Taylor, P. and Thackwray, R. (2001c) *Managing for Investors in People*, 2nd edn. London: Kogan Page.

Tennant, M. (1999) Is learning transferable?, in D. Boud and J. Garrick (eds) *Understanding Learning at Work*. London: Routledge.

Thackwray, B. (1994) *University Staff: A Worthwhile Investment?*, in P.T. Knight (ed.) *University-Wide Change, Staff and Curriculum Development*. SEDA Paper 83. Birmingham: Staff and Educational Development Association.

Thackwray, B. (1997) *The Effective Evaluation of Training and Development in Higher Education*. London: Kogan Page.

Thackwray, R. (1998) *Investors in People in Universities and Colleges*. London: Investors in People UK.

Thackwray, R. (2000) *The 'New' National Investors in People Standard*. UCoSDA Briefing Paper 78. Sheffield: UCoSDA.

THETO (1999) *Labour Market Information Project: A Survey of Human Resource Development, Qualifications and Skills within the Higher Education Sector*. Sheffield: THETO.

THETO (2000a) *National Occupational Standards for Higher Education Managers and Administrators*, Sheffield: THETO.

THETO (2000c) Higher Education Qualification and Standards Frameworks: A project funded by the Qualifications and Curriculum Authority.

Thorne, M. and Cuthbert, R. (1996) Autonomy, bureaucracy and competition: the ABC of control in higher education, in R. Cuthbert (ed.) *Working in Higher Education*. Buckingham: SRHE/Open University Press.

Tichy, N.M., Fombrun, C.J. and Devanna, M.A. (1982) Strategic human resource management, *Sloan Management Review* 23(2): 47–61.

Timmons, Jeffry A. (1999) *New Venture Creation: Entrepreneurship for the 21st Century*. IRWIN/McGraw-Hill.

Tobias, S. (1990) *They're Not Dumb, They're Different: Stalking the Second Tier*. Tucson, AZ: Research Corporation.

Trow, M. (1974) *Problems in the Transition from Elite to Mass Higher Education*. Paris: OECD.

Trow, M. (1994) Managerialism and the academic profession: the case of England, *Higher Education Policy*, 7(2).

Trowler, P., Saunders, M., and Knight, P. (2003) *Change Thinking, Change Practices*. York: LTSN Generic Centre.

Tuckett, A. and Sargant, N. (1999) *Marking Time: The NIACE Survey on Adult Participation in Learning 1999*. Leicester: NIACE.

United Nations Educational, Scientific, and Cultural Organization (1972) Learning to Be: the world of education today and tomorrow (Fauré report). Paris: UNESCO.

Universities' and Colleges' Staff Development Agency (1994) *Higher Education Management and Leadership: Towards a National Framework for Preparation and Development*. Sheffield: UCoSDA.

Universities' and Colleges' Staff Development Agency (2000) UCoSDA *Survey of Central Staff Development Units, Final Report*. Sheffield: HESDA.

Universities UK (2001a) *Higher Education. Facts and Figures*. London: Universities UK.

Universities UK (2001b) Universities UK statement on widening participation. www.universitiesuk.ac.uk/insight/show.asp?sp=3 (accessed 17 November 2001).

Upton, N., Sexton, D. and Moore, C. (1995) Have we made a difference? An examination of career activity of entrepreneurial majors since 1981. Houston, Texas: Working paper, Baylor University. Available from http://hsb.baylor.edu/cel/ifb/research/babpap.htm.

Van de Ven, A.H. (1992). Suggestions for studying strategy process: a research note, *Strategic Management Journal*, 13: 169–88.

Van den Elsen, W. and Anderson, W. (1999) *Nijmegen University Project Report: UFB* (VSNU Netherlands).

Vesper, K.H. (1985) *Entrepreneurship Education 1985*. Wellesley, MA: Babson College.

Vesper, K.H. (1993) *Entrepreneurship Education 1993*. Los Angeles: UCLA.

Warner, D. and Palfreyman, D. (1996) *Higher Education Management*. Buckingham: SRHE/Open University Press.

Warren, A. (2002) ALTO and the EFFECTS evaluation strategy, in C. Rust (ed.) *Proceedings of the 9th International Improving Student Learning Symposium*. Oxford: Oxford Centre for Staff and Learning Development.

Watson, D. and Taylor, R. (1997) *Lifelong Learning and the University*. London: Taylor and Francis.

Webb, G. (1996) *Understanding Staff Development*. Buckingham: SRHE/Open University Press.

Webb G. (2001) The accreditation of university teachers: an interested view, in D. Woodhouse (ed.) *The Profession of Tertiary Teaching: Contemporary International Debate on Accreditation*. Wellington: New Zealand Universities Academic Audit Unit.

Weeks, P. (2000) Benchmarking in higher education: an Australian case study, *Innovations in Education and Training International*, 37(1): 59–67.

Weick, K. (1976) Educational organisations as loosely coupled systems, *Administrative Science Quarterly*, 21(1).

Weimer, M. (1998) Effectiveness and ethics: the right issue but the wrong questions, *International Journal for Academic Development*, 3(2): 108–10.

Weimer, M. and Lenze, L.F. (1991) Instructional interventions: a review of the literature on efforts to improve instruction, in J. Smart (ed.) *Higher Education: A Handbook of Theory and Practice*. New York: Agathon.

Wenger, E.C. (1998) *Communities of Practice: Learning Meaning and Identity*. Cambridge: Cambridge University Press.

West, R. (chair) (1998) *Learning for Life: Review of higher education financing and policy (Final Report)*, Department of Employment, Education, Training and Youth Affairs, Canberra.

Wilkinson, A., Redman, T. and Snape, E. (1993) *Quality and the Manager: An IM Report*. Corby: Institute of Management.

Williams, D. and Triller, F. (2000) *Sharing Experiences of Investors in People's Assessment*, Briefing Paper 79. Sheffield: HESDA.

Wills, S. and Alexander, S. (2000) Managing the introduction of technology in teaching and learning, in T. Evans and D. Nation (eds) *Changing University Teaching: Reflections on Creating Educational Technologies*. London: Kogan Page.

Wilson, D.A. and Morley, M. (2001) The Internal Quality Award at Loughborough University, in M. Box and R. Thackwray (eds) *Investors in People in Higher Education* (2nd edn). Sheffield: HESDA.

Wineburg, S.S. (1991) Historical problem solving: study of the cognitive processes used in the evaluation of documentary and pictorial evidence, *Journal of Educational Psychology*, 83(1): 73–87.

Wineburg, S.S. (1992) Probing the depths of students' historical knowledge, *AHA Perspectives*, 30(3): 1–24.

Woodhouse, D. (1998) Auditing research and the teaching research nexus, *New Zealand Journal of Educational Studies*, 33(1): 39–53.

Woodhouse D. (1999) Quality and quality assurance, in J. Knight and H. de Wit (eds) *Quality and Internationalisation in Higher Education*. Paris: OECD.

Yorke, M. (2001) *Assessment: A Guide for Senior Managers*, LTSN Generic Centre Assessment Series No. 1. York: LTSN.

Young, M.F.D. (1999) *The Curriculum of The Future*. London: Falmer Press.

Zacks, R. (2000) The TR university research scorecard. *MIT Enterprise Technology Review*, from http://www.techreview.com/magazine/ju100/zacks.asp

Index

The Society for Research into Higher Education

The Society for Research into Higher Education (SRHE), an international body, exists to stimulate and coordinate research into all aspects of higher education. It aims to improve the quality of higher education through the encouragement of debate and publication on issues of policy, on the organization and management of higher education institutions, and on the curriculum, teaching and learning methods.

The Society is entirely independent and receives no subsidies, although individual events often receive sponsorship from business or industry. The Society is financed through corporate and individual subscriptions and has members from many parts of the world. It is an NGO of UNESCO.

Under the imprint *SRHE & Open University Press*, the Society is a specialist publisher of research, having over 80 titles in print. In addition to *SRHE News*, the Society's newsletter, the Society publishes three journals: *Studies in Higher Education* (three issues a year), *Higher Education Quarterly* and *Research into Higher Education Abstracts* (three issues a year).

The Society runs frequent conferences, consultations, seminars and other events. The annual conference in December is organized at and with a higher education institution. There are a growing number of networks which focus on particular areas of interest, including:

Access
Assessment
Consultants
Curriculum Development
Eastern European
Educational Development Research
FE/HE
Funding
Graduate Employment

Learning Environment
Legal Education
Managing Innovation
New Technology for Learning
Postgraduate Issues
Quantitative Studies
Student Development
Vocational Qualifications

Benefits to members

Individual

- The opportunity to participate in the Society's networks
- Reduced rates for the annual conferences
- Free copies of *Research into Higher Education Abstracts*

- Reduced rates for *Studies in Higher Education*
- Reduced rates for *Higher Education Quarterly*
- Free copy of *Register of Members' Research Interests* – includes valuable reference material on research being pursued by the Society's members
- Free copy of occasional in-house publications, e.g. *The Thirtieth Anniversary Seminars Presented by the Vice-Presidents*
- Free copies of *SRHE News* which informs members of the Society's activities and provides a calendar of events, with additional material provided in regular mailings
- A 35 per cent discount on all SRHE/Open University Press books
- The opportunity for you to apply for the annual research grants
  - Inclusion of your research in the *Register of Members' Research Interests*

Corporate

- Reduced rates for the annual conference
- The opportunity for members of the Institution to attend SRHE's network events at reduced rates
  - Free copies of *Research into Higher Education Abstracts*
- Free copies of *Studies in Higher Education*
- Free copies of *Register of Members' Research Interests* – includes valuable reference material on research being pursued by the Society's members
- Free copy of occasional in-house publications
- Free copies of *SRHE News*
- A 35 per cent discount on all SRHE/Open University Press books
- The opportunity for members of the Institution to submit applications for the Society's research grants
- The opportunity to work with the Society and co-host conferences
- The opportunity to include in the *Register of Members' Research Interests* your Institution's research into aspects of higher education

Membership details: SRHE, 76 Portland Place, London W1B 1NT, UK Tel: 020 7637 2766. Fax: 020 7637 2781. email: srhe@mailbox.ulcc.ac.uk world wide web: http://www.srhe.ac.uk./srhe/
Catalogue: SRHE & Open University Press, McGraw-Hill Education, McGraw-Hill House, Shoppenhangers Road, Maidenhead, Berkshire SL6 2QL. Tel: 01628 502500. Fax: 01628 770224. email: enquiries@openup.co.uk – web: www.openup.co.uk

MANAGING THE LEARNING UNIVERSITY

Chris Duke

This book debunks prevailing modern management theories and fashions as applied to higher education. At the same time it provides practical guidance for a clear and easily understood set of principles as to how universities and colleges can be re-energized and their staff mobilized to be effective in meeting the growing and changing needs of the global knowledge society. It is anchored in knowledge of management and organizational theory and in the literature about higher education which is critiqued from a clear theoretical perspective based on and tested through long experience of university management and leadership.

Chris Duke offers challenging advice for managers in tertiary and higher education – from self-managing knowledge workers who may feel themselves to be the new academic proletariat, through to institutional heads, some of whose attempts to manage using strategic planning, management-by-objectives and other techniques seriously unravel because they fail to benefit from the talents and networks which make up the rich 'underlife' of the institution. Loss of institutional memory and failure to tap tacit know-how and mobilize commitment through genuine consultation and shared participatory management inhibits organizational learning and generates apathy – or drives staff dedication and creativity into oppositional channels.

Managing the Learning University indicates how higher education institutions can link and network their internal energies with external opportunities and partners to be successful and dynamic learning organizations. It points the way to enabling an enterprising and valued university to thrive in hard times, and to be a community where it is actually a pleasure to work.

Contents
Introduction: who manages what? – Changing universities – Managing and people in post-modern times – Managing what abiding university? – Managing through cooperation – Managing the academic enterprise – Managing people and resources – Managing communication and using information technology – Is the learning university manageable? – References – Index.

176pp   0 335 20765 0 (Paperback)   0 335 20766 9 (Hardback)

DEPARTMENTAL LEADERSHIP IN HIGHER EDUCATION

Peter T. Knight and Paul R. Trowler

This book is primarily aimed at those who have, or will have, a role in leading departments or teams in higher education institutions. It examines the ways in which mainstream leadership thinking does – and does not – apply to departments and teams in HEIs and suggests that departmental leadership is critical to institutional well-being. A series of substantive chapters explores assessment, learning and teaching, research and scholarship, administration and continuing professional development, and the final chapter discusses the ways in which individuals learn how to lead. The book offers a way of looking at the practice of leading rather than presenting a selection of tips or tools for leadership, but is studded with fascinating views from departmental leaders and extensive practical advice.

Contents

Preface – Contexts – Changing – Leadership theory, leadership practice – Leading in higher education departments – Learning from other places – Issues – Leading and assessment – Leading learning and teaching – Leading research and scholarship – Administration and positioning – Continuing professional development – Learning to lead – Conclusion – References – Index.

224pp   0 335 20675 1 (Paperback)   0 335 20676 X (Hardback)

RECONSTRUCTING PROFESSIONALISM IN UNIVERSITY TEACHING

Melanie Walker (Ed.)

- How can academics carve out new and effective ways of working with students against a background of constant change and policy pressure?
- How can university teachers both enhance student learning and realize their own educational values?
- What might be the shape of a new professionalism in university teaching?

At the heart of this book is a small group of academics from very different disciplines making sense of their teaching situations. We witness each of their struggles and celebrations in designing a new course, engaging a large first year class, introducing a mentoring programme, nurturing independent learning through project work, using debates to develop students' critical thinking, and evaluating the success of their teaching.

This book is the story of a higher education project, and central to the story are the attempts of university teachers to enact a critical professionalism in their everyday lives in teaching and learning; and also their development of a shared and collaborative dialogue. Each of the team seeks not only to improve their practice of teaching but also to explore amongst themselves what kind of professional they want to be and how to realize it in their work with students.

Reconstructing Professionalism in University Teaching reveals how academics working together on researching their own teaching can both improve their students' learning and start to redefine their own professional roles.

Contents

Acknowledgements – Notes on contributors – Preface – Part one: Towards a new professionalism in university teaching – Mapping our higher education projects – Action research for equity in teaching and learning – Collaboration within a community of practice – Part two: Teachers and learners in action – Introducing a mentoring programme – Using debates in developing students' critical thinking – Engaging a large first year class – Measuring performance: some alternative indicators – Designing a new course – Learning independently through project work – Part three: Endings and beginnings – Reconstructing professionalism in university teaching: doing otherwise – Index.

224pp   0 335 20816 9 (Paperback)   0 335 20817 7 (Hardback)